New Naldrett Press

CAPITALISTS, CLOWNS, AND CLERKS,
Choir-boys, Cops and Crooks:

Alan Naldrett

ISBN: 9781091002333

DEDICATION

This book is dedicated to all the Capitalists, Clowns, and Clerks, Choir-boys, Cops and Crooks, the Medical Healers, Religious Kneelers, Real-Estate Dealers, and Mafia Squealers. Also, the Potato Patch Rakers, Union Breakers, Auto Makers, Basketball Takers, and Political Fakers: The Mayors of Detroit.

TABLE OF CONTENTS

17. James A. Van Dyke—Railroad Mayor
18. Frederick Buhl—First of the Buhl Brothers
19. Charles Howard—Shipping Agent and Mayor
20. John Ladue—Leather Merchant Mayor
21. Zachariah Chandler—Better to Be Senator
22. John H. Harmon—Printer and Mayor
23. Oliver Moulton Hyde—Hardware Merchant Mayor
24. Henry Ledyard—Jack-of-all Trades Mayor
25. John Patton—Carriage Maker Mayor
26. Christian H. Buhl—Hatter Mayor
27. William C. Duncan—Brewer Mayor
28. Kirkland C. Barker—Tobacco Tycoon Mayor
29. Merrill I. Mills—Gunpowder and Stove Merchant Mayor
30. William W. Wheaton—Grocer Mayor
31. Hugh Moffat—Church Builder Mayor
32. Alexander Lewis—Canadian Mayor
33. George C. Langdon—Malter Mayor
34. William G. Thompson—Baseball Team Owner and Barroom Brawler
35. Stephen Benedict Grummond—General Store Mayor
36. Marvin H. Chamberlain—Liquor and Tobacco Mayor
37. John Pridgeon—Marine Mayor
38. Hazen S. Pingree—Potato Patch Pingree
39. William Richert—Fill-in-Mayor
40. William C. Maybury—Detroit Bicentennial Mayor
41. George P. Codd—Baseball Pitcher and Mayor
42. William Barlum Thompson—Meat Market Mayor
43. Philip Breitmeyer—Florist Mayor
44. Oscar Marx—Optical Mayor
45. James J. Couzens—Ford Pioneer Turned Mayor and Governor
46. John C. Lodge—More than a Freeway
47. Frank Ellsworth Doremus—Bare-Footed Mayor

ACKNOWLEDGEMENTS

I wish to thank all the teachers in school and college who had me write essays instead of taking tests. It really helped with my writing. I also want to thank Lynn Lyon, Dave Castle, my great family, the Historical Society of Michigan, Detroit Historical Society, and everybody else who helped with the writing. I especially want to thank Gail Zabowski for major editing and suggestions!

Most of the photos are public domain, from Wikipedia, or shot by me (such as the gravesites). Thanks to everyone that allowed me use of their photos (most are credited by the photo).

Please feel free to let me know information you think should be included, mistakes or misconceptions that possibly need to be corrected, or other pertinent information at alannaldrett@gmail.com.

FOREWORD

The major details about a city's mayors and information about their lives would usually give one a fair idea of an area's history. In Detroit's case, that is only about 66% correct, since Detroit was founded in 1701 by French explorers, and for its first 100 years Detroit was a fort, a port, and a trading post. In these years Detroit was governed by territorial governments run by French, and then, after the French and Indian War, English governors.

DETROIT-THE FIRST CENTURY

Samuel de Champlain, the founder of Quebec, sent Etienne Brule to the Great Lakes area to explore the Michigan area in 1618. French explorer Adrien Joliet passed through and camped around Detroit in 1669. These were the first recorded times Europeans were in the Detroit area.

The area of Detroit and environs were explored on or around August 10, 1679 by René-Robert Cavelier, Sieur de La Salle, a guy who could never fit his whole name on a ship. Instead, he named his ship the Griffon and sailed down the Detroit River. To name the lake and river nearby, LaSalle and his companion Father Louis Hennepin chose St. Clair, since it was St. Claire's feast day. This is counter to what many sources say was the source of the name. Some say it was named for the first Territorial Governor assigned to the area, Arthur St. Clair.

Etching of René-Robert Cavelier, Sieur de La Salle, who explored the Detroit area

The territory was claimed and governed by France as part of the "New France" territory. The French had been in North America (the "New World") since Jacques Cartier sailed the Gulf of St. Lawrence in 1534. They mostly occupied the territory to trade with the Native Americans and maintain a burgeoning fur industry. French Voyageurs would canoe through the area, trading with the natives, and inter-marrying with the Native Americans.

Postage stamp honoring Cadillac's landing in Detroit.

CADILLAC FOUNDS DETROIT

Cadillac received a charter from the French crown to build a fort and settlement to help protect the French fur industry from the British and the Indians. Sailing to the New World, on July 24, 1701, Antoine de Lamothe Cadillac established a trading post on the Detroit River. He and his 100-man crew built

Fort Pontchartrain du Détroit out of logs, and then built Ste. Anne de Detroit Catholic Church, the first building of Detroit.

Statue of Cadillac in Detroit's Hart Plaza.

Cadillac was the first administrator of Detroit. He had full authority from the powers-that-be in France to regulate commerce (including alcohol), build needed structures, and supervise the Indian tribes in the area. He issued land grants around the city but required the payment of rent from the people he issued the grants to, as well as a percentage of their crops.

Cadillac was at the center of many early stories of the area. In one Cadillac is warned by a fortune teller to "Beware the

Nain Rouge." Later when Cadillac and his wife are out on the town in Detroit, they sight the Nain Rouge (French for "Red Devil"). Cadillac kicks him, assuring bad luck for himself.

The Nain Rouge, who shows up in Detroit throughout its history when there are bad times.

Cadillac had major problems after that, no doubt due to kicking the Nain Rouge. He got sent to Louisiana, recalled to France and spent time in the Bastille for "abuse of authority" (like requiring a percentage of tenant's crops after charging them rent).

He was released and spent his final days as governor of a small area in France. Ever since this Cadillac incident, it has been said that the Nain Rouge appears whenever Detroit is about to have a crisis. It's one of the oldest stories of Detroit mythology and there is now a parade every spring in which the Nain Rouge is chased out of the city.

Cadillac left for Louisiana in 1710 but left a memorable

legacy in Michigan. The Cadillac automobile, the city of Cadillac, Cadillac Square in Detroit, and many other places bear his name in memory of his founding of Detroit.

In 1712, the town and fort were successfully defended against the Fox and Sauk Indians during the *Fox War*. The town grew to more than 600 inhabitants by 1760, when the British took over the fort during the French and Indian War. At the end of the war, the English took over the French settlements in the New World and kept Detroit.

Successfully fending off *Pontiac's Rebellion* in 1763, the territory was ceded to the United States by the British in 1783 under the Treaty of Paris after the Revolutionary War. However, it wasn't until about 1796 that the U.S. actually took possession of the territory.

In the 1700s England also had explorers, like John Cabot, that allowed England to claim large parts of the New World. Since England and France had spent the last centuries fighting each other over one thing or another, it didn't take long for the Seven Years War to erupt. The New World had its own version and name for the war—the French and Indian War. When England triumphed in 1763, the Treaty of Paris awarded them France's claims in North America.

England's original intent in the New World was to award the territory that included Michigan to the Native Americans and just concentrate on the French colony of Quebec they had received from France.

In 1787 Congress passed the Northwest Ordinance, and Michigan was a part of the lands called the Northwest Territory. The first governor of the Northwest Territories was General Arthur St. Clair, who was a British officer during the French and Indian War and then joined the American colonies during the Revolutionary War.

Arthur St. Clair had been President of the Continental Congress when the Northwest Ordinance was passed and then was named the first Territorial Governor of the Northwest Territory. He was recalled by President Washington in 1802 after a disastrous Indian battle and replaced by Charles Willing Byrd through 1803.

The Northwest Territory in 1787

The battle that St. Clair lost was called, strangely enough, St. Clair's Defeat. He lost almost 1,000 men (out of about 4,000 total) to a group of many tribes of Indians—called the Western Confederacy of American Indians.

The Indian leaders and tribes included Little Turtle of the Miami tribe, Buckongahelas of the Delaware tribe, and Blue Jacket of the Shawnees. They were joined by Potawatomi tribe members, and the whole confederation of Indians involved in the battle numbered over a thousand.

Oil portrait of Arthur St. Clair, first Governor of the Northwest Territory and unfortunate namesake of the "St. Clair's Defeat" Battle

The resulting 1802 loss was called "the most decisive defeat in the history of the American military" and was the largest victory ever won by American Indians.

Most of the Michigan territory was still governed by the British, who had refused to vacate the area after the Revolutionary War and were supporting the hostile Indians. Finally, in 1794, General "Mad Anthony" Wayne bought his troops to the area of a recent storm, which had knocked down several trees.

Called the Battle of Fallen Timbers, Wayne and his men were able to push the hostile Indians out. Wayne had them sign the Treaty of Greenville which ceded the area that is now Ohio to the United States. The British finally left the area shortly thereafter. The U.S. took possession of the territory and a territorial legislature was established in 1802.

Sections of the Northwest Territory became states, including Ohio in 1803, Indiana in 1816, and Illinois in 1818. The area that was left was chiefly the areas that became Michigan and Wisconsin. It was named the Michigan Territory in 1805, (the area had briefly been part of the Indiana Territory since 1800) and Detroit was named the Territorial Capital.

The first Territorial Governor of the Michigan Territory was William Hull. He was Governor until his fateful surrender of Detroit to the British in 1812. After that, Lewis Cass held the position.

The Michigan Territorial Governors were:

William Hull	March 1, 1805 to August 16, 1812
Henry Proctor (British Governor)	August 24, 1812 to September 28, 1813
Lewis Cass	October 13, 1813 to August 6, 1831
George Bryan Porter	August 6, 1831 to July 6, 1834

| Stevens T. Mason | July 6, 1834 to September 15, 1835 |
| John S. Horner | September 15, 1835 to July 3, 1836 |

The Territorial Governor had an assistant, the Territorial Secretary. The Michigan Territorial Secretaries were:

Stanley Griswold	March 1, 1805 to March 18, 1808
Reuben Atwater	March 18, 1808 to October 15, 1814
William Woodbridge	October 15, 1814 to January 15, 1828
James Witherell	January 15, 1828 to May 20, 1830
John T. Mason	May 20, 1830 to July 12, 1831
Stevens T. Mason	July 12, 1831 to September 15, 1835

In 1820 Lewis Cass took a 45-member crew around Michigan to explore it and dispel the "swampy wasteland" myth, helping to set the stage for Michigan to attract enough people to reach 60,000, the amount needed to petition for statehood.

When Cass became Secretary of War in President Andrew Jackson's cabinet, George Porter was appointed the new Governor of the Michigan Territory. Unfortuneatly, he died in the Cholera epidemic in 1834, on one of his few visits to the area. The Territorial Secretary John Mason's son Stevens had been doing much of the governing in the Michigan Territory.

John Mason got called to Texas and Stevens was left to pretty much run the state since Porter was an absentee Governor. Mason was named Territorial Secretary, and then finally Territorial Governor when Porter died.

Although the most famous picture of General William Hull is a rare profile shot (most were full-face then), it's not true that this is one of his mug shots. An almost profile shot of Lewis Cass is next. The next Governor was George B. Porter, cholera victim of 1834, and then Stevens Mason, who was replaced by "Little Jack" Horner, much disparaged governor who was pelted with a rain of vegetables whenever he was seen on the street.

George Porter's tombstone in Elm-wood Cemetery

Statehood Prelude-the Toledo War

Michigan didn't become an official state until 1837, although the state flag says 1835, the date Governor Stevens Mason thought Michigan *should've* become a state. In between 1835 and 1837, Michigan was involved in the "Toledo War," and was in a limbo between being a territory and becoming a state.

The conflict began when there was a territorial misunderstanding because of the fallibility of early maps. Although the most southern portion of Michigan clearly belonged to Michigan, Ohio claimed it as part of their boundary when they became a state in 1803. Michigan's claim was according to the Northwest Ordinance, passed by Congress much earlier, in 1787.

Because of the success of the Erie Canal, Toledo's area became a prized territory due to its position on the Maumee River. Although there had long been misunderstandings about whether the territory was the property of the state of Ohio or the territory of Michigan, it all came to a head in 1835, once Michigan reached the population requirements to become a state. The would-be new state now had to submit boundaries.

Included in the boundary claims of the Michigan territory

was the Maumee River area that became Toledo, Ohio. Ohio also claimed the same area, and had it written in the state boundaries in their constitution when they became a state. Ohio successfully blocked Michigan's statehood bid because of this misunderstanding, and both areas put together militias to fight it out in 1835.

With very few casualties except livestock and vegetable gardens, at one point both militias planned to engage with each other but both sides got lost in the Great Black Swamp. The closest they got to any true conflict was when both sides yelled taunts at each other across the Maumee River.

After spending 1836 in territorial limbo, at a building with faulty heat in the dead of January, the fledgling state came to an agreement dubbed the "Frostbitten Convention." Michigan would concede all rights to the Toledo Strip, in return for the western and central portion of the Upper Peninsula. The Sault Ste. Marie area was already undisputedly Michigan's.

Once Michigan became a bona-fide state, the history of Detroit's mayors continued. Stevens Mason had been elected Michigan's first governor, headquartered in Detroit, prior to the Toledo War conclusion and became Michigan's first and youngest Governor. For a background on early Detroit history, short bios on Stevens Mason and William Woodbridge are fundamental, since they are examples of the two of the largest, diverging influences in Detroit government.

Stevens Mason—Don't Call Him Boy Governor

The first thing to know about "Boy Governor" Stevens Thomson Mason (1811-1843) was to never let him hear you call him Boy Governor. After this "insult" was printed in the Whig-leaning *Western Emigrant* newspaper, Mason saw the reporter, George Corselius, on Jefferson Avenue in Detroit and had a brief discussion. This led to a full-fledged fight, which by all accounts was won by Mason. Corselius went on to start the *Michigan Whig* newspaper. Mason was a Democrat.

Stevens Thomson Mason (1811-1843) was born in Virginia and then moved to Lexington, Kentucky, where he spent his youth. He attended Transylvania University and then in 1830 when he was 19, he followed the family to the Michigan Territory. Mason's father John Mason had been named the Secretary of the Michigan Territory, second-in-command to the Governor.

Stevens was taught how to do his father's job, and when John Mason was sent to Texas, Stevens took over the job. Technically, the Governor, George Porter was in charge, however, he spent all his time in Pennsylvania tending his business there. In a cruel twist of fate, he contracted cholera during the 1834 epidemic and died in one of his few ventures to the Michigan Territory. This left Mason still in charge and with the title Acting Governor.

Mason led the territory into becoming a certified state, even though the Toledo War was a big roadblock. When Mason continued the animosities with Ohio over the title to the Toledo Strip, President Andrew Jackson fired him and replaced him with John Horner (after two others refused the position).

This turned out to be a mistake, especially for John Horner, soon nicknamed "Little Jack" (Horner). The people of Michigan were at first wary of one so young as Mason becoming the head of the government. But that changed, and Mason had the people behind him when they saw how vigilantly he worked on Michigan's behalf.

When Jackson fired Mason, the Michiganders took it out on Horner. He was burned in effigy and pelted with vegetables whenever he made a personal appearance. After being threatened with tar and feathering, he fled to Wisconsin and was Governor of the Wisconsin Territory when Michigan became a separate state.

Mason's popularity carried over when Michigan held their first Governmental election. It was a bit premature since Michigan wasn't quite a state yet, but Mason handily beat his Whig opponent, William Woodbridge. Woodbridge never forgot the defeat and continued to dog Mason all through his term. His biggest slap in the face was when he tried to pass an age limit for Governor that would have excluded Mason for being too young.

Mason persevered, and Michigan was finally declared an official state in January 1837. Mason had a stormy term as Governor. He was ambitious, launching three canal projects, and road and railroad commitments. Even though this put Michigan in dire financial straits, Mason was re-elected to a second term.

In his second term, Mason went to New York to negotiate a loan for Michigan and met Julia Phelps. They fell in love and married, and Julia moved back to Michigan with Mason. However, with all the new projects and loans, Michigan's debt was astronomical, much to the chagrin of the Whig Party. Mason was defeated by William Woodbridge in his bid for re-election and so Mason moved with his wife to New York.

Mason started practicing law and was beginning to do well when he contracted Scarlet Fever and died in 1843. He was only 31.

He was at first interred in New York, but a state-wide movement in 1905 had his body exhumed and re-buried in Detroit's Capitol Square, where a statue of Mason was erected in bronze. The bronze came from the melted-down cannons of Fort Michilimackinac. Capitol Park was the location of the original Michigan Capitol Building.

Capitol Square in the early 1900s.

The city of Mason, Michigan, and Mason County are named for Stevens Mason.

William Woodbridge, Certified Curmudgeon

If Stevens Mason could be said to have had an "arch-enemy," it would be William Woodbridge, who succeeded Mason as Michigan's first Governor from the Whig Party. Woodbridge had Mason's job of Territorial Secretary when Cass was still Governor and seemed to resent the young Mason's authority. Woodbridge criticized Mason every chance he could. Woodbridge even admitted that he wanted to try to get Mason jailed and worked towards it.

William Woodbridge (1780-1861) was born in Norwich, Connecticut on August 20, 1780. In 1791 he moved with his family in Marietta, Ohio. Having completed most of his schooling in Connecticut, Woodbridge began working in a law office in Marietta and met Lewis Cass, whose family was residing in Marietta. Woodbridge met and married Juliana Trumbull, daughter of poet John Trumbull, who Trumbull Street in Detroit is named for.

When he was 16, his father sent him back to Connecticut to continue his education. Returning to Marietta in 1806, he passed the Ohio bar and began practicing law in Marietta. But there wasn't a lot of work in Marietta, so when Lewis Cass offered to make him Territorial Secretary of the Michigan Territory while Cass was Governor, Woodbridge accepted.

In 1819 Woodbridge was elected the Michigan Territories' representative to Congress. He then returned to his job as Territorial Secretary until 1828, when President John Quincy Adams appointed him to the Michigan Territorial Supreme Court. In 1838 he was elected to the State Senate as a Whig and became a thorn in Governor Mason's side, raising objections to everything that Mason proposed and taking every opportunity to put roadblocks in front of everything Mason suggested. When Michigan's first constitution was being written, Woodbridge tried to get a passage in it that stated the Governor had to be at least 30 years old. Governor Mason was 25 at the time.

In 1840 William Woodbridge was elected to be Michigan's second Governor. In 1841 he was elected to the U.S. Senate and resigned as Governor. His Lieutenant Governor, James Wright Gordon, assumed the position. Woodbridge remained Senator for his entire six-year term and didn't run for re-election when it was over.

While in the Senate Woodbridge was Chairman of the Committee on Public Lands in the 28th Congress in 1843 and 1844, and the Committee on Patents and the Patent Office in the 29th Congress, 1845 and 1846.

Upon retirement, Woodbridge spent much of his time fighting the City of Detroit from encroaching on his large farm. He was able to hang on to the property until his death on October 20, 1861. He was buried in Detroit's Elmwood Cemetery.

The Woodbridge neighborhood is named for him, as is Woodbridge Avenue, Woodbridge Township in Hillsdale County, and Woodbridge Elementary School in Zeeland, Michigan.

Great Fire of 1805

Most of the physical remains of Detroit's first 104 years were unfortunately wiped out by the Great Fire of 1805. The settlement's early years were influenced by the Native American events of the time, including the Fox-Sauk Indian Wars. Also affecting Detroit's early history was the Revolutionary War and the War of 1812, when Detroit was taken by the British.

After the War of 1812, when Detroit once again became the property of the United States, the mayoral system began—albeit in a very different form than the first Board of Trustees system.

Detroit History in a Nutshell

The history of Detroit's mayors begins around 1801, but the first two, Solomon Sibley and Elijah Brush were mayors in name only and quickly resigned when they realized this.

The first actual, not just ceremonial, mayor of Detroit was John R. Williams. He was the first mayor of the City Charter of 1825—which he also wrote. The City Charter also named the city's ruling body the "Common Council."

The Great Fire of 1805 in Detroit.

In the beginning of Detroit's civil government, mayors served only a year. Later, the terms would be extended to two years, and then four years. Therefore, Detroit has had over sixty mayors in the almost 200 years the mayoral system has been in place. Many were mayor for one year only and some were like John R. Williams, who became mayor of Detroit on five non-consecutive occasions, each time a year or less.

As Detroit grew in population after the Erie Canal opened in 1825, it lost its reputation as a marshy swampland where nothing would grow. In 1828 Detroit was named the capital of the Northwest Territory. As the population increased, so did the identity of the city. It was the first capital of Michigan when it became a state in 1837.

At first just a port, Detroit became a manufacturing center in the 1850s, becoming known at various times for the manufacture of stoves, pharmaceuticals, garden seeds, and even cigars. After 1860, Detroit was listed as one of the Top 20 largest cities in the United States. Detroit was full of trees, and considered one of the most beautiful cities in the U.S. It was dubbed "The Paris of the Midwest."

Wars, Riots, and Insurrections in Detroit

From the earliest times, Detroit was an upstart town. In 1833 Detroit had its first riot, with black settlers battling the Wayne County Sheriff, John Wilson, when a fugitive slave couple, Thornton and Ruth Blackburn, were jailed. Wilson was killed in the melee and the Blackburns escaped to safety in Canada.

In 1835 Detroit was a gathering place for disgruntled settlers who were angry that Ohio was blocking Michigan from becoming a state because Michigan wouldn't rescind its claim on the area that is now Toledo. The Toledo War was the result and Detroit was a focal point because it was the capital of the Northwest Territories, and then of the State of Michigan.

This conflict with Ohio over who owned Toledo kept Michigan from getting to be a state in 1835. Militias were formed, and threats bandied back and forth.

In 1837 the Toledo War was resolved with Michigan giving up Toledo in exchange for the western portion of the Upper Peninsula. Not much later, Detroit had one of the "Hunter's Lodges" of the Patriot War, a skirmish with Canadian and American settlers together wanting to free Canada from British rule and have it join the U.S.

In 1849, "middle-class" citizens didn't like the railroad tracks going through their neighborhoods and tore up the tracks along Gratiot Highway.

In the 1850s there were the "whorehouse wars," where stone-throwing white people would attack brothels in German neighborhoods that catered to black men. Often the buildings were torched.

In 1863, soldiers fired on a group of white people attempting to lynch a black man, William Faulkner. One man was killed, and then an angry white mob descended on the black area of the city now known as Greektown. They burned about 30 buildings while hindering the firemen trying to put out the blazes.

In 1891, a strike by trolley employees led to three days of rioting. Stones were thrown at trolleys, rails were ripped up, and horses were unhitched. The rioters threw paving stones at and fought with the police.

In 1894, a group of Polish workers and others were upset about pay cuts and attacked the Wayne County sheriff and his deputies. Three people were killed.

In 1942, about a thousand white people gathered at the opening of the Sojourner Truth housing project. Police battled protesters for hours, with numerous injuries.

In 1943, 34 people were killed in a race riot that began around Belle Isle. Racial violence continued for two days as white business owners had their windows broken on Hastings Street. Police were responsible for shooting 17 out of the 25 black people killed.

Other examples of Detroit's unruliness include the birth of the Bernstein Brothers at 404 Gratiot Avenue, in the city. They became the first members of the Purple Gang, a gangster outfit that was the most infamous of the criminal gangs in the 1920s. They ran a protection racket and had a large control over illegal alcohol imports during Prohibition. They helped to provide Chicago's Al Capone with a liquor supply.

As time went on, the Jewish Purple Gang of the 1920s was supplanted with the Italian Mafia gangs of the 1930s. Organized crime in 1930 gave Detroit the moniker "Murder City" for the first time, as large amounts of gangland shootings occurred.

Becoming the Motor City

When automobile manufacturing caused Detroit to become the Motor City in 1900, the population doubled and quadrupled, until finally, at its peak in the early 1950s, Detroit grew to become the fourth largest city in the United States with over 2 million people.

As Detroit grew, it developed big city problems that sometimes the mayors would be able to fix. However, in many cases the mayors *were* the problem. Detroit is often considered to have three great mayors—Hazen Pingree, James Couzens, and Frank Murphy. But they also have four that might make anybody's list of the Worst Mayors Ever. This list of mayors would probably include Richard Reading ("Double Dip Rick"), Charles Bowles (first big-city mayor in the U.S. to be removed from office), Louis Miriani (jailed for tax evasion after his term), and Kwame Kilpatrick (who as of 2019 is still in federal prison serving a 28-year sentence for embezzlement, extortion, racketeering, and other crimes).

Motor City to Murder City

In the early years of the 20th Century, when Detroit was plagued with organized crime, there were also other subversive groups exerting influence in the city. These included the Ku Klux Klan and the Black Legion. Add to that the bootleggers, prostitutes, blind pigs, and gambling den owners that were "independent operators," while paying off the authorities, and you have an excellent picture of an "open city."

In the 1930s, as the number of auto companies dwindled from many to just a few, jobs began to dwindle as well. At this time the labor unions began operating. The auto manufacturers all resisted unionization, causing many monumental battles within the city.

One of the more interesting occurrences in Michigan labor history was when the Governor of Michigan, Frank Murphy, a former Detroit mayor, called out the National Guard to stop a riot at the General Motors' Flint sit-down strike. Unlike previous insurrections however, Murphy didn't call out the Guard to aid the factory owners, but to protect the workers from the factory owners. This was a turning point in the recognition of the United Auto Workers (UAW) union.

World War II arrives, and Detroit becomes the "Arsenal of Democracy." After the war, Detroit is hailed as a "Model City" and there is slum clearance, and new construction, but no new public housing. Neighborhood "covenants" keep real estate agents from showing blacks housing in the "white area." All seems well but there is trouble bubbling up under the surface. Finally, in July 1967, the U.S.'s largest riot occurs in Detroit and rages for five days, until it was finally broken up by the National Guard and U.S. Army.

Riots and Racial Turmoil

"White flight," which had been occurring for a while before the riot, continued at a quicker rate after July 1967 as white people left the city and moved to the suburbs. Before long, Detroit had a black mayor who was as antagonistic towards the suburbs as they are against him.

In 1984, another riot broke out in Detroit as the Detroit Tigers won baseball's World Series. Cars were overturned and set on fire.

As the century came to an end, it seemed there was more wrong about Detroit than there was good. An epidemic of crack cocaine helped turn Detroit once more into the "Murder City," with record-breaking homicide rates.

As the crack epidemic receded, Detroit also had a problem on the day before Halloween each year, commonly known as "Devil's Night." On this night, youths would torch the many vacant (and some not vacant) houses of the city. This problem was lessened and then ceased after the "Detroit Angels" started operating in the early 1990s under Mayor Archer. The Angels were neighborhood volunteers who drove around their area keeping an eye out for arsonists. Devil's Night was re-christened "Angel's Night."

A Corrupt Mayor and Bankruptcy

As Detroit suffered financial woes under new mayor Kwame Kilpatrick, behind the scenes Kilpatrick and his friends and family were bilking the city. After Kwame's forced resignation, the Detroit Common Council under Acting Mayor Kenneth Cockerel began to go out of control, singing songs during meetings that included Councilwoman Martha Reeves, from Motown's Martha and the Vandellas. Common Council member Monica Conyers, wife of U.S. Representative John Conyers, went to jail for accepting a bribe while on the Council.

Finally, the city is settling down under Mayor Dave Bing, and then the bankruptcy happens! The city is declared bankrupt in 2013 and has a financial manager appointed by the Governor of Michigan running things for a while. Detroit finally emerges from the bankruptcy in 2015.

New Renaissance

The city is now in a new renaissance stage, shedding billions in debt. Long vacant downtown skyscrapers are being rehabilitated, and the city that brought the country autos, an Arsenal of Democracy, Motown and electronic music is starting to thrive, with new restaurants and new residents.

As Detroit rebuilds, it remembers the city motto, created by esteemed pioneer Father Gabriel Richards after the Great Fire of 1805: ""Speramus meliora; resurgent cineribus," which translates to— "We hope for better things; it shall arise from the ashes."

The Earliest "Mayors"

In 1802 Detroit was incorporated as a village and in 1805 it became the seat of the Northwest Territory. Also, in 1805, the Great Detroit Fire occurred, destroying most remnants of the town's structures from the 1700s. Detroit was rebuilt and re-platted by Judge Augustus Woodward. Governing of the town was originally by a Board of Trustees, with the chairman of the board as the highest position.

The first chairman was James Henry (1771-1812), in 1802. He was born in Pennsylvania and moved to Detroit in 1798, establishing a tannery. He was appointed in 1802 and elected later that year. His other offices included justice of the peace in 1798; supervisor of Michigan roads in 1801; overseer of the poor, 1802; Judge of the Court of Quarter Sessions, 1802; Wayne County commissioner, 1804; Wayne County Tax Assessor, 1807; and Associate Judge of the Court of Huron and Detroit in 1807.

The next chairman of the board was John Mays (1756-1829), who moved to Detroit from England in 1778. He was a Justice of the Court of Common Pleas in 1788 and became Chief Justice from 1800 until 1807. When he was appointed one of five of the first Detroit Board of Trustees, he became the second chairman, from 1803 until 1804. (For a complete list, see the Appendix at the end of the book.)

When Detroit was surrendered to the British in the War of 1812, Mays took possession of the American flag, raising the same one up again when the U.S. took back Detroit.

Upon ratification of Detroit's 1824 Charter, Mayors of Detroit served one-year terms. After 1857 the term was doubled to two years.

John Mays

Solomon and Sarah Sibley

C HAPTER ONE— SOLOMON SIBLEY—FIRST MAYOR OF DETROIT AND WORTHY GENTLEMAN

The third Chairman of the Board of Trustees of Detroit was Solomon Sibley (1769-1846), who was born October 7, 1869 in Sutton, Massachusetts. He went to Rhode Island College, now Brown University, and graduated in 1794. After stints in Marietta and Cincinnati, Ohio, he received a land grant from President James Madison and moved to Detroit in 1797, the year it was first freed from British control. As one of only two lawyers in Detroit at that time, he had a rough life, riding his horse down rough-hewn Indian trails to get to court in Cincinnati or Chillicothe, Ohio.

He married Sarah Whipple Strout, and they had eight children, one of which was noted Army officer Ebenezer Sibley, and another was the future Governor of Minnesota, Henry Hastings Sibley. Solomon's daughter Katherine married another Mayor of Detroit, Charles C. Trowbridge.

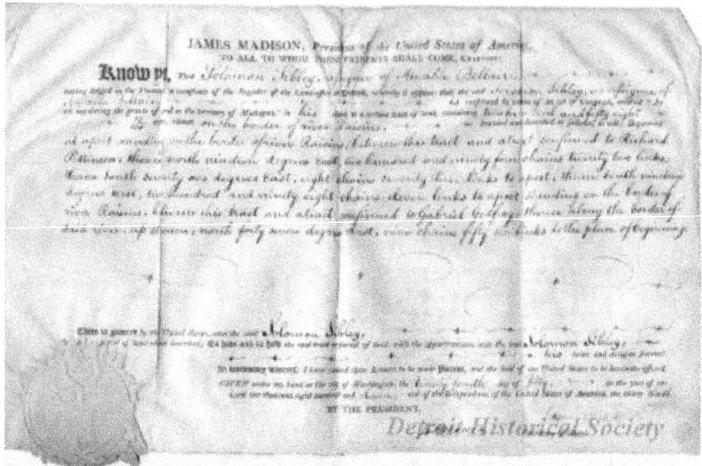

President Madison's land grant to Solomon Sibley (Courtesy of Detroit Historical Society)

In December 1798, Sibley was a delegate to the Northwest Territory Legislature. He was elected in a Detroit tavern and the runner-up, James May, protested that Sibley had won by providing alcohol to everybody. Nevertheless, Sibley represented Wayne County in the first meeting of the legislature.

In 1802 Sibley was instrumental in getting Detroit incorporated as a village and was one of the five on the first Detroit Board of Trustees. He served as Chairman from 1804 until 1805. Robert Wilkinson was elected in 1805, but the Great Fire of Detroit in 1805 effectively ended local government.

Sibley Helps with Charter, Becomes Mayor

Solomon assisted when Judge Augustus Woodward and Territorial Governor William Hull replaced the original charter in 1806 with one that called for them to appoint a mayor. The first mayor they appointed was Solomon Sibley. He resigned the office after realizing that the Territorial Governor was still making all the decisions.

After serving in the War of 1812 as a Captain in the Michigan Militia, he was appointed the Auditor of the Territory from 1814 to 1817, and then President James Madison appointed him as the U.S. Federal Attorney from 1815 to 1823. From 1821 to 1823 he was the Delegate to Congress from Michigan. In 1823 Madison appointed him Chief Justice of the Supreme Court of the Michigan Territory. Sibley retired in 1837, after helping draft legislation for Michigan's statehood. He also helped raise funds for the founding of the University of Michigan.

In 1823, Sibley bought a limestone quarry south of the Detroit city limits in Wayne County. Solomon (and later his sons) developed the mining operations that had been going on at the site since 1749. A small village named Sibley grew around the quarry and was a station on the Canada Southern Railroad called the Sibley Station. Sibley's post office was started in 1903 and in 1920 Sibley was incorporated as a village. In 1929 it was annexed by the City of Trenton, with the village area now known as the Sibley Section.

The Founding of Pontiac

Solomon and his wife Sarah helped get the town of Pontiac, Michigan started. They bought land there and supervised the building of the first structures in the early 1800s. Their first building began as a log cabin in 1819 and is the oldest house in Oakland County, Michigan. It is now called the Sibley-Hoyt House.

Sibley-Hoyt house in Pontiac

In 1825 they sold 50 acres to Elizabeth (Lisette) Denison Forth, who became the first black woman to own land in Michigan. Living to be 114, Ms. Forth became quite wealthy due to smart investments. She used some of her money to endow churches.

Elizabeth Denison Forth

Solomon had the Sibley House in Detroit built, but died before moving in. His wife Sarah and two unmarried daughters lived in the house until Sarah died in 1851. The house, at 976 E. Jefferson in Detroit, is one of the oldest residences in the city.

The Sibley House in Detroit

When the surveyor-general remarked that the soil of Michigan was all swampy and sandy, Solomon grew a pear in his own orchard that weighed thirty ounces (almost two pounds), was seven and a half inches long, and fourteen and a half inches in circumference, proving the surveyor very wrong! Because of false reports like the surveyor's, Michigan was not settled until over 30 years after similar-but-without-the-Great Lakes Ohio.

Solomon Sibley died in Detroit in 1846 and was buried in Detroit's Elmwood Cemetery. His death was declared a day of mourning, and Supreme Court Justices and other law personnel wore black armbands for a month after his death. Sibley Street in Detroit was named for him.

Solomon Sibley gravesite

Elijah Brush, Mayor of Detroit 1806

C HAPTER TWO-
ELIJAH BRUSH
—BRUSH STREET
NAMESAKE

The next person to be appointed mayor—and then resign the position for the same reason as Sibley—was Elijah Brush (1773-1813). He was mayor briefly in 1806. He owned the ribbon farm (a long, narrow strip of land with water frontage) that ran along what is now Brush Street.

Brush was born May 10, 1773 in Bennington, Vermont, went to Dartmouth College and graduated in 1798 with a law degree. He moved to Detroit in 1798. He was the United States Attorney from 1811 to 1814 and Treasurer of the Michigan Territory from 1806 until 1813.

Brush resigned as Mayor for the same reason that Sibley did —the mayor had no duties and was a symbolic position only.

Brush served in the War of 1812 as a Lieutenant Colonel and was taken prisoner by the British. He was sent to Toronto, was returned in 1813, and died shortly thereafter. He was buried in Elmwood Cemetery.

Brush Park in the late 1800s.

His son, Edmund A. Brush, subdivided the area in 1835, and
by 1850 it was one of the earliest exclusive areas of Detroit, Brush Park. Some mansions from that era still sur-
vive.

Alan Naldrett

Both plaques are on Brush's Elmwood Cemetery gravesite

There was a period with no mayors—the period of 1806 to

1812, when it was ruled by Governor William Hull, and during the War of 1812, when Governor Hull gave up the City of Detroit to the British and it was ruled by British military officers.

General Hull Gives Away Detroit

Detroit was "recaptured" by the British during the War of 1812. It was a totally bloodless surrender to the English due to a subterfuge perpetrated by the Shawnee Indian chief Tecumseh and British officer Sir Isaac Brock.

Tecumseh had his warriors circle the fort, emitting blood-curdling screams and war whoops. As they circled the fort numerous times, Hull was duped into thinking that there were many more Indians and British than there actually were. In truth, the people in the fort outnumbered the attackers. In response, Hull simply surrendered, much to the consternation of Lewis Cass, William Woodbridge, and the other soldiers in the fort.

Cass and others later testified at William Hull's trial. Hull was convicted of four counts of cowardice, seven counts of neglect of duty, and "unofficer-like" conduct. He was sentenced to be executed by firing squad, but his sentence was commuted by President Madison because of Hull's Revolutionary War service and due to his advanced age (he was sixty).

American General William Hull

While the British occupied Detroit, one of the British officers in charge was General Henry Proctor. Proctor banished
30 of Detroit's residents from Detroit for disagreeing with
his views on the War of 1812. The remaining Detroiters then
named streets after the thirty people banished.

Detroit is Returned to the U.S.

After the war ended and Detroit was returned to the U.S.
in 1815, Detroit was incorporated as a city and resumed the
Board of Trustees form of government. This time, the chair-
men of the board included George McDougall (1816–1817),
Abraham Edwards (1817–1818), John R. Williams (1818–
1819), James McCloskey (1819–1820), James Abbott (1820–
1821 and 1823–1824), and A. G. Whitney (1821–1822 and
1822–1823).

John R. Williams, Mayor of Detroit 1824, 1825, 1829, 1830, 1844-46

C HAPTER THREE —JOHN R. WILLIAMS—THE OTHER FIRST MAYOR

John R. Williams (1782-1854) wrote a new city charter in 1824 and conveniently became the first mayor of Detroit under the new charter. Mayors served one-year terms with no pay under this document and so there was a new mayor every year. This caused Detroit to have a LOT of mayors, though many would run for Mayor again and win after their initial term.

The government was a Mayor-City Council type, with the City Council named the Common Council. The Common Council consisted of 16 members, two from each of the eight wards in Detroit.

Business with Millionaire Uncle Louis

Besides being the first mayor under the 1824 Charter, Williams was also the fourth and the thirteenth mayor and had multiple terms, serving in the years 1829, 1830, 1844 and 1846.

His uncle on his mother's side was an early Detroit pioneer and one of Michigan's first millionaires, Joseph Campau. His father was Thomas Williams, who was a merchant, landowner, Justice of the Peace, Notary Public, town crier, and the man who conducted the 1782 Census.

John Williams was born May 4, 1782 in Detroit. He added the "R" to his name later to distinguish himself from another John Williams in Detroit. From 1796-1799 he was in the Territorial Militia. He quit in 1799 to form a trade partnership with another Campau uncle, Louis Campau, Sr. (Louis Campau, Jr., his son, went on to settle Saginaw and Grand Rapids.) Williams became an agent for fur traders, and only spoke French until he was in his 20s.

While in Canada procuring supplies for his company, Williams got into a duel with and wounded Robert Cavalier, Sieur La Salle. For this he was jailed for several months in Montreal, Canada.

During the War of 1812 Williams served as the Captain of an artillery company where he was taken prisoner and once again briefly imprisoned. He survived the War and was also a Brigadier General in the Black Hawk War. At his death in 1854 he was the senior Major General of the state militia. He was often referred to as "General Williams" due to his position in the Black Hawk War. A plaque at his gravesite denotes his Black Hawk War service.

Founding the Detroit Free Press

In 1802, when Detroit was incorporated as a township, he was named Town Clerk. In 1803 he built his own store which burned but was rebuilt. In 1804 he married Mary Mott, and they had ten children together. In 1831, along with his Uncle Joseph Campau, Andrew Mack and Sheldon McKnight, he started the Democratic Free Press and Michigan Intelligencer, later to become the Detroit Free Press. He is credited with the book, *Godfrey of Rheims, a Humanist of the Eleventh Century*.

During Williams' mayoral term in 1845 the main competitor of the Detroit Free Press, the Detroit News, started.

In 1823 Williams wanted to represent Michigan in Congress. The candidates were Williams, John Biddle (later Mayor), and Wayne County Sheriff Austin Wing. Williams thought he had the whole election in the bag, because he was the only Catholic running and figured he would get all their votes. But that plan went out the window when popular Catholic Priest Father Gabriel Richards decided to run.

Father Richards won, and Richards came in last. In anger, Williams and his Uncle Louis Campau quit the Catholic Church. Consequently, their Catholic relatives are buried in Mt. Elliot Cemetery, while Williams and Campau are buried across the fence in Protesant Elmwood Cemetery.

John R. was a merchant, landowner, and president of a bank. He was bilingual in English and French (he grew up speaking French and didn't learn English until he was in his 20s) and was politically conservative, opposing municipal spending and taxes. He was the first Mayor of Detroit under the charter of 1824.

The election of 1825 put John Williams in office and his first year as Mayor was 1826. During this period the Erie Canal opened and a wave of German and other immigrants came to Detroit. Roads were also improved between Detroit and Toledo, Chicago, and St. Joseph. Also during his first mayoral term, the U.S. closed Fort Shelby and dismantled it in 1826, giving the land to the city.

In 1825 Williams was elected with 102 votes, with the other votes going to five other candidates. In 1829, 1830, 1844 and 1846 he was repeatedly elected to yearly terms as Mayor.

Elected again in 1830, it was during this term that the Irish began to emigrate to Detroit, settling west of Woodward Avenue in an area known as Corktown.

Serving two more terms as mayor in 1844 and 1846 Williams governed during the time that the U.S. built Fort Wayne in Detroit in 1825 (because of increasing problems in the area with the British), and Michigan became the first state to abolish capital punishment.

Fort Wayne in Detroit, constructed in 1825 during John R. Williams mayoral term.

When he died at

the age of 72 in 1854, he was buried in Elmwood Cemetery. He was pre-deceased by his wife, Mary Mott, in 1805. She was buried in the St. Anne's Church cemetery. They had ten children together.

John R. Street is a major Detroit roadway named for him (he named it himself!), as is Williams Street. The two streets used to cross, but Williams Street has diminished to only a block long, no longer crossing its namesake John R. There is also an elementary school named for John R. Williams in Detroit.

John

R. Williams gravesite in Elmwood Cemetery.

CHAPTER FOUR— HENRY JACKSON HUNT —FIRST DETROIT MAYOR TO

DIE IN OFFICE

Henry J. Hunt, Mayor of Detroit in 1826

Henry Jackson Hunt (1788-1826) was a businessman who was born September 14, 1788 in Watertown, Massachusetts. He was the eldest son of a Revolutionary War Colonel, Thomas Hunt, who served in the Battle of Lexington and was wounded at the Battle of Bunker Hill. Thomas and family moved to Fort Wayne, Indiana, and then on to Detroit with "Mad" Anthony Wayne's army in 1800.

Thomas Hunt was transferred to St. Louis in 1805 and died in Belle Foutain, Missouri, in August 1809. This left Henry the "head of the family." His mother Eunice and young Henry were left to raise his ten other children.

Henry J. Hunt married Ann McIntosh from Canada in 1811 and they had no children (perhaps because after helping raise eight brothers and two sisters, Henry didn't care to have any children). But Hunt's brother Samuel named his son Henry

Jackson Hunt after Mayor Hunt. The nephew Henry Hunt became a famous Brigadier General in the Civil War.

Upon the end of the war, Henry resigned his commission and opened a general store. He also practiced law with his brother-in-law Major Abraham Edwards. Henry's sister Ruth had married Major Abraham Edwards who was the deputy quartermaster of Detroit during the War of 1812. Hunt continued to start businesses and successfully owned several mercantile and real estate enterprises.

Partnership With Lewis Cass

One of Hunt's businesses was a grist mill, which he owned in partnership with Michigan Territorial Governor Lewis Cass. The mill was powered by a treadmill worked by oxen and was located on the the outskirts of the city at the edge of the Cass farm. (Lewis Cass once remarked that Henry Hunt and his wife Ann were the "handsomest couple in Detroit.")

In 1815 and 1816 Hunt was appointed one of the Wayne County Court Judges, and in 1817 he served as Detroit City Assessor. In 1818 Hunt's father-in-law William "Angus" McIntosh moved to Scotland when through a series of unexpected deaths he became the Earl of Moy of Scotland! McIntosh left Henry as a director of the Bank of Michigan.

Hunt became a trustee of the University of Michigan in 1821 and helped to organize the "Protestant Society." In 1819 he was a delegate to Congress. He became one of the "Trustees of the Corporation of Detroit" in 1823.

In 1826 Hunt was elected Mayor of Detroit as a Democrat, defeating William Woodbridge 105 to 92 for the two-year term. (Woodbridge went on to be a Michigan Senator and Governor.) Detroit's population was about 2,000 in 1826.

Becomes First Mayor to Die in Office

Unfortunately, Hunt died of cholera on September 15, 1826 before he could complete the mayoral term. He was the first Mayor to die in office. Jonathan Kearsley, the City Recorder, executed the duties of the mayor upon Hunt's death until the next annual election.

Hunt was thought at the time to have contracted cholera by entering a cemetery chiefly occupied by cholera victims. Although the likelihood of this is debatable, the cemetery in question was probably the City Cemetery, also called the Clinton Street Cemetery, at Gratiot and Clinton Street. These bodies were removed to Elmwood later on, and the plot of land is where the Eastern Market is now. Henry's wife Ann lived until 1856, and she is buried in Elmwood Cemetery, right across from the chapel.

Henry J. Hunt's autograph is the rarest of all Detroit mayors, with only one known signature surviving. Many old sources incorrectly call him "Henry I. Hunt" due to the way he signed his middle intial. Hunt Street in Detroit is named for him.

C HAPTER FIVE— JONATHAN KEARSLEY —THIRTY YEARS AT THE SAME JOB

Jonathan Kearsley (1786-1859) first became Mayor of Detroit due to Henry Jackson Hunt's untimely death from cholera in September 1826.

Kearsley was born in Middletown, Pennsylvania on August 20, 1786 and went to Washington (now called Washington and Jefferson) College in 1811.

Loses Leg in War of 1812

The next year the War of 1812 began and Kearsley joined up as a First Lieutenant in the Second Artillery Corps. He rose to the rank of Major and fought in the Battle of Stoney Creek, the Battle of Crysler's Farm, and the Battle of Chippewa, which followed the Capture of Fort Erie. It was during the Battle of Chippewa that he was wounded in the leg and had to have it amputated. The operation was done poorly, and Kearsley suffered pain for the rest of his life.

In 1814 he was appointed Collector of Internal Revenue. In

57

1815 he married Margaret Hetich and they had three children. In Virginia he held the title of Collector of Revenue Taxes from 1817-1819. He moved to Detroit and became the Receiver of Public Monies, an office he held for a total of thirty years. When Margaret died he married Rachel Valentine.

After being appointed to fill out Henry J. Hunt's 1826 term, Kearsley was elected in his own right in 1829. He served on the Board of Trustees of the University of Michigan from 1827-1837, and then after the college charter was re-organized, he served on the Board of Regents from 1838 until 1852. He was defeated by 541 votes for mayoral reelection by Whig candidate DeGarmo Jones in 1839.

After he died on August 31, 1859 at the age of 73, the Kearsley Community School District was named for him. In Genesee County, Kearsley Township was also named for him. He was buried in Elmwood Cemetery next to his second wife Rachel Valentine, who he predeceased by just six months.

John Biddle and his wife Eliza Falconer Biddle (Portraits by Thomas Sully, 1818), John was Mayor of Detroit 1827-1828.

C HAPTER SIX
—JOHN BIDDLE
—PENNSYLVANIA
NOBILITY

John Biddle (1792-1859) was the fourth mayor of Detroit under the 1824 charter. He was born in Philadelphia, PA, the son of Hannah and Charles Biddle, and graduated from Princeton College in New Jersey. He was from a well-known and prominent Pennsylvania family, known for its military officers and political figures. He was the second mayor in a row born in Pennsylvania, the same as Jonathan Kearsley.

Like many early Detroit mayors, Biddle served in the military. In his case, he was in the U.S. Army during the War of 1812. Upon enlisting, he was promoted to Second Lieutenant and in March 1813 was promoted to First Lieutenant.

Serving mostly on the Niagara front, Biddle was promoted to Captain of the 42nd Infantry in October 1813 and became assistant inspector general with the rank of Major from 1817 to 1821. He was the Commander for Fort Shelby in Detroit for a short time. He was often referred to as Major

Biddle after his military service. In fact, it says "Major" on his tombstone. He had a little trouble in 1820 when he was convicted of the assault of Thomas Vickery and fined fifteen dollars.

Indian Agent, Paymaster, Register of the Land for the Michigan Territory

Biddle left the military and accepted a position as Indian Agent and Paymaster at Green Bay, Wisconsin in 1821. In 1823 he moved back to Detroit as Register of the Land for the Michigan Territory. He continued in this position until Michigan achieved statehood in 1837.

While he was still Register of the Land for the Michigan Territory, he became Mayor of Detroit in 1827 and 1828. While he was Mayor, Detroit's county, Wayne was divided into townships. They were: Brownstown, Bucklin, Ecorse, Hamtramck, Huron, Manguagon, Plymouth Springwells, and Detroit.

One of the few remaining, intact land offices such as the one Biddle worked at is in White Pigeon, Michigan.

He was succeeded as Mayor by Jonathan Kearsley. Biddle then served as a Delegate from the Territory of Michigan to the 21st Congress of the U.S. from 1829 until 1831. He was Detroit's first mayor from the Whig Party.

Biddle ran unsuccessfully as a member of the Whig Party for the U.S. Senate and for the Michigan governorship in 1835 but became Speaker of the Michigan House of Representatives in 1841. He was also a Trustee of the University of Michigan. He served on various civic committees, including a stint as President of the Historical Society of Michigan in 1837.

Founding of Wyandotte

He and his wife, Eliza Falconer, had four children. They spent a lot of time on the 1,800 acres (according to some accounts, 2,200) south of Detroit which Biddle acquired in 1818. It had been the site of a Native-American village, Maquaqua. Biddle built a large estate on the land that was finished in 1835. He named the estate "Wyandotte" for the Indian tribe that once dwelled in the area. This became the name of the surrounding town founded in 1854. The Eureka Iron Corporation bought the Biddle land and platted it, forming the Village of Wyandotte. The main road through Wyandotte is named Biddle Street.

President of the Michigan Central Railroad and Owner of the Biddle House

John Biddle was the President of the Michigan Central Railroad and the first President of the Farmers' and Mechanics' Bank from 1829 to 1837. In 1851 Biddle commissioned a hotel to be built on the busy corner of Randolph Street and Jefferson Avenue, the former site of General William Hull's residence. The hotel was named the Biddle House and for many years was the most elegant of Detroit's hotels with many famous guests, including General Ulysses Grant, President Andrew Johnson, and Admiral David Farragut. Later, it was used as one of the nation's first auto showrooms by William Metzger.

Different views of the Biddle House on Jefferson Avenue in Detroit, 1850s and 1860s

In 1826, John Biddle retired to his Wyandotte estate and also spent time at another estate of his up north in St. Louis, Michigan. Additionally, the family had a home in Pennsylvania and often travelled to Paris, France. In 1859, the Biddles went to White Sulphur Springs, in what is now West Virginia, for Eliza's health. John Biddle died there in August and was returned to Detroit to be buried in Elmwood Cemetery. Biddle Street in Detroit was named for him.

JOHN BIDDLE
MAJ 42 US INF
AIG PA
WAR OF 1812
MAR 2 1792   AUG 21 1859

John Biddle's monuments in Elmwood Cemetery

Alan Naldrett

Marshal Chapin, Mayor of Detroit in 1831

C HAPTER SEVEN —DR. MARSHALL CHAPIN—PROPRIETER OF DETROIT'S FIRST DRUG STORE

Marshall Chapin (1798-1838) was born in Bernardston, Massachusetts on February 27, 1798, and was one of nine children of Dr. Caleb Chapin and his wife Mary. When the family moved to New Caledonia, New York, Marshall went to Geneva Academy and received a medical degree in 1819.

Chapin lived briefly in Buffalo, New York, where he studied medicine with an uncle, and then moved to Detroit and opened the town's first drug store, located on the south side of Jefferson near Griswold. He shared the building with John Palmer, who sold dry goods.

Chapin also started a successful practice in Detroit as a private physician. In 1823 he married Mary Crosby and they had four children together—Louisa, Helen, Charles and Marshall. Also in 1823 they built a large house on Woodbridge Street, between Randolph and Bates Streets (by some accounts, Brush and Beaubien).

Chapin later moved to Fort Street, buying the whole block between Cass and First Streets. He purchased the large lot for $105 from the land office and built a house.

During the 1820s there were about 900 people living in Detroit, with most houses located on either Woodbridge Street or along the Detroit River. Savage Indians and wolves kept the townspeople always on the alert.

Official Detroit City Physician

He was appointed the physician for Fort Shelby by Lewis Cass and was a city alderman in 1826 and 1827. The alderman was the second highest office in city government, after the mayor. During the two major cholera outbreaks in Detroit in 1832 and 1834, he was appointed the City Physician. The first epidemic in 1832 was started by 200 infected sailors who had just come in from the East Coast. A major amount of the population succumbed to the disease. Chapin never took payment for his physician services from people to whom it would be a hardship.

In 1831 Chapin was elected Mayor of Detroit as a member of the Whig Party. During his mayoral term the population was about 2,300—the 35th largest in the U.S.

In 1832 Chapin was the Chief Engineer for the Detroit Fire Department and was kept busy during the Cholera epidemic. In 1833 he was again elected Mayor of Detroit. While he was Mayor in 1833 mail began to be available from the East Coast on a daily basis.

Detroit's First Riot

Also, in 1833, the "Blackburn incident" occurred. A runaway black slave and his wife, Thornton and Ruth Blackburn, were living in Detroit when they were captured by a Kentucky bounty hunter who was going to return them to the Kentucky farm they had escaped from. Many black Detroiters armed themselves and helped the couple escape jail and flee to Ontario, Canada.

After surviving two cholera epidemics, Chapin died of heart disease at the age of 40 on August 25, 1838 and was buried in Elmwood Cemetery. His drug store was operated by his sons after Chapin's death. The business survived into the 1880's. Chapin Street in Detroit was probably named for Marshal Chapin, although some sources say Austin or David Chapin.

Marshal Chapin Gravesite in Elmwood Cemetery

Area of Cass Expedition of 1831 where Trowbridge was Recording Secretary.

Charles C. Trowbridge, Mayor of Detroit in 1834.

C HAPTER EIGHT —CHARLES TROWBRIDGE —EXPLORER, BUSINESSMAN, AND MAYOR

Charles Christopher Trowbridge (1800-1883) was a part of Lewis Cass's Expedition of 1820. This was undertaken because Cass wanted to demonstrate that Michigan was not the swampy wasteland it was said to be. One widely-read source claimed that Michigan only had one acre in 1,000 suitable for farming and Cass was happy to prove this information wrong with his expedition.

In 1837 Trowbridge was one of the people who influenced Michigan to end the Toledo War by giving Toledo to Ohio in return for the Upper Peninsula. From his travels, Trowbridge knew that the Upper Peninsula had many mineral and lumber resources.

Charles Christopher Trowbridge was born December 29, 1800 in Albany, New York, to a Revolutionary War veteran, Luther Trowbridge, who fought at the Battle of Lexington and the Battle of Saratoga. Charles was the youngest of six children born to Luther and his wife Elizabeth.

In 1813 Trowbridge was apprenticed to businessman Horatio Ross of Owego, New York to learn merchandising—until Ross's business failed in 1818. Trowbridge decided to check out the Michigan area and ended up in Detroit. He secured a federal appointment as a Deputy United States Marshal and a Deputy Clerk of Courts for Michigan. In 1820 he worked on the decennial census.

With such a quick and prodigious rise, Trowbridge caught the notice of soon-to-be Territorial Governor, Lewis Cass. Cass was tired of hearing about the bad reputation suffered by the Territory of Michigan. This was widely thought to be spread by soldiers stationed around the area. For instance, in the Fort Saginaw area in 1822, the fort was abandoned after just one year. The fort commander, Major Daniel Baker, complained about the pestilent swamp, mosquitos, and malaria, and ended his rant with, "Nothing but Indians, muskrats, and bull frogs could possibly subsist here." He was echoing what previous pioneers had claimed about Michigan, pioneers who had never traveled inland much beyond the lakefronts.

Lewis Cass knew from the early maps that the whole area of Michigan was surrounded by water. Water transportation was the main way to get around back in the 1800s, yet Ohio, which had no Great Lakes or other comparable features (the only large waterway was the Ohio River), became a state in 1803. Unfortunately, in the 1820s Michigan, which is surrounded by water, was not even close to attracting enough settlers to qualify for statehood. This was mainly due to the "pestilent swamp" reputation.

Trowbridge Accompanies Cass on 1820 Expedition

In 1820, Lewis Cass and crew, including Henry Schoolcraft, and future Mayor of Detroit Charles Trowbridge, explored the area between the Great Lakes and the tributaries of the Mississippi River. Trowbridge served as Cass's secretary and Schoolcraft was the mineralogist. Their explorations included the Upper Peninsula, and parts of Wisconsin and Minnesota. They discovered numerous riches in the natural resources, including the minerals and lumber of the area. At one point they viewed the Ontonagon Boulder, a giant boulder of native copper, revered by the Native Americans. The discovery of the copper boulder by the Cass Expedition helped start Michigan's copper mining boom. The boulder is now in the Smithsonian Museum in Washington, D.C.

The Ontonagon Boulder was visited by the Cass Expedition in Michigan's Upper Peninsula

When Cass returned and spread the news about his expedition, more settlers started to come to Michigan. In 1825, the Erie Canal opened, and a flood of people moved to Michigan from the New York area.

In 1834 Trowbridge was elected Mayor of Detroit (with no opposition) as a member of the National Republican Party. He arranged for the construction of Detroit's first city hall. It was built on Woodward at Cadillac Square. It lasted until the 1870s, when in 1877 a new building was erected. This was also the year of the start of Detroit's second cholera epidemic in which many Detroiters died.

Detroit's first real estate tax was imposed at this time and a sewer system was planned. Limits were placed on the number of stores selling liquor in the city. By 1835 Michigan's population had surpassed 60,000, the magic number needed to apply for statehood.

Trowbridge Suggests Exchange of Toledo for the Upper Peninsula

Ohio blocked Michigan's bid for statehood because Michigan would not cede the area of Toledo (then named Port Lawrence) to Ohio. By January 1837 Michigan was tired of the border dispute and ready to bargain. Lucius Lyon, who with Trowbridge had been on the 1820 Cass Expedition, was also aware of the natural resources of the Upper Peninsula, and with the support of Trowbridge, successfully suggested that Michigan be given the Upper Peninsula in return for giving up the rights to the mouth of the Maumee River, which became Toledo.

Trowbridge befriended and studied the Native Americans he met along the way and could speak the Cherokee language fluently. He became an assistant in what was then called the "Indian Department" for the federal government and helped negotiate a treaty with the Menominee and Winnebago Indian tribes.

Charles Trowbridge married Catherine Sibley, the daughter of prominent citizen and first Mayor of Detroit, Solomon Sibley. Trowbridge built what is now the oldest residence in Detroit at 1380 E. Jefferson Street. Twenty-two years later the same families would build the second-oldest residence, the Sibley House, down the street at 976 E. Jefferson. The families are all buried in the same area of Elmwood Cemetery.

Founder of Allegan, Michigan

Trowbridge, besides helping to develop Detroit, was also one of the founders of Allegan, Michigan. He had business interests in banking and railroads and in 1833 he was the alderman of Detroit, and in 1834, during the cholera epidemic, was elected Mayor. He quit abruptly during his term and Andrew Mack finished it. During this time George Porter, the Territorial Governor, contracted and died of cholera in one of his infrequent visits to the area.

The Trowbridge House at 1380 E. Jefferson, the oldest residential house in Detroit.

In 1835 Trowbridge ran as the Whig Party candidate in the first Michigan gubernatorial election (before Michigan was even a bona fide state) but lost to Democrat Stevens T. Mason. He became President of the Michigan State Bank in 1844, until the bank was dissolved in 1853.　　　Trowbridge was President of the Detroit and Milwaukee Railway Company, and a Director of the Detroit and St. Joseph Railway Company. He also served as President of the Board of Public Charities, as well as on the boards of other charitable organizations.

He died in 1883 at the age of 82 and was interred in Elmwood Cemetery. Trowbridge Avenue in Detroit is named for him.

Charles Trowbridge gravesite in Elmwood Cemetery.

Andrew Mack, Mayor of Detroit in 1834

CHAPTER NINE —ANDREW MACK—MAYOR OF DETROIT AND MACK'S PLACE

Andrew Mack (1780-1854) was born November 18, 1780 in New London, Connecticut, and became a sailor while still young, sailing around the world *three* times as captain of his own ship!

He purchased a herd of Merino sheep in 1808, shipped them from Spain, and herded them from the East Coast westward to Cincinnati, Ohio. (Merino sheep are considered by many to have the softest and finest wool of any sheep.) When he arrived in Cincinnati he established a wool factory and a hotel.

During the War of 1812 he became a Captain and then a Colonel and so was often called "Colonel Mack" for the rest of his life. When the war was over he returned to Cincinnati and was elected a member of the Cincinnati City Council. He was a Senator in the Ohio State Assembly in 1827-1828 and ran unsuccessfully for Mayor of Cincinnati in 1829.

In 1829, President Andrew Jackson appointed Mack the Customs Collector for Detroit. He held this post for ten years and became quite wealthy. In 1831, he was part of a consortium that purchased the *Democratic Free Press and Intelligencer* from the original publisher. Mack bought the equipment and presses of the *Oakland Chronicle* and moved it to Detroit. The newspaper became the *Detroit Free Press.*

Brief Term as Mayor of Detroit

In 1830 Mack opened what was long considered the most fashionable hotel in Detroit, the Mansion House Hotel. He was especially lauded for the compassion he showed cholera victims, when so many other establishments were closed to them.

He married Amelia and had a son, Andrew Augustus Mack,

and an adopted daughter.

In 1834, during the midst of the cholera epidemic, Mayor Trowbridge abruptly quit. Mack won the run-off election and became Mayor of Detroit. During his short term the Common Council voted to move to better quarters until a new City Hall could be built and also decided to hire an accountant to prepare a bookkeeping system for the city. Also, the "city watch" was disbanded after several its members were either neglecting their duties or showing up intoxicated.

While Mayor, in March 1835 Mack presided over a public meeting that protested Ohio's efforts to claim the area around the "Toledo Strip." The Toledo Strip was the area around present day Toledo, Ohio that was ceded to the Michigan Territory in the Northwest Ordinance. Ohio had claimed ownership over the area in its 1806 State Constitution.

While Mayor, Mack was nominated by the Democratic-Republican Party for Michigan Governor but lost to Stevens Mason. Mack unsuccessfully ran for re-election for Detroit mayor in 1836 and 1837. In 1839 he was elected to represent Wayne County in the Michigan State Legislature.

Looking for a change of venue, Andrew Mack moved to what is now the Marysville, Michigan area. He opened a general store which he called Mack's Place. He bought a sawmill on the St. Clair River that had been built by partners Meldrum and Park on Meldrum's Creek. After they sold the mill to Andrew Mack, the creek was known as Mack's Creek. Mack also opened a fuel stop for freighters on the St. Clair River.

Mack's Place became a center of commerce for the area and was given a post office from 1849 until Mack's death on July 12, 1854. The post office was then transferred to Vicksburg and renamed Marysville.

When Mack died, he and his wife Amelia were buried on their property which now adjoins the Riverlawn Cemetery. The portion they are buried on is now part of the Marysville Golf Course. There is a Mack Road in both Detroit and Marysville. Some accounts say the one in Detroit is named for Andrew, others say it's for John Mack of Hamtramck.

Andrew and Amelia Mack gravesite on Marysville Golf Course.

Alan Naldrett

Levi Cook, Mayor of Detroit 1835-1836

C HAPTER TEN— LEVI COOK— TOLEDO WAR MAYOR

Levi Cook (1792-1866) was probably the most civic-minded mayor of Detroit. He was born December 16, 1792 in Bellingham, Massachusetts, the son of a farmer. He taught school in Massachusetts and then entered the fur trade in Buffalo, New York. He came to Detroit in 1815 where he taught school for a year.

In his first year in Detroit, he began his public service by becoming a Trustee of the city while still working as a school-teacher. The next year he managed a general store. In 1822 he became the City Treasurer, and from 1824 to 1827 he was a Wayne County Commissioner. He was a Colonel in the Michigan Militia during the Indian Wars and became a director of the Farmers and Mechanics Bank in 1829. He became the President of the bank from 1838 to 1845.

He opened an unsuccessful grocery business, but then started a successful dry goods business with his brother Orville. He married Eliza Sanderson, but the couple had no children. Having no children of his own to educate, Cook paid for many children of his cohorts to continue higher education.

In 1827 and 1828 he was the Superintendent of the City Poor and was also Alderman-at-Large in 1828. He was Treasurer of the Michigan Territory from 1830 to 1836 and was also Chief Engineer of the Detroit Fire Department during the same period. In 1834 he was Supervisor of Detroit.

Levi's friends always marveled at Cook's propensity to serve in various municipal offices. "Where most people complain" one of Cook's friends noted, "Levi just runs for office and changes it." Cook held more than 20 offices in Detroit and Michigan government and often occupied four or five at a time.

In 1832 he became Mayor as a member of the National Republican (Whig) Party. While mayor he still served as the City Clerk. He ran unopposed for mayor in 1832 and served during the first cholera epidemic suffered by Detroiters. In the 1832 epidemic, popular and notable Catholic Priest Father Gabriel Richards died.

Mayor Cook, with city physician Marshall Chapin, helped establish guidelines to prevent cholera from taking hold in the city. They issued regulations for ship and boat traffic on the Detroit River. Passengers could not get within 100 feet of the harbor without being checked by the Detroit Public Health Department.

Residents were instructed to whitewash their houses, clean yards, and fill or drain stagnant water holes or pools to prevent the spread of cholera.

Despite the precautions, cholera was said to be spread from the returning troops of 1832's Black Hawk War, a skirmish between Indian Chief Black Hawk and the Sauks, Meskwakis, and Kickapoo Indian tribes, vs. the U.S. It was established that returning troops on the steamer the *Henry Clay* released the cholera bacteria into the city, despite the city's efforts to prevent it. A sailor jumped ship into the city. Eventually, cholera would kill 7 to 10% of Detroit's population in 1832.

A lot of residents thought the cholera was caused by a "miasma" in the air, which they combatted by burning barrels of pitch at every street corner. This added to the macabre atmosphere, as men with carts went through the streets calling for people to "bring out their dead."

Cook established standing committees on claims and accounts, ways and means, fires, streets, and health in 1832. Cook was re-elected in 1835, besting Andrew Mack, and 1836, beating John Biddle. He was mayor during the years of the "Toledo War" and led the fight to protect Detroit from foreign militias.

During his mayoral term in 1836 the Detroit Municipal Water Works Department was established, with a new city sewer system. The same year a new City Hall was opened with an open-air market on the ground floor. How many City Halls can boast an open-air market?

During his final mayoral term in 1836, streets were required to have street signs, the first underground sewer was built, and in September 1836 the Common Council drew up a new charter with revised bylaws and ordinances for the city.

On January 26, 1837, Cook led Detroit's celebrations when Michigan finally became an official state.

Elected to the House of Representatives

After being Mayor, in 1838 Cook was elected to serve in the U.S. House of Representatives, representing Wayne County. As a businessman, he became a Director of the Farmer's and Mechanic's Bank in 1829 and served as President of the bank from 1838 to 1845. In 1845 he became President of the Bank of St. Clair.

He was predeceased by his wife Eliza when he died on December 2, 1866. They had no children. He was buried in Elmwood Cemetery. Cook Street in Detroit is named for him.

Alan Naldrett

Levi Cook gravesite in Elmwood Cemetery, Detroit.

Henry Howard, Mayor of Detroit

C HAPTER ELEVEN —HENRY HOWARD— MERCHANT MAYOR

Henry Howard (1791-1878) was born September 15, 1801 in Hinsdale, Massachusetts and later moved to Geneva, New York with Ralph Wadhams. He entered into a partnership with Wadhams to form a dry goods business, Howard and Wadhams. It was located on the "Smart Block" of Detroit at Jefferson and Woodward, opening in 1823. They also had a warehouse at the foot of Randolph Street.

Looking to get into the lumber business, Howard and Wadhams bought land and a sawmill on the Black River called Clyde Mills, in St. Clair County. Wadhams moved to the area to manage the business and a small settlement, called Wadhams, grew around the mill. The settlement is still there.

However, by 1835 the mill was in the red, having accrued $30,000 worth of debt. On top of the mill's struggles, the Panic of 1837 hit. The mill went into receivership and was sold to its creditors in 1839.

During this time Henry Howard continued to live in Detroit. He was City Alderman in 1833 and 1834, and along with Charles Trowbridge and Territorial Secretary Stevens Mason, worked on a committee dedicated to limiting the number of places licensed to serve alcohol in the city.

Howard and Wadhams Dry Goods Store c1843 in the "Smart Block" in Detroit

Howard became Mayor in 1837 as a Democrat. This was the year of the Panic of 1837 and the year Michigan was finally declared a state. He defeated Whig candidate Marshall Chapin, 682 to 411. The population of Detroit was about 7,000 at that time.

Not long after he was elected mayor a smallpox epidemic broke out in the city. The Common Council passed a resolution to provide everyone with smallpox vaccine who couldn't afford it.

During this time, a "city watch" of 200 armed men was set up by Mayor Howard and Governor Mason to guard against public insurrection during the 1837-1838 "Patriot War" at the Michigan-Canadian border. Problems handled by the city watch included false fire alarms, weapons discharged in the city limits, and other civil difficulties. The city adopted a policy of strict neutrality on the Patriot War, however there was a battle in Windsor, Ontario, in Canada, right across the Detroit River from Detroit. The campaign to add Ontario to the U.S. petered out by 1839.

Because of the Panic of 1837, the Common Council issued $10,000 in small script to be issued and $5,000 in paper script to meet the city's debts.

In 1837 the route for the Detroit and St. Joseph Railroad (forerunner of the Michigan Central Railroad) was approved. In 1838 the route for the Detroit and Pontiac Railroad was approved.

One of the ordinances passed during the Howard administration and signed by Howard were prohibitions against occupying any part of the street, or erecting a tent or shanty, shop-table, or other tables or obstructions, for the purposes of retail sales of liquor, cakes, pies, or other food, or merchandise. A fine of $5.00 for each offense would be charged.

First Michigan Treasurer

Howard became Michigan's first State Treasurer, from 1836 to 1839 and State Auditor General from 1839 to 1840. He was a Democrat while in Detroit but switched to the Republican Party later in life. He and Andrew Mack were the only Democratic Mayors of Detroit between the years of 1831 to 1842, the nine others were all members of the Whig Party.

He moved to Buffalo, New York in 1840 to become Treasurer of the Buffalo Savings Bank, a position he held for thirty years. He died in Buffalo on July '15, 1878 at the age of 76.

Augustus Porter, Mayor of Detroit 1838-1839

C HAPTER TWELVE —AUGUSTUS S. PORTER— PREFERRED SENATOR TO MAYOR

Augustus Seymour Porter (1798-1872) was born January 18, 1798 in Canandaigua, New York to a family that were well-to-do and prominent in the U.S. His uncle was Peter Buell Porter (1773–1844), the United States Secretary of War under John Quincy Adams.

Moved to Detroit from New York to Practice Law

Porter first attended Canandaigua Academy and then graduated from Union College in Schenectady, New York in 1818. He practiced law in New York until 1827, when he moved to Detroit. He was admitted to the Michigan bar and began to practice law there.

Resigns as Mayor of Detroit to Run for Senate

In 1830 he became the Recorder for Detroit. In 1837, the year Michigan became a state, he was the Treasurer of the

Michigan Pioneer Society. In 1838 he successfully ran for Mayor of Detroit as a Whig. He resigned as Mayor in March 1839 to successfully run for the U.S. Senate, replacing Lucius Lyon and becoming the second person to represent Michigan in the Senate. He served from 1840 to 1845. Asher Bates replaced Porter as Acting Mayor of Detroit.

Porter married his first wife, Sarah Mansfield, in 1822. She died giving birth to their only child in 1824. The child also died shortly after his mother. In 1832 Porter married another Sarah, Sarah Barnard, and they had two daughters.

In 1848 Porter relocated to Niagara Falls, New York, to a residence owned by his father. He died there in 1872 and was buried in Oakwood Cemetery in Niagara Falls.   There is a Porter Street in Detroit, possibly named for him or early Governor George Porter.

Augustus Porter burial memorial in Niagara Falls, New York.

Asher B. Bates, Mayor of Detroit 1839

CHAPTER THIRTEEN—ASHER B. BATES—SHORTEST MAYORAL TERM

When Augustus Porter left his Detroit Mayoral office to serve in the U.S. Senate, he had one month left on his term, March to April 1839. Asher Brown Bates (May 2, 1810 – June 1, 1873) became Acting Mayor to fill out the term until the next election.

Bates was born May 2, 1810 in Le Roy, New York, in Genesee County. Like his predecessor, Augustus Porter, Bates attended Union College in New York and graduated in 1828. He moved to Detroit in 1831 and was admitted to the bar. He served as Detroit's Justice of the Peace, City Attorney, and City Recorder. He was also an agent for the *Protection Insurance Company* of Hartford, Connecticut.

He had a few law firms and partners, the first one being *Farnsworth and Bates*. He married Lucille Beals in 1832; she died in 1839. He then married Elizabeth Judd in 1843.

Detroit Mayor for a Month

In 1839 Bates finished the Mayoral term of Augustus Porter, who had been elected to the U.S. Senate. The term was for only one month, putting Bates into the running for the record-holder of shortest Mayoral Term for the City of Detroit. He was a member of the Whig Party.

Bates briefly moved to Jackson County, Michigan, and then in 1848 he moved to Hawaii. He was the Attorney General for Hawaii and served on the Privy Council 1849-1853, and as an attorney for the King of Hawaii (Hawaii was still a monarchy). He was the Registrar of Conveyances from 1849 to 1859, and a Notary Public for the Island of Oahu.

Although he had become a citizen of the Kingdom of Hawaii, he moved to San Francisco, California in 1863 to become a bankruptcy judge. He died of leprosy (contracted while living in Hawaii) in San Francisco in 1873. He was buried in Buell Cemetery in LeRoy, Genesee County, New York.

Asher

B. Bates in Buell Cemetery, Genesee County, New York

De Garmo Jones, Mayor of Detroit 1839

C HAPTER FOURTEEN —DE GARMO JONES—THE MAYOR WHO BUILT THE CAPITOL BUILDING

De Garmo Jones (1787-1846) was born in Albany, New York on November 11, 1787. He worked providing provisions to the troops during the War of 1812 as a "sutler," a person who maintains a store on a military base. It was then that he passed through Detroit with General William Henry Harrison.

Jones took up permanent residence in Detroit in 1818, arriving on the steamship *Walk-in-the-Water*, the first steamship on the Detroit River. When Jones married New Yorker Catherine Annin in 1819, she moved to Detroit. They had seven children.

Jones Developed Many Businesses

The De Garmo Jones family purchased a farm between

what is now 3rd and 4th Street. Besides the farm, Jones had wide-ranging business interests. He was one of the first directors of the railway company that became the Michigan Central Railroad, and one of the first stockholders of the Bank of Michigan. He owned and developed copper mines near Lake Superior, and had interests in warehousing, shipping, and construction companies. He erected the first plaster mill in the state. A company he had an interest in built the first Michigan Capitol Building in Detroit in 1832.

The first Michigan Capitol Building was a brick structure, built in the Greek Revival Style, with a portico (porch) and Ionic columns. The central tower rose to 140 feet and could be seen all over the city. It was first known as the Territorial Capitol Building and was located at the corner of Griswold and State Street, now Capitol Park. When the capital city of Michigan was changed to Lansing, the building became the Union School, Detroit's first high school and library.

Michigan Capitol Building in Detroit in later years when it was the Capitol Union School

Jones served as Detroit's Alderman in 1827, 1830, and 1838, and Michigan Adjutant-General in 1829. In 1839 he was elected Mayor of Detroit as a Whig, defeating Jonathan Kearsley. In 1840 and 1841 Jones finished his public service as a member of the Michigan State Senate.

When Jones died in Detroit on November 14, 1846 at the age of 59, his estate was appraised at more than $250,000. His able widow Catherine invested wisely, and when she died in 1865, the value of the estate had doubled to over $500,000. There was at one time a Jones Drive in Detroit, but it has since been renamed Plaza Drive.

De Garmo Jones family monument and personal monument in Elmwood Cemetery.

ZINA PITCHER
(From a family portrait)

Dr. Zina Pitcher, Mayor of Detroit 1840, 1841, and 1843

C HAPTER FIFTEEN —ZINA PITCHER —M.D. AND MAYOR

Dr. Zina Pitcher (1797-1872) was born in Washington County, New York, at Fort Edwards on April 12, 1797. He went to the "common schools," the public schools of the day (as opposed to private or parochial schools). At the age of twenty he began medical studies at Castleton School and then continued at Woodstock, Vermont, where he graduated with a medical degree in 1822. It was said he used Indian burial sites to study anatomy.

In 1824 he married Ann Sheldon, who was from a prominent Kalamazoo family. They had two children, Nathaniel and Rose. When Ann died in 1864, Pitcher married Emily Backus from Rochester, New York. Their only child, Sidney, died in infancy.

Becomes Surgeon of the U.S. Army

President James Madison appointed Pitcher Assistant Surgeon in the U.S. Army in 1823. President Andrew Jackson promoted him to Surgeon in 1829. In 1835 he was named President of the Army Medical Board. Because of these appointments he became well-traveled throughout the United

States. He worked among the various Indian tribes and authored many journal articles on the value of various Indian medicines.

In 1836 Dr. Pitcher moved to Detroit and in 1837, until 1852, was a member of the Board of Regents of the University of Michigan. He was instrumental in organizing the medical department at U of M.

Mayor of Detroit Three Times

In 1840, 1841, and 1843 he was elected Mayor of Detroit. The population of Detroit was over 9,000 persons at that time.

During his 1843 term, the Michigan Convention of Colored Citizens met in Detroit and the Underground Railroad intensified their involvement in the area. Over a 30-year period, it was estimated that over 45,000 slaves were assisted in escaping to freedom in Canada through Michigan.

Detroit was a major nexus for escaped slaves to go through on their way to freedom in Canada, where the U.S. Fugitive Slave Act of 1850 wasn't in effect. The act required slaves to be returned when found, even if in a free state (like Michigan).

In 2001 the Gateway to Freedom monument was installed in De-

troit's Hart Plaza.

The companion to the Gateway to Freedom monument is the Tower of Freedom, located across the Detroit River in Windsor. Both are by the same sculptor, Ed Dwight.

The Tower to Freedom in Windsor, Ontario by Ed Dwight.

Abolitionists on the Underground Railroad had to be secretive. If caught helping slaves escape they could be fined heavily and imprisoned. A series of signals involving lamps and flags was devised. Houses would have secret rooms to hide the escaped slaves until they could be helped across the border. Two of the locations in Detroit were the First Congregational Church, and the Second Baptist Church, which has a tunnel leading to the bar next door. Detroit was often the most exciting stop on the Railroad, since it was usually the last stop before freedom.

Across the street from the Fort Street Presbyterian Church, this bar has a tunnel leading there. It was used to hide people in the Underground Railroad days, and to transport liquor during the Purple Gang days.

Dr. Pitcher was known as the "Father of Free Education" in Detroit and considered it his crowning achievement as Mayor. He had the Common Council petition the State Legislature for the right to have free public schools in Detroit.

In 1845 Dr. Pitcher was the Wayne County Physician and in 1847 the Detroit City Physician. From 1848 to 1867 Pitcher was the physician and surgeon for St. Mary's Hospital in Detroit, and from 1857 to 1861 he did the same for, and also oversaw the United States Marine Hospital in Detroit.

MARINE HOSPITAL.

U.S. Marine Hospital at the SW corner of Jefferson at Mt. Elliot, one of the hospitals Dr. Pitcher was at.

Throughout his civil career he kept his private practice as a physician and was well-regarded as such. He conducted medical research and had numerous scholarly papers published as well as founding a few medical journals. He was the tenth President of the American Medical Association (AMA). He also helped organize the State Insane Asylum at Kalamazoo.

He was lauded for his patience and kindness as well as his skills as a surgeon. When he died in 1872 he left a son and a daughter and had a street named for him in Detroit and Ann Arbor. The Detroit Pitcher Street was changed to Stimson Street in 1905 and Martin Luther King Drive in the late 1960s. There is a Pitcher Elementary School in Detroit named for him.

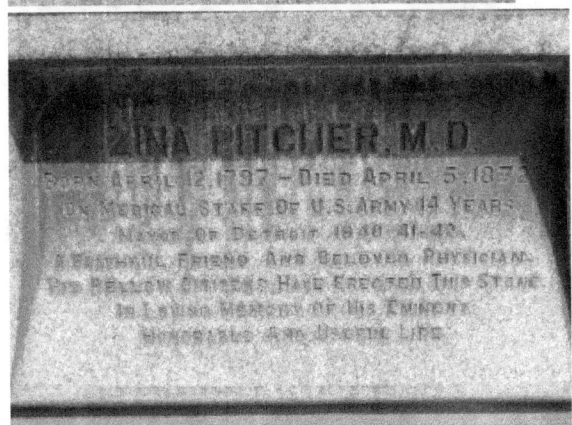

Zina Pitcher gravestone in Elmwood Cemetery.

Douglass Houghton (Courtesy of the University of Michigan), Mayor of Detroit 1842

C HAPTER SIXTEEN —DOUGLASS HOUGHTON—STATE GEOLOGIST AND DETROIT MAYOR

While Douglass Houghton (1809-1845) is probably better known for his explorations and geological efforts on behalf of Michigan, he also served one term as Mayor of Detroit in 1842.

Houghton was born in Troy, New York on September 21, 1809, to Judge Jacob Houghton and his wife, Mary. The family moved to Fredonia, New York, where Douglass grew up and developed an interest in science and geology. He did experiments and had slight scarring on his face from his early research into gunpowder. He earned a medical degree at Rensselaer Institute in 1829 and the next year started teaching there as an Assistant Professor of Chemistry and Natural History.

Comes to Detroit to Deliver Lectures and Decides to Stay

In November 1830 he arrived in Detroit to deliver a series of lectures. This was at the request of Lucius Lyon, later Michigan's first Senator. Houghton spoke in the Lecture Room of the Old Council House on Jefferson Avenue. The lectures were very popular, and Houghton subsequently moved to Detroit and became one of the most admired people in the city.

In 1831, he went with the federal expedition to find the source of the Missouri River as the surgeon and botanist. When he returned, later in 1831, he settled in Detroit and started a practice as a physician.

In 1833 he married his Fredonia sweetheart Harriet Stevens and they established their home at 19 Wayne Street in Detroit. They had three children—Hattie, Mary, and Douglass, Jr., over the next few years.

Douglass Houghton mineral-hunting in Michigan's Upper Peninsula.

As Doctor, Treated Cholera Victims Indiscriminately

In 1834 Houghton indiscriminately treated victims of the cholera epidemic, regardless of race or social class, at great risk to himself. Houghton worked with 3-time Detroit Mayor

Zina Pitcher. About one-eighth of the citizens of Detroit died because of the epidemic.

In 1837 Houghton was named the State Geologist for the State of Michigan, a position he held until his death. He was a member of the *National Institute* in Washington, the *Boston Society of Natural History,* and many other literary and scientific institutions. He used his geology, botany, and medical connections to promote the natural resources of Michigan and helped to bring commerce and business to the state. He became the second teacher employed by the University of Michigan.

Plaque in the Kewanee Peninsula honoring Houghton, who did a lot of exploring in the area.

In 1842 Houghton was, unbeknownst to him, elected Mayor of Detroit for the Democratic Party while he was away on expedition. Nominated without his knowledge, he was elected Mayor over Whig opponent John R. Williams, 624 to 474. Nevertheless, he served with distinction and consented to a second annual term in 1843. During his tenure, the Detroit Public School System began.

Houghton explored the Kewanee Peninsula and wrote extensively on it and the minerals of Michigan. He said about the life of an explorer:

> *"Wading the streams by day, tortured by swarms of mosqui-*

tos at night—often short of provisions, and often drenched by rain—were it not that courage is uplifted by the love of science, both for its own sake and the good it is to accomplish, the task of the pioneer explorer would be hard indeed."

Untimely Drowning Death

In 1845, Houghton drowned in Lake Superior, near the mouth of the Eagle River at the top of the Upper Peninsula, when his small boat capsized in a violent storm. His body washed to shore in May 1846 and was buried in Elmwood Cemetery. He was only 36 and was much mourned and missed.

Named for him is Houghton Lake, Houghton County, Douglass Houghton Falls, and the City of Houghton, home of Michigan Technological University, which is where Houghton donated his vast mineral collection. Also named for him is *Houghton's Goldenrod*, a plant which Houghton discovered in the Upper Peninsula during his 1839 expedition.

After Houghton's mayoral term, John R. Williams served his third, nonconsecutive term as Mayor.

The Houghton family plot in Elmwood Cemetery. Douglass, his wife, and three children are all buried there.

James A. Van Dyke, Mayor of Detroit 1847

C HAPTER SEVENTEEN —JAMES A. VAN DYKE —RAILROAD MAYOR

James A. Van Dyke (1813-1855) was born in Mercerberg, Pennsylvania on December 10, 1813, and graduated from Madison College in Union Town, Pennsylvania. He studied law in Chambersburg, Pennsylvania, and at Hagerstown and Baltimore, Maryland.

In 1834 he moved to Pittsburgh, Pennsylvania and then on to Detroit, where he was admitted to the Michigan bar after studying in the A.D. Fraser Law firm. He entered private law practice in 1835 with Charles W. Whipple until 1838, when Whipple became a Judge on the Supreme Court. Van Dyke then entered into a partnership with E.B. Harrington until Harrington died in 1844. Van Dyke then entered into partnership with H. H. Emmons until 1852. Van Dyke then became the attorney for the Michigan Central Railroad.

In 1835 and 1839 Van Dyke was appointed City Attorney for Detroit and in 1840 he was the Wayne County Prosecuting Attorney. He was a City Alderman in 1843 and 1844. One of his goals was to get the city on a sound financial basis, as he worked on the City Council's Ways and Means Committee.

Stabilized City Finances as Mayor

In 1847 he was elected Mayor of Detroit as a Whig. He felt that after his mayoral term he had succeeded in stabilizing the city's finances.

Described as a brilliant orator, Van Dyke was President of the Fire Department from 1847 to 1851 and was instrumental in its early organization. He was on the Board of the Detroit Water Commissioners from 1853 until his death on May 7, 1855. He was only 42 when he died and converted to Catholicism on his deathbed. Some of his children became priests and one became a lawyer.

Detroit and Macomb County's Van Dyke Avenue was named for him, as well as the defunct village of Van Dyke, now part of Warren, Michigan.

Capitalists, Clowns, and Crooks, Choir-boys, Cops and Clerks: The May-

Frederick Buhl, Mayor of Detroit in 1848

CHAPTER EIGHTEEN —FREDERICK BUHL—FIRST OF THE BUHL BROTHERS

Frederick Buhl (1806-1890) was the first of the Buhl brothers to be elected Mayor of Detroit. He was born in Butler County, Pennsylvania, on November 20, 1806, and went to Pittsburgh, hoping to learn the jewelry business at age 16. Unfortuneatly, he had to quit the trade due to ill health. He moved to Detroit in 1833.

His brother Christian moved to Detroit at the same time. Christian was trained in millinery or "hat making." The two brothers formed a partnership to sell hats, and then diversified by buying and selling furs as F & C H Buhl Co. They became one of the largest fur shippers in the country.

Becomes a Titan of Industry

As Detroit turned more to industry, so did the Buhl brothers. They founded the *Detroit Locomotive Works,* and then the *Buhl Iron Works,* later to become the *Detroit Copper and Brass firm.*

In 1868, the brothers turned to property development.

They built an attractive office building at Griswold and Congress Street in Detroit on the site where the parade grounds for Fort Shelby had been. It was a popular place for law firms to rent offices and the area became the foundation of the financial district.

By the third generation of the Buhl family, it was determined that a larger building would be more serviceable. In 1925 the old building was torn down and a 26-story skyscraper, known as the Buhl Building, was constructed in its place. It was built in the "cruciform" style to capture natural light and was designed by architect Wirt Rowland, also known for designing Detroit's art deco Guardian Building.

The Buhl Brothers partnership lasted for 20 years, until Christian retired in 1853. Frederick continued as F. Buhl and Co. until 1887, when his son Walter took over the business.

Frederick Buhl was one of the Directors of the Michigan State Bank, and of the Second National Bank of Detroit. He was President of the Fort Wayne & Elmwood Railway Co. and of Harper's Hospital. In 1847 he was one of the founders of the Merchant's Exchange and Board of Trade and President of the Board

In 1848 Buhl was elected Mayor of Detroit. This was the same year that the State Capitol was moved from Detroit to Lansing. Also built in 1848 was the Saints Peter and Paul Church, now the oldest, still extant, church in Detroit.

The Buhl Stamping Co. building in the 1840s.

Frederick Buhl was married to Matilda Beatty from his home county in Pennsylvania. Together they had six children. Buhl continued working at his enterprises until his death on May 12, 1890. He was buried in Elmwood Cemetery. Buhl Avenue in Detroit is named for him.

Buhl Trading Company and factory in the Corktown section of Detroit.

The Buhl Building and the St. Peter and Paul Church

Frederick Buhl gravesite in Elmwood Cemetery.

Capitalists, Clowns, and Crooks, Choir-boys, Cops and Clerks: The May-

Charles Howard, Mayor of Detroit 1849-1850

CHAPTER NINETEEN —CHARLES HOWARD—SHIPPING AGENT AND MAYOR

Charles Howard (1804-1884) was born in Chenango County, New York on August 7, 1804, and moved with his family to Port Jervis, New York. Upon reaching adulthood he moved to Sackett's Harbor in New York where he became a schooner captain.

He then became a shipping and forwarding commission merchant in Oswego, New York, for the *Alvin & Bronson Company*. This company became *Bronson, Crocker & Co.*, and then Charles Howard was made a partner and the business name changed to *Bronson, Crocker, & Howard*. They were located at the foot of Randolph Street.

Father of Playwright Bronson Howard

In 1834 Charles married Margaret Vosburg and the couple had two children, daughter Mrs. William Waterman, and a son, famed actor and playwright Bronson Howard.

Poster of a movie written by famed playwright, Bronson Howard, son of Mayor Charles Howard.

In 1840 Howard moved to Detroit to open a branch office for *Bronson, Crocker, & Howard*. In 1848, he started a partnership with N. P. Stewart and became a railroad contractor, purchasing a substantial portion of the Detroit and Milwaukee Railroad. In 1854 he dissolved the partnership with Stewart and started one with his brother Sebre Howard. He was also President of the Farmer's and Mechanics Bank and the Peninsular Bank.

The State Fair started in 1849, when Charles Howard was Mayor. Pictured is the 1914 Fair.

Eventful Mayoral Reign

In 1848 Howard was elected Mayor of Detroit as a Democrat and served in 1849. He defeated Whig candidate Buckminster Wright 1,326 to 1,226. While he was Mayor the first telegraph message in Detroit was sent, from Detroit to Buffalo. Also, the first Michigan State Fair was held in Detroit in 1849. Many Scandinavians immigrated to Detroit and the Upper Peninsula in 1849 and a great number of them went into toolmaking.

During Howard's mayoral tenure, citizen antipathy against the railroads resulted in the destruction of tracks along Gratiot Avenue. The perpetrators justified their actions by claiming that the trains were a hazard. Some train tracks were rerouted because of this protest.

While mayor, he obtained public support for building a new school building, and he hired an official city physician. He also dealt with a cholera epidemic from June to September 1849 which took over 300 lives.

While mayor, Howard was host to President Millard Fillmore and historian George Bancroft when they visited Detroit.

After his mayoral term, in the 1850s, he headed a railroad construction firm, S. and C. Howard Company. He also served on the Board of Directors of the Detroit and Pontiac Railroad.   When the Peninsular Bank failed during the Panic of 1857, he quit as its President. In 1858 he moved to New York with his brother and started "Howard Brothers Firearms." They were in business from 1863 to 1874.

In 1879 he returned to Detroit and resided with his daughter and son-in-law, William Waterman, a real estate broker. Howard died in 1883, of lung congestion, in the Waterman home. He was 79. Howard Street in Detroit was named for him.

Charles Howard gravesite in Elmwood Cemetery.

John Ladue was Mayor of Detroit in 1850.

C HAPTER TWENTY —JOHN LADUE—LEATHER MERCHANT MAYOR

John Thomas Ladue (1803-1854) was born in Lansingburg, New York on November 18, 1803, to Peter and Mary Ladue. He married Mary Angel in 1827. While still in New York, he operated a business with his brother Andrew.

In 1847 he came to Detroit as a wool and Moroccan Leather merchant and opened a large tannery on Rivard Street. He had a store on Michigan Avenue near the Campus Martius. He was well-liked and trusted among the businessmen and so was nominated to run for Mayor of Detroit in 1850. This was just a few years after he had moved to town. Ladue was a Democrat and defeated the Whig candidate, David Smith—1,420 to 1,352.

In 1850 the main business of Detroit was shipping. The population topped 21,000. One notable occurrence was the so-called "Whorehouse Wars." This "war" was in actuality white citizens in German neighborhoods throwing stones at patrons going in and out of brothels catering to black men. Often the buildings would be burnt.

Ladue Calls Military to Restore Order

Ladue was lauded for calling the military in to restore order during a turmoil in 1850 caused by the arrest of fugitive slaves. Ladue called a town meeting and raised $500 to purchase the slave from his owner and free him.

Also, during Ladue's tenure in 1850, the first Temple Beth El was established in Detroit. They are the oldest Jewish congregation in Michigan.

Bernard Stroh moved from Kirn, Germany to escape the German Revolution in 1850. Settling in Detroit, he founded what became the most famous of Detroit's breweries, Stroh's Brewery, makers of Stroh's "Bohemian Style" beer.

Stroh's Brewery

Ladue didn't run for reelection after his single term but

went back to private life and managing his businesses. He died at home on December 8, 1854 at the age of 51, survived by his four children—John, Charlotte, George, and Austin. He was buried in Elmwood Cemetery.

John Ladue gravesite in Elmwood Cemetery.

Alan Naldrett

Zachariah Chandler, Mayor of Detroit 1851-1852

C HAPTER TWENTY-ONE—ZACHARIAH CHANDLER—BETTER KNOWN AS SENATOR

Zachariah Chandler (1813-1879) was one of the many politicians who made the transition from the Whig Party, to the Republican Party, which had its first official meeting in Jackson, Michigan in 1854. He was Mayor of Detroit from 1851 to 1852 and gained great renown when he served in the U.S. Senate as well.

Chandler was born on December 10, 1813 in New Bedford, New Hampshire to farmer Samuel and his wife Margaret. He was the sixth of seven children. He attended New Bedford Public Schools until age fifteen, when he began attending Derry and Pembroke Academy. Afterward, he taught for a semester in a rural schoolhouse and then moved to Nashua where he worked as a clerk in a general store.

Started with a General Store

Chandler moved to Detroit in 1833 and opened his own general store, in partnership with his brother-in-law Franklin Moore. In 1836 he bought out his partner and became sole owner of the business, becoming the first business in Detroit to sell over $50,000 worth of goods in one year. After 1840, Chandler put his focus on wholesale selling instead of retailing.

Doing well at wholesaling, Chandler further invested in road-building companies, banks, railroads, timber land, and downtown real estate. In 1844 he married Letitia Grace Douglass of New York on December 10. They had one child, Mary, born in 1848.

Zachariah's uncles Benjamin Orr and Thomas Chandler both served in the U.S. Congress, helping to inspire him to become politically active. In the late 1830s, as his wealth grew, he started contributing money and time to the Whig Party and became a delegate to their convention in 1850.

Elected Mayor of Detroit as a Whig

In 1851, the Whig Party selected Chandler as their candidate for Mayor of Detroit. Chandler beat his Democratic opponent, former Mayor John R. Williams, 1,909 to 1,558. While Mayor, Chandler was head of the Common Council, which was composed of mostly Democrats. The council had 16 seats, two from each of the eight wards in the city.

Chandler had a contentious term as mayor, mostly due to the Democratic majority. There was a scandal of sorts when the council hired a new city printer who was a Whig, at a meeting in which few Democrats were in attendance. Otherwise, Chandler spent his energies while mayor working on the city budget and physical improvements. He never ran again for mayor after his single term.

In 1941, during his short term as mayor, the Detroit Gas Light Company installed gas lighting in homes using pipes laid beneath the principal streets.

Chandler was the Whig candidate for Michigan Governor in 1852 but lost to Democratic candidate Robert McClelland. This was his last time running as a Whig.

Helps Found the Republican Party

In 1854, Chandler helped start the Republican Party. The meeting was held outside in Jackson, Michigan, since there were too many people to fit in the planned hall, which was hot and stuffy anyways. They held the meeting outside "under the oaks," where there was plenty of room. The #1 platform of the new party was the abolishment of slavery.

In 1857 Chandler was chosen to be in the Senate, which is what he was most well-known for. He served three terms, from 1857 to 1875, and also briefly in 1879. Serving during the Civil War, he was on the Committee on the Conduct of the War. He supported blacks being given the vote and the Wade-Davis bill of 1863 (a reconstruction bill pocket-vetoed by Lincoln).

He successfully sponsored a bill to have the federal government widen and deepen the St. Clair Flats in 1861. He was chairman of the Senate Commerce Committee and did much to improve the waterways of the nation.

St. Clair Flats in Southeast Michigan

Chandler was the Secretary of Interior from 1875 to 1876, and then the Republican Party National Chairman also in 1876. In 1878 he was reelected to Congress but died on November 1, 1879 of a cerebral hemorrhage before completing his term. He was in a Chicago hotel while campaigning for Republican candidates there. He was buried in Elmwood Cemetery. Chandler Park, Chandler Park Drive, and Chandler Avenue were all named for him.

Zachariah Chandler gravesite in Elmwood Cemetery.

John H. Harmon, Mayor of Detroit 1852-1853

CHAPTER TWENTY-TWO— JOHN H. HARMON— PRINTER AND MAYOR

John Hanchett Harmon (1819-1888) was born June 21, 1819 in Portage, Ohio to Mary and John Harmon, a newspaper publisher. John, Jr. got ink in his veins from working in his father's print shop and helping with the Ravenna, Ohio newspaper that his father owned.

In 1838 John, Jr. moved to Detroit as the assistant to Lucius V. Bearce, a "General" in the Patriot War, also known as the "Rebellion." This was an insurrection of Americans and Canadians who were trying to rid the North American continent of the British army and annex Canadian territory to the United States.

The Patriot War's Battle of Windsor

Harmon took part in the Battle of Windsor, often considered the closing of the Patriot War. In this battle, 140 Americans and Canadians crossed over the Detroit River to Windsor. Harmon personally helped burn the British barracks in Windsor and set fire to the steam boat the *Thames*. Twenty people died in the conflict. After the hostilities Harmon got a job with the *Detroit Free Press*. In 1841 he married Sarah Rood and they had three children. In 1850, he joined the Michigan State Militia, becoming a colonel.

Owner of the Detroit Free Press

In 1842 he became editor, one of the publishers, and one-third owner of the *Detroit Free Press*. In 1853 he became the sole owner of the newspaper and but sold it after just one year in 1854.

While working as a publisher and journalist, John H. Harmon became prosperous and influential in the politics of the day. He was an imposing presence at six-feet in height with jet-black hair.

Two-Term Mayor of Detroit

In 1847 he became a City Alderman and was again an Alderman in 1848. In 1852 he was elected Mayor of Detroit as a Democrat and re-elected in 1853. At that time the population of Detroit was more than 26,000, and there were about 4,600 buildings in the city—600 brick and 4,000 made of wood. During Harmon's mayoral term, George B. Russell founded the *Detroit Car and Manufacturing Company* to build railroad cars.

After his mayoral term, President Franklin Pierce appointed Harmon to be Collector of the Port of Detroit. Harmon held this job for four years, spending most of his time in Washington, D.C. when Congress was in session.

After his appointment ended with Pierce's Presidential term, Harmon stuck around Washington as an early version of a lobbyist. He was influential with members of the Democratic Party and knew most of the prominent politicians of the day. But unfortunately, he developed a drinking problem.

Returning to Detroit, he suffered a decline in his fortune due to his generosity while drinking. Therefore, he returned to work at the *Free Press*. He conquered his demons and became a complete abstainer before he died in a hotel in Detroit in 1888. He was buried in Elmwood Cemetery. Harmon Street in Detroit was named for him.

John Harmon and his wife's tombstones are missing but their kids are still there in Elmwood.

Oliver Moulton Hyde

C HAPTER TWENTY-THREE---OLIVER MOULTON HYDE —HARDWARE MERCHANT MAYOR

Oliver M. Hyde (1804-1870) was another prosperous, self-made businessman who became Mayor. He was born on March 10, 1804 in Sudbury, Vermont and was educated at the village school and Castleton Seminary. He married Julia Ann Sprague in 1827. Moving to Castleton, Vermont, he opened a dry goods store. In 1834, he sold the store to move to Mt. Hope, New York to establish and manage two blast furnaces.

Hardware Store on Woodward Avenue

Hyde moved to Detroit in 1838 and opened a hardware store on Woodward Avenue. Besides hardware, he began manufacturing and selling counter scales. He then added a foundry and machine shop on Atwater Street near the foot of Dequindre

Street and manufactured marine engines, steam hardware, and steamboat machinery.

Hyde was affectionally called "Uncle Oliver" and it was said that "he could provide anything from a mousetrap to a meeting house."

In 1852 Hyde began a floating dry-dock business, which entails providing "a narrow basin or vessel that can be flooded to allow a load to be floated in, then drained to allow that load to come to rest on a dry platform." Dry docks are used for the maintenance, repair, and construction of boats and ships.

In 1852, he built a steam sawmill in Saginaw, Michigan, on the west bank of the Saginaw River, across from what was then a town named East Saginaw.

Hyde married Julia Sprague of Poultney, Vermont and they had a house in Detroit at Michigan Avenue and Griswold Street, at the spot where the David Whitney Building is today.

Elected Mayor Three Times

Hyde was a generous man—he was involved in extensive charity work and loaned or gave away a substantial portion of his fortune. Elected many times to the Detroit City Council, Hyde also served three terms as mayor, in 1852, 1854 and 1855.

During Hyde's mayoral administration the first railroad connection between New York and Detroit was completed. The Soo Locks also opened at this time. Many Italians immigrated to Detroit and settled on the east side of the city. Hyde also got the ball rolling on establishing the Detroit House of Corrections.

Like previous Mayor John H. Harmon, Hyde was appointed Collector of the Port of Detroit by President Zachary Taylor and President Millard Fillmore after his mayoral term. Hyde was the last Whig Mayor of Detroit. Like most Whigs, he switched to the Republican Party when the Whig Party ended.

In 1863 he suffered a debilitating stroke and was confined to his house. He had another stroke in 1867. However, he continued to provide public service and to support recruiting during the Civil War. He died in 1870, leaving three children, and was buried in Elmwood Cemetery.

Oliver Moulton Hyde monument in Elmwood Cemetery

Henry Ledyard, young and old, Mayor of Detroit 1855-1856

C HAPTER TWENTY-FOUR—HENRY LEDYARD—JACK-OF-ALL-TRADES MAYOR

Henry Ledyard (1812-1880) was Mayor of Detroit in 1855, in between Oliver Moulton Hyde's two terms. He was also a state senator, and U.S. Asst. Secretary of State under Lewis Cass.

Ledyard was born March 5, 1812 in New York City into a distinguished family that included a Governor of New Jersey and a U.S. Supreme Court Justice. He graduated from New York's Columbia College (later University) with a law degree in 1830.

Assistant to Lewis Cass

He began practicing law and met Lewis Cass, who had just been appointed as Minister to France. Cass asked Ledyard to be his assistant, and Ledyard agreed, going to Paris with Cass and taking charge of the American Embassy in France. In 1839 he married Cass's daughter Matilda. The couple had five children together.

Ledyard returned to the United States in 1844 and, still

working for Lewis Cass, managed the Cass property holdings. He was a founder of the State Savings Bank, Elmwood Cemetery, and a member of the Board of Education. He was one of the original commissioners on the Wayne County Board of Commissioners.

Building Plank Roads and Serving as Mayor

Ledyard started a company that constructed one of the first major plank roads in Michigan. In 1849-1850 he was Alderman for the city and in 1855 he served his lone mayoral term, during which waves of Italian and Polish immigrants arrived in the city.

In July and August of 1855, three treaties with neighboring Indian tribes were signed in Detroit. They included a treaty with the Ottawa and Chippewa tribes, and treaties with the Sault Ste. Marie, Saginaw, and Swan Creek Chippewa. Up north, the Soo Locks were completed, making travel from Detroit easier.

In 1855 Detroit had 49 hotels, of "various grades." There were three Presbyterian churches, three Methodist churches, a Congregational church, a Unitarian Church, and several Catholic churches including the Mariners Church, the Cathedral of Saints Peter and Paul, and St. Paul's Church. There were 28 churches in all, five soda and small beer factories, nine soap and candle factories, 24 private schools, 25 public schools, 333 stores, 345 mechanic shops, 260 grocery stores, 131 boarding houses, 24 private meat markets, 24 warehouses, four public bathing establishments, 49 taverns, and 17 breweries. Detroit also had four banks, 21 bakeries, and many other businesses in the middle of the 19th Century.

In 1857 Ledyard was elected as a Democrat to the State Legislature but resigned when his father-in-law Lewis Cass was made Secretary of State and once again wanted Ledyard to be his assistant. Ledyard remained in Washington, D.C. until 1861.

He moved to Newport, Rhode Island and was President of the Newport Hospital and the Newport Library. He died in 1880 at the age of 68 while vacationing in London, England. He was buried in Newport, Rhode Island.

Henry

Ledyard's gravesite in Newport, Rhode Island

John S. Patton, Mayor of Detroit, 1858-1859

C HAPTER TWENTY-FIVE—JOHN S. PATTON—CARRIAGE MAKER MAYOR

John S. Patton (1822-1900) was born March 1, 1822 in County Down, Ireland, the son of James and Eliza Patton. In 1830, John and James moved to the United States and settled in Albany, New York; in 1831 the rest of the family joined them there.

When he was 17 in 1839, Patton was apprenticed to a carriage maker. In 1843 he moved to Detroit and worked for other carriage makers. In 1845 he opened his own carriage construction business and factory. In the same year he married Eliza Anderson and they had five children. His carriage factory burned down in 1848, but Patton rebuilt, and the business once again prospered.

Chief of the Fire Department

Patton became known in the Detroit community as a learned man with thespian skills, including his "proper" use of Irish and Scottish brogues. He was Chief Engineer of the Detroit Fire Department 1852-1854 and was President of the Detroit Fire Department from 1855 to 1857.

Two-Term Mayor

As a Democrat, he was elected as City Alderman in 1853 and 1854 and was Mayor of Detroit in 1858 and 1859. During his mayoral term, on March 12, abolitionists Frederick Douglass and John Brown met at the home of William Webb. This led to the Harper's Ferry conflict in West Virginia at the federal militia, where Brown was captured and later hanged.

During Patton's mayoral term the Sewer Commission was formed, and the first paved streets were constructed. Also, the first streetcar line was laid, and ordinances were adopted to control waste, garbage, and pollutants dumped into the rivers and streams. Additionally, laws were enacted to curb prostitution, and the fire department took steps to hire permanent fire fighters for the city, as opposed to volunteer forces.

In 1859, the first billiards world championship was held in Detroit.

Patton next became the Wayne County Auditor from 1864 to 1869, Wayne County Sheriff 1869-1871, Justice of the Peace from 1880 to 1892, and United States Consul to Amherstburg, Ontario 1893 to 1897.

Patton died on November 15, 1900 and was buried in Elmwood Cemetery with full Masonic honors. He was survived by five children.

Patton family gravestone in Elmwood Cemetery.

Christian Buhl, Mayor of Detroit 1860-1861

C HAPTER TWENTY-SIX—CHRISTIAN BUHL—HATTER MAYOR

Christian Henry Buhl (1810-1894) was the brother of Mayor Frederick Buhl, who was Mayor in 1848. Christian's mayoral term was 1860-1861, during the American Civil War. They were the only pair of brothers to be Mayor of Detroit (Henry Howard and Charles Howard were not related).

Christian was born May 9, 1810 in Zelienople, Pennsylvania, which is 28 miles north of Pittsburgh. His father, also named Christian, was a hat maker from Bavaria, Germany and taught his son Christian the business.

Starting with Hats, Moving on to Copper and Brass

Christian moved to Detroit in 1833 with his brother Frederick, who he formed a partnership with, making and selling hats. The brothers branched out into furs and factories. They founded the Detroit Copper and Brass Company and the Peninsular Car Company, which manufactured railroad cars.

Christian married Caroline Delong of Utica, New York in 1842. The couple had five children, only two of which, Theodore and Frank, outlived their parents.

In 1853, Frederick decided to retire after 20 years in partnership with his brother. Christian then quit the fur business, and went into business with Charles Ducharme, opening a wholesale hardware business. When Ducharme died, Buhl brought his sons Theodore and Frank into the business and the company was renamed *Buhl, Sons & Co.* Christian was also part-owner of the *Sharon Iron Works* and the *Detroit Locomotive Works.* The latter became the *Buhl Iron Works.*

The Buhl Iron Works at 3rd and Larned Streets in Detroit

The *Sharon Iron Works* was in Sharon, Pennsylvania and the Buhls became involved with steel with the *Buhl Steel Works of Sharon.* Christian's son Frank moved to Sharon to manage the family's businesses and built the Buhl Mansion there.

The Buhl Mansion in Sharon, Pennsylvania.

Christian Buhl was invested in railroads, including the *Detroit, Eel River, & Illinois Railroad*, and the *Detroit, Hillsdale, & Indiana Railroad*. Christian was also President of the Detroit National Bank and on the boards of the Michigan State Bank and the Second National Bank of Detroit.

Buhl and Sons Hardware, 1891

The Buhl Block in Detroit

First Republican Mayor of Detroit

Christian was originally a member of the Whig Party, like his brother Frederick. He was elected to Detroit's Common Council for the 2nd Ward as a Whig in 1851. But as the Whig Party diminished and the northern Whigs joined the Republican Party, so did Christian. In 1851 he was elected a city alderman as a Republican. In 1860 he was elected the first Republican Mayor of Detroit. A new charter changed the mayoral term to two years instead of one.

Civil War Mayor

In 1861, Christian's first year as Mayor, the Civil War began. Michigan sent one of the first volunteer regiments to Washington, D.C. to defend the Union. By the end of the war, an estimated 14,753 Michigan soldiers had died in the Civil War. This was roughly one in six of everyone who served. While 4,448 deaths were due to combat, the rest were due to disease.

In Buhl's first year as mayor, Detroit's only high school began to accept women. In 1861, Buhl's second year as mayor, the Volunteer Fire Department of Detroit began to be replaced with paid personnel. A new Detroit City Hall began construction.

In 1885 Buhl donated a substantial law library to the University of Michigan, worth more than $15,000. Upon his death he willed another $10,000 to the library. He donated large amounts to the Detroit Institute of Art and served as a Trustee to the Detroit Medical College.

Christian Buhl died in 1894 at the age of 83 and was interred in Elmwood Cemetery. Buhl Avenue in Detroit is named for him (or his brother Frederick, or both of them).

Christian Buhl mausoleum

William C. Duncan, Detroit Mayor 1862-1863

C HAPTER TWENTY-SEVEN— WILLIAM C. DUNCAN —BREWER MAYOR

William Chamberlain Duncan (1820-1877) was born May 18, 1820 in Lyons, New York, a transplanted New Yorker like many of Detroit's early mayors. The Duncan family moved to Rochester, New York in 1825 and William stayed there until 1841. He then got a job as a steward on one of the passenger steam boats that sailed the Great Lakes. One of the ships he worked on was the *Julia Palmer.* It was the first "side-wheel" steamer on the Great Lakes when it first appeared on Lake Superior in 1836.

From Sailor to Brewer

Duncan moved to Detroit in 1849 and became a brewer. His Duncan Brewery was one of the city's largest. From 1852 to 1862 his William C. Duncan Brewery was the city's largest. From 1862 to 1865 it was called Duncan Central Brewery and then became George Langdon & Co. Brewery from 1865 to 1872. George Langdon became Mayor of Detroit 14 years later.

DUNCAN'S CENTRAL BREWERY,

Opposite M. C. R. R. Depot, Woodbridge Street,

DETROIT, - - - - - - - - - MICHIGAN.

 WILLIAM C. DUNCAN,

MANUFACTURER OF

BEER, PALE & AMBER ALES

For Shipping and City Use!

AND DEALER IN

BARLEY, MALT AND HOPS.

The finest qualities of Stock Ales for Shipping, and the most delicate Pale Ale for family use, always on hand in large or small packages.

William C. Duncan advertisement in the Detroit City Directory and Advertising Gazetteer of Michigan for 1855-56.

Duncan's brewery was located at 186 Woodbridge Street by the Michigan Central Railroad yard and produced pale and amber ales, and porter and stout beer. His advertisements read, "the most delicate Pale Ale for family use" apparently denoting a time when beer drinking was not just for adults. William was partners with brother Elison in operating a malthouse at River and Fourth Streets.

He sold the brewery to Nathan Williams and George C. Langdon, another future Detroit mayor, in 1864.

Duncan advertised his brewery as across from the Michigan Central Railroad Station, seen in the front of the photo. Duncan's brewery is to the left of the chimney in the picture.

Duncan made a lot of friends, as only a brewer could, and was elected City Alderman in 1852, serving until 1857. When the revision of the City Charter created the position of Council President, he was the first elected to that office.

In 1862 he was elected Mayor of Detroit as a Democrat, serving in 1862 and 1863, while the country was still engaged in the Civil War. In 1863, anti-draft and race riots occurred in Detroit and other cities. Draftees resented being conscripted into military service on what they felt was on behalf of Southern blacks. (The Emancipation Proclamation had just been released.) This was the editorial line fomented by *The Detroit Free Press*, the Democratic Party newspaper. This was not the first time the newspaper had caused violence through its reporting.

On June 15, 1862 Mayor Duncan was at a rally in Detroit's Campus Martius to recruit Michigan men to enlist in Michigan's 24th Artillery Division. Suddenly, the grandstand was rushed by anti-draft protesters. The dignitaries had to make a run for it to the safety of the Russell House.

Anti-Draft Riot

The riot in Detroit started on March 6, 1863 and the *Detroit Free Press* wrote that it was "the bloodiest day that ever dawned upon Detroit."

The *Detroit Free Press* ran inflammatory articles claiming that blacks would take jobs away from white laborers. The black community was attacked, and 35 buildings were destroyed by fire, and more were damaged. At least two people were killed—one black and one white. More than 200 people, mostly black, were left homeless.

The Michigan Legislature recommended that the community be compensated, but the Detroit City Council wouldn't approve it. What they DID approve was a full-time police force, which remained almost full-time white until into well into the 20th Century.

During Duncan's two-year term, Harper Hospital in Detroit was founded as a military hospital, and Fannie Richards opened the first private school for black women. The regiment called the First Michigan Colored Troops by George DeBaptiste and John D. Richard was formed. The 1,400 men joined the Union Army and became the 102nd U.S. Colored Troop. The Canadian border was heavily patrolled to prevent citizens from avoiding military duty.

First Streetcar Service in Detroit

The first streetcar (pulled by horses) began to operate at the corner of Jefferson and Woodward in Detroit in 1863. A ride cost a nickel.

When Duncan's term ended in 1863, he was elected to the Michigan Legislature as a State Senator. In 1865 he ended his term and began in the banking business as Duncan, Kibbee, & Co. He terminated his banking employment due to ill health and went to Europe.

Duncan made his return to Detroit political life in 1873, as a member of the newly-created Board of Estimates. The Board of Estimates included representatives of the Common Council and the Mayor's office. The board was involved with land use and taxation. Duncan was asked by the Democrats to run for Mayor again but refused due to his ill-health.

He lived on until 1877, when he died, unmarried and childless, at the age of 57. He was buried in Detroit's Elmwood Cemetery.

William Duncan memorial in Elmwood Cemetery.

Kirkland C. Barker-Detroit Mayor 1864-1865

CHAPTER TWENTY-EIGHT —KIRKLAND C. BARKER—TOBACCO TYCOON

Kirkland C. Baker (1819-1875) was born September 8, 1819 in East Schuyler, New York, in Herkimer County. He went to the local school until he was 14, when he was sent to a "manual labor" school in Whitesboro, New York where he worked a number of hours each day to pay for his schooling. Upon graduation at age 16 he started working in a store in Frankfort, New York, where he stayed for a year.

Barker next worked another year at a store in Utica, New York. When he was 18 he moved to Cleveland, Ohio and worked in a public warehouse. He was often put in charge of vessels traveling to New York. Barker married Jennette Bedell of Ann Arbor in 1847 and the couple had three children.

Because of Barker's skill in navigating sailing vessels, he was elected Commodore of the Yacht Club.

Traveling Tobacco Salesman

Barker moved to Detroit and worked as a traveling salesman for a tobacco firm in Logansport, Indiana. He then started his own tobacco business, establishing branches in New York City and Detroit, with a factory in Jersey City, New Jersey. The business failed and Barker started over again.

He then founded *K.C. Barker & Co.* (later to become the *American Eagle Tobacco Company*) and was successful enough to pay off all the debts of the previous business.

K.C. Barker & Co. Tobacco Advertisements

An American Eagle Tobacco Co. pocket tin.

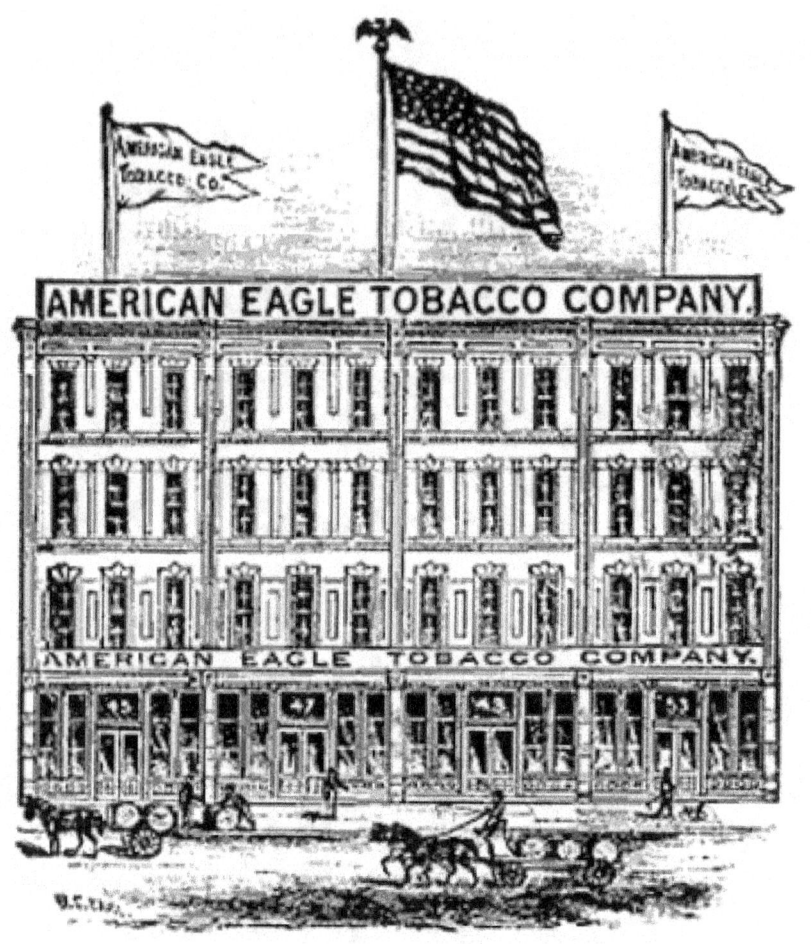

American Eagle Tobacco Company Building on Atwater Street.

Barker's tobacco company was one of the first in Detroit. They processed plug chewing tobaccos, smoking tobaccos, and pipe blends. Some of the "fine cut" brands were Bijah's Joy, Crown of Joy, Clipper, and American Eagle. The smoking brands included Mackinaw, Universal Favorite, and Canada Mixture. The company processed over a million and a half pounds of tobacco per year and shipped to every city in the United States, as well as China and Brazil.

Barker Starts Public Life

Barker was elected Detroit Alderman in 1863, and in 1864,

174

the last year of the Civil War, was elected to a two-year Mayoral term. One Civil War matter that occurred in the Detroit area was the Philo Parsons Incident. The Philo Parsons was a side-wheeler ship on the Detroit River that was hijacked by Confederate forces in a plan to take the USS Michigan on Lake Erie from the Union. From there the plan was to free Confederate prisoners on Johnson Island, in Sandusky, Ohio. Mayor Barker was instrumental in heading off the piracy.

Barker was also involved in stopping a conspiracy by Canadian Confederate sympathizers to upset the 1864 national election by burning U.S. border cities near Canada. He hoped the confusion would delay or stop the election.

While he was Mayor, Bessemer Steel was first produced at *Eureka Iron Works* in Wyandotte, Michigan and Richard Trevelick formed the Detroit Trades Assembly, Detroit's first central labor organization. The Michigan State Equal Rights League Convention met in Detroit in 1865.

In 1865 the Detroit Public Library opened with 5,000 books and the Detroit Police Department was established. The Michigan State Equal Rights League Convention was held in Detroit in 1865 during Barker's term.

In October, 1864, word reached Barker from the U.S. Consul in Toronto, Ontario that there was a plot to burn Detroit. Barker instituted Detroit's first night patrols to protect the city and made plans to have a permanent, paid night police force.

After his mayoral term was over, Barker brought his brother and his son into the tobacco business and retired to a home on Grosse Ile.

Friend of Colonel Custer

He was an avid outdoorsman and became President of the Detroit Audobon Society. He was active in the Detroit Horseman's Club, and was elected Commodore of the Detroit Yacht Club. One of the racehorses he owned was named Ericsson, a world-record holding trotting horse.

One of Barker's best friends was Colonel George Armstrong Custer, who would visit Barker on Grosse Ile accompianed by his wife Libby. Barker met Custer before the Civil War and became a lifelong friend, even though he was 20 years older than Custer. Custer once said that Barker was a "liberal and high-minded gentleman, whom I am proud to number among my warmest friends."

Barker gave Custer two hunting dogs, Maida and Blucher, who were frequently mentioned in Custer's memoirs of Kansas City in 1867 to 1869. Custer wrote about a buffalo hunt that he organized in 1869 that included Barker and many of his Grosse Ile friends.

Tragically, Barker was in his boat near his Grosse Ile home when he had a stroke and drowned at the age of 55. Barker's yacht, the Cora, had been well-known in Grosse Ile. The best accounting of the accident was in the book by Isabelle E. Swan, *The Deep Roots: A History of Grosse Ile to July 6, 1876*, published in 1976.

Ms. Swan wrote, "While being readied for entry in the International Boat Club regatta, Mr. Barker's racing yacht Cora lay at anchor off Stony Island May 20. Aboard the Mattie, which carried three tons of ballast for the Cora that morning, were Mr. Barker, Frederick Dudgeon, Manly Webb (sailing master of the Cora), and fourteen-year-old Peter Miller, son of Mr. Barker's gardener. The Mattie capsized; all were thrown overboard and drowned." K.C. Barker was buried in Elmwood Cemetery. Barker Street in Detroit is named for him.

Kirkland C. Barker house on Grosse Ile, Michigan

Individual stone for K.C. Barker

K.C. Barker in Elmwood Cemetery. Most of the lettering on the Barker family stone is worn and illegible.

Merrill I. Wills, Mayor of Detroit 1866-1867

CHAPTER TWENTY-NINE —MERILL I. MILLS— GUNPOWDER AND STOVE MERCHANT

Merrill I. Mills (1819-1892) was born in Canton, Connecticut to Isaac and Asenath Merrill Mills. Merrill went against his parents' wishes for him to go to college and instead joined his father's gunpowder firm in 1833. He moved to Alabama in 1838 to administer the business there, and moved back in 1840 when his father's health began to fail.

Layover in Detroit Becomes Permanent

In 1845 Mills decided to start a new business out west and set sail for Fort Wayne, Indiana. Icy waters closing the water routes forced a layover in Detroit. Mills liked the area and decided to stay and open a general store. He also started successfully trading in furs and in 1850 started manufacturing cigars. He founded the company *Nevins & Mills* to manage his businesses in 1861 and in 1878 he started the Banner Tobacco

Company. He married Cynthia Barbour and had two children, Merrill B. Mills and Ella Mills.

In 1867 Mills founded the Detroit Stove Works with partners Jeremiah and James Dwyer, and hardware czar Charles DuCharme. The Upper Peninisula discoveries of iron ore were a boon to Detroit industry. Detroit started producing many iron products, including wheels for railroad cars, ships, marine engines, and cast iron stoves.

The Detroit Stove Works was one of the three large stove manufacturers that made Detroit the "Stove Capital of the World." The other two were the Michigan Stove Company and the Peninsular Stove Company.

The Peninsular Stove Co. sold nice-looking, or-nate but rugged stoves.

In 1872 Mills started the Michigan Stove Company. The Detroit Stove Works and the Michigan Stove Company merged to form the Detroit-Michigan Stove Company and some of their most well-known stove brands were Garland, Laurel, and Jewel.

A large, 25 feet high, 30 feet long, and 20 feet wide Garland Stove was built to advertise the stove company at the Chicago World's Columbian Exposition of 1893. The "World's Largest Stove" was then returned to Detroit and sat on the stove company's property. It was later taken to the entrance to Belle Isle, and eventually the Michigan State Fairgrounds, where it was restored in 1998 but unfortuneatly was struck by lighting in 2011 and burned to the ground.

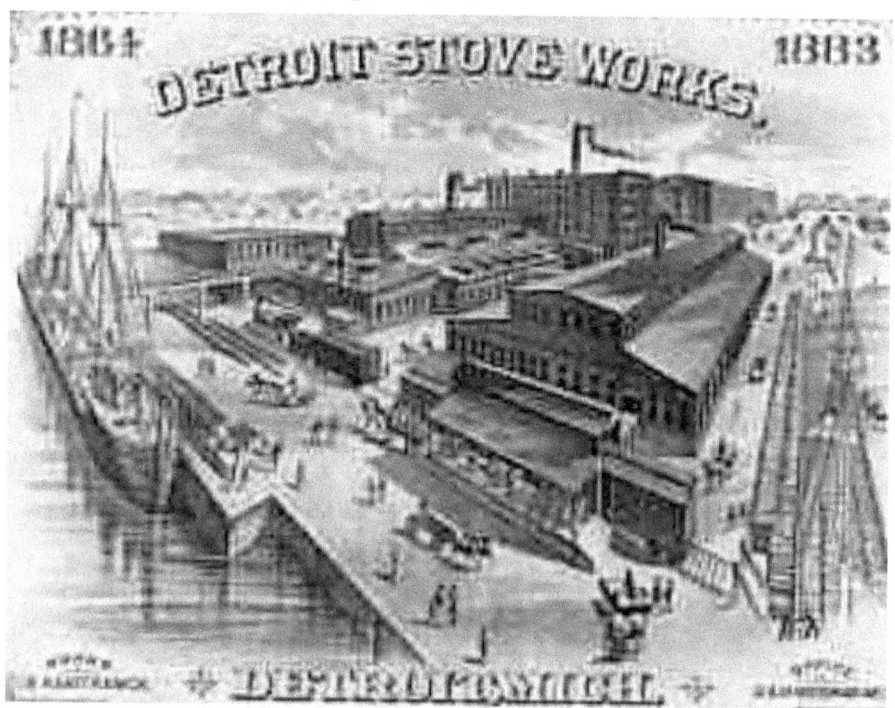

The Detroit Stove Works in 1883.

The giant Garland Stove in happier days.

Mills also had interests in the Detroit Fire and Marine Insurance Company, the Detroit First National Bank, the Frankfort Furnace Company, the Eldredge Sewing Machine Co. of Chicago, and he was President of the Transit Railway Company of Detroit.

Mills was a Democrat, and chaired the Michigan Democratic State Committee in 1856 and 1857. He was on the Detroit Board of Estimates and in 1878 was the Michigan delegate to the Democratic Convention. Mills conducted a lot of fund-raising for the Union Army during the Civil War.

Major Detroit Industries Form

In 1865 Mills was elected Mayor of Detroit for the 1866-1867 term, besting Republican Henry P. Bridge by a vote of 3,851 to 2,958. During his mayoral term, Reconstruction started in the South.

During his term, pharmacist James Vernor returned home from the Civil War in 1866 and discovered that a cask of ginger ale had transformed into a "Deliciously Different" drink. He marketed it as Vernor's Ginger Ale and it became one of the country's first soft drinks.

In 1867 the D.M. Ferry Seed Co. was founded. The company would turn Detroit into a well-known seed center. Besides the seeds and stoves, Detroit was also known as a pharmaceutical center with companies like Parke-Davis headquartered in the city. It had grown into the nineteenth largest city in the U.S. with almost 70,000 people by the 1860s.

Heath issues caused Mills to retire from public life and his businesses in 1880. His son Merrill took over supervising his various enterprises. In 1882 Mills died and was buried in Woodlawn Cemetery. His estate was valued at over a million dollars in the days when a million dollars was a huge chunk of change.

Mills Mausoleum in Detroit's Woodlawn Cemetery.

Alan Naldrett

William W. Wheaton—Mayor of Detroit 1868 to 1871

CHAPTER THIRTY —WILLIAM W. WHEATON—GROCER MAYOR—NEVER ON STAR TREK

William W. Wheaton (1833-1891) was born in New Haven, Connecticut on April 5, 1833, to John, a Revolutionary War officer, and Orit Wheaton. When his father died in 1844, Wheaton was left at the age of eleven to help care for the family. He went to school in New Haven and Hartford, Connecticut. At the age of 16 he started working for wholesalers Charles H. Northam & Co.

Professional Grocer

He worked for Northam Grocers for four years and then moved to Detroit and got a job with Moore, Foote & Co., wholesale grocers in 1853. By 1855 he was ready to venture out on his own and he became the junior partner in Farrand & Wheaton, selling groceries and pharmaceutical supplies. In 1859 he bought out his partner and the company became Wheaton & Co.

He later got involved with other partners, branching out with other merchandise. His companies included Wheaton & Peek in 1862, W. Heaton, Leonard, and Burr in 1863, and Wheaton & Poppleton in 1869. In 1873 he became the treasurer and general manager of the Marquette and Pacific Rolling Mill Company.

Two-Time Mayor

When Democrat Will Wheaton (not the *Star Trek* actor) ran for Mayor of Detroit in 1868, he beat his Republican opponent George C. Codd 4,271 to 3,909. The population of Detroit was 68,827 at the time. He was reelected in 1870, beating his Republican opponent John D. Standish 4,813 to 4,102. While he was mayor a new City Hall was built, and black children were first allowed in public schools.

He was later chairman of the Democratic State Committee and was State Representative in 1889. He died in Detroit on November 11, 1891 and was buried in Elmwood Cemetery.

William Wheaton tombstone, front and back.

Alan Naldrett

Hugh Moffat, Mayor of Detroit 1872-1875

CHAPTER THIRTY-ONE—HUGH MOFFAT—SCOTTISH CHURCH BUILDER MAYOR

Hugh Moffat (1810-1884) was born in Coldstream, Scotland. He emigrated to America and first settled in Albany, New York. In 1838 he relocated to Detroit, obtaining carpentry work. He soon built up a successful business as a builder and contractor and in 1852 branched out into the lumber trade. He purchased large tracts of land that was laden with lumber in northern Michigan and built a sawmill.

Hugh Moffat's sawmill at the foot of Dubois Street in Detroit.

Moffat the Master Builder

One of the structures built by Moffat and his companies include the Mariner's Church, which has since been moved to Hart Plaza in Detroit from its original location at Woodbridge and Woodward Avenue. Other grand structures he built, that have since been demolished, include St. Paul's Church, the Biddle House, and the Moffat Block, built in 1871.

Moffat was married three times, outliving all his wives. He had five children: Isabella, Margaret, Alice, William, and Addison. Addison joined him in the lumber business.

The Old Mariner's Church in Hart Plaza was moved in 1955 after a campaign to save it by the Detroit News. It was moved from its original location at Woodward and Woodbridge to Hart Plaza at the nexus of Woodward and Jefferson.

The Old Mariner's Church in Detroit was built by Moffat and immortalized in a Gordon Lightfoot song about the sinking of the steamship the *Edmund Fitzgerald.*

In a musty old hall in Detroit they prayed,
In the Maritime Sailors' Cathedral
The church bell chimed till it rang twenty-nine times
For each man on the Edmund Fitzgerald.

-Gordon Lightfoot's *Wreck of the Edmund Fitzgerald.*

Moffat was opinionated and broke with his Scottish Presbyterian Church during the Civil War when the minister could not tell him whether slavery was morally right or wrong. He continued to be a firebrand and quick-tempered. He was well-known in Detroit, if not always well-liked. He was known as "conservative and penny-pinching," but also as "Honest Hugh Moffat."

Penny-Pinching Mayor

Moffat was elected Mayor as a Republican in 1871. He beat his Democratic opponent William Foxen 5,522 to 4,695. Moffat ran on a platform of curtailing Common Council spending and vetoed many bills due to their cost. Moffat vetoed 28 of 120 measures in one year from Detroit's Common Council. One issue he vetoed many times was the petitions of tavern-owners to open on Sundays.

Detroit Michigan Soldiers' and Sailors' Monument in the Campus Martius of Detroit.

In 1872 Moffat presided over the unveiling of the Michigan Soldiers' and Sailors' Monument. The monument was started in 1867 and was in the city's Campus Martius area.

In 1873 Moffat ran for reelection against Democrat Charles A. Garrison and beat him 5,560 to 4,178. The total population of Detroit in 1870 was more than 79,000; by 1874 it topped 100,000.

During the 1870s Detroit made the transition from a farming and port community to an industrial one. An 1874 report listed Detroit's leading industries and its output production. They were:

- Iron and Metal Works-$11,128,500
- Tobacco and Cigars-$4,000,000
- Flour and Feed Mills-$1,830,000
- Breweries and Malt Houses-$1,116,000
- Lasts and Shoes (A last is a mechanical form that has a shape like that of a human foot)-$986,000
- Furniture-$725,000
- Stoves-$625,000
- Boiler Shops-$585,000
- Rail Car Building

After his mayoral terms, Moffat continued to be a thorn in the side of his Democratic opponents but didn't run for any more public offices. He preferred concentrating on his lumber business.

Hugh Moffat died at the age of 74 on August 6, 1884, after a long illness at his home. He died not long after his son Addison and was buried in Elmwood Cemetery.

The Moffat Block, built in 1871, was at the southwest corner of Fort and Griswold Streets in Detroit. It was razed in 1922.

Hugh Moffat's gravesite in Elmwood Cemetery.

Alan Naldrett

Alexander Lewis, Mayor in 1876 and 1877

C HAPTER THIRTY-TWO— ALEXANDER LEWIS— CANADIAN MAYOR

Alexander Lewis (1822-1908) was born on April 5, 1822, in Sandwich (now Windsor), Ontario of a Welsh father (Thomas) and French Catholic mother (Jeanette). Alexander completed his schooling in Canada, before crossing the border into Detroit in 1837, the year of Michigan's statehood.

Lewis started with a job as a clerk at the age of 11 at his brother Samuel's store. The store was *E. W. Cole & Co.* general store and Lewis made $4 a month. He worked there until 1839. He then joined the firm of the *G. and J.G. Hill Drug Co.* in Pontiac. By 1842 he had formed his own freight-forwarding and commission company.

In 1862 he attained even more success with a flour and grain business. He was on the board of many financial institutions, including the Detroit Gas Company, on which he served as president, and the Detroit Public Library. His far-ranging business ventures included insurance, wholesale goods, and real estate.

His associations included becoming the Director of the Detroit Fire & Marine Insurance Company, a Director of the Detroit National Bank, President of the Detroit Gas Light Company, Director of the Detroit Iron and Wires Company, and in 1862 he was President of the Detroit Board of Trade.

He married Elizabeth Ingersoll in 1850 and they had thirteen children, only eight of whom survived. Many of his children were involved in their father's businesses.

Police Commissioner and Law-and-Order Mayor

Lewis was Detroit's Police Commissioner for ten years, from 1865 to 1875. In 1875 he was elected Mayor as a member of the Democratic Party, besting his Republican opponent William G. Thompson 7,367 to 5,691. He ran on a "law-and-order" plank.

Lewis served one term as Mayor and during his term he readied the city for the nation's Centennial Celebration in 1876. While he was Mayor the Detroit Opera House opened in 1877. On the first floor, J.L. Hudson built his first store, which would later dominate Detroit's merchant area. Also, in 1877 telephone service began in Detroit with 124 subscribers. Detroit was the first city to assign phone numbers. The Detroit College, now the University of Detroit/Mercy College opened in 1877.

Lewis was Chairman of the Democratic State Committee after he was Mayor and was a State Representative in 1889. By 1884 he had retired, owning a substantial amount of downtown Detroit property. He died on November 11, 1891 in Detroit at the age of 85 and was buried in Elmwood Cemetery.

Alexander Lewis Gravesite in Elmwood Cemetery

Alan Naldrett

George C. Langdon, Mayor of Detroit 1878-1879

C HAPTER THIRTY-THREE—GEORGE C. LANGDON— MALSTER MAYOR

George Curtis Langdon (1833-1909) was born in Geneva, New York and attended school in Batavia, New York and Farmington, Connecticut. When he was 18 he became a clerk for the wholesale firm of *Lord, Warren, Slater & Co*. When he returned to Geneva, his father sent him to Flint, Michigan to work on a farm.

Master's Degree in Bookkeeping

After working on the Flint farm for three years, he went to Detroit and attended Gregory Commercial College, studying bookkeeping. Graduating with a master's degree in Bookkeeping in 1858, he started doing accounting for a copper smelting firm, and then went to work at a bank. He took on a partner and began dealing in flour and grain. This led him to connect with brewers and maltsters.

In 1864 he and a partner, Nathan Williams, purchased what had been Mayor Duncan's brewery, *Duncan Central Brewery,* and renamed it *Langdon & Co.* He bought out his partner in 1870 and became sole owner. He sold the brewery to become a maltster, the one who prepares the malt from grain, often to a brewer's specifications. As a maltster he made a very comfortable living.

Belle Isle

In 1878 he was elected as Mayor of Detroit as a Democrat, beating the Republican opponent John Greusel 6,905 to 5,480. He is mainly remembered for the purchase of Belle Isle during his administration. Becoming one of the most famous city parks, it was designed by Frederick Law Olmstead, who also designed Boston's Emerald Necklace Park, Central Park in New York, Chicago's White City Exposition, and many others.

Belle Isle Grand Canal

After serving as mayor, Langdon had some financial problems and had to return to work, becoming a clerk in City Hall. He died in his birthplace, Geneva, New York, in June 1909. His body was returned to Detroit and buried in Woodmere Cemetery.

George Langdon gravesite in Woodmere Cemetery.

William G. Thompson, Mayor of Detroit, 1880 to 1883

C HAPTER THIRTY-FOUR—WILLIAM G. THOMPSON—BASEBALL TEAM OWNER AND BARROOM BRAWLER

William Gillon Thompson (1842-1904) was born in Lancaster, Pennsylvania on July 23, 1842, and educated at Amherst College. In 1861 he left school in his senior year and joined the 4th Pennsylvania Cavalry of the Union Army and fought in the Civil War. He was stationed in Detroit during the winter of 1861 to 1862. During the Battle of Chancellorsville, he was severely wounded and was then promoted to first lieutenant for his bravery.

When his enlistment was over he moved to Toledo, Ohio where his mother lived. In Ohio he enlisted in a lancer regiment with the rank of first lieutenant. (Lancer regiments originally used lances but by the Civil War era "Lancer Calvary" was a historical name used for armored divisions.) He further served with units in New Jersey and Michigan.

Columbia Law Degree and Detroit Law Firm

When he was mustered out, Thompson moved to New York City and studied law at the Columbia College of Law, now Columbia University. He then moved to Detroit to join the law firm D. B. and H. M. Duffield. In 1867 he was admitted to the bar and married Adelaide (Lillie) Brush, granddaughter of Elijah Brush. The couple had one daughter, Adele, before Adelaide died in 1876.

Thompson was described as slight in height and meticulous about his appearance, with his hair carefully parted in the middle, and his handlebar mustache freshly waxed and trimmed. He dressed smartly and carried his chewing tobacco in a silver tobacco box.

Besides practicing law, Thompson had other civic and business interests. He served on the Board of Estimates in 1873 and built the Hotel Ste. Claire on the Campus Martius in Detroit in 1879. He was a City Alderman in 1874 and 1875 and a delegate to the Republican National Convention from Michigan in 1876 and 1880. He was on the Board of Directors for Recreation Park. While Mayor he was elected President of the Detroit Jockey Club.

Recreation Park in the 1880s.

Recreation Park was between Brady and Willis Streets in Detroit and had its entrance on Brady Street. The park hosted women's basketball besides Detroit's first baseball team.

Detroit's First Baseball Team

In 1881 Thompson became the President of Detroit's first major-league baseball team, the Detroit Wolverines. It had long been discussed that Detroit should have a baseball team. Thompson was instrumental in getting Detroit the franchise from its previous sponsors. Waiting until he became mayor to make the contact to the National League, he used the Detroit Mayor letterhead to make the successful request. The Detroit Wolverines played in Detroit for the National League from 1881 to 1888.

Pharmacy tycoon Frederick Stearns purchased the team in 1885 and then bought the Buffalo Bisons so he could get the best ballplayers of the day, known as "The Big Four." They were Dan Brouthers, Jack Rowe, Hardy Richardson, and Deacon White. He also purchased a great hitter, Sam Thompson, who was admitted to the Baseball Hall of Fame by the Veteran's Committee, as was Dan Brouthers and Deacon White.

Stearns added the "Big Four" and Thompson to the Wolverines. With the new players, the Wolverines won the National League championship, and then the 15-game World Series in 1887, beating the St. Louis Browns.

The *Detroit Wolverines* played one more year before disbanding at the end of 1888. A new pay structure made the league not profitable for Detroit, which was still a relatively small city with a little over 110,000 residents. Their place in the National League was filled by the *Cleveland Spiders* in 1889.

The Detroit Wolverines pictured at the Boston South End Grounds in 1888.

Thompson Serves Two Terms as Mayor

Thompson was defeated in his quest for the Mayor's office in 1876 but was successful in 1880, defeating Democrat George C. Langdon 8,587 to 6,480. This was despite the opposition of the Detroit Free Press, who constantly gave the Republican Thompson bad press, reflecting on his "untrustworthy character." He was reelected in 1882, besting Democrat William Brodie 8,060 to 6,649.

The first opera house of Detroit, started in 1869, burnt in 1886. Thompson helped get the "Grand Opera House" rebuilt.

In February 1886 Thompson was at Swan's Bar on Woodward Avenue when he got into a political argument with Edward Bagard. Bagard hit Thompson soundly in the head with his cane, causing Thompson to be hospitalized.

Brawling at the Train Station

After his first wife Adelaide died, three years later in 1878

Thompson married Adele Campau, granddaughter of Joseph Campau. The marriage did not go well, and in 1888 the couple began divorce proceedings. The proceedings were very acrimonious, and Adele's brother Daniel Campau warned Thompson that he "must not talk about his wife hereafter in barrooms and other public places, as he has been doing."

Thompson once more *did* talk about his ex-wife, and the two had a public brawl at the Michigan Central Train Station. Eyewitness accounts stated that both men injured the other "quite grievously." Campau struck first, hitting Thompson on the head with his cane. The two men pummeled each other, and both were hospitalized, although reportedly Thompson got the worst of it. Thompson had been able to keep the barroom brawl two years previously out of the papers, but wasn't so lucky with this one, as even the New York Times reported on the brawl.

First Michigan Central train station in Detroit, where Campau and Thompson brawled.

Thompson disagreed with the Republican platform and switched parties from the Republicans to the Democrats. This split the party into two factions, one led by Thompson and the other by his brother-in-law and barroom opponent, Daniel Campau. Although he sought the nomination, Thompson was not nominated for Mayor by the Democrats. He was unsuccessful again in 1891, but in 1894 he switched back to the Republicans and was elected to the State Senate.

In 1904 Thompson was hit by a bicycle rider in downtown Detroit. Never fully recovering, he died in a sanitarium in Yonkers, New York on July 20, 1904, and was buried in the family plot in Princeton, New Jersey.

William Thompson gravesite in Princeton, New Jersey

Stephen B. Grummond, Mayor of Detroit 1884 to 1885

CHAPTER THIRTY-FIVE—STEPHEN B. GRUMMOND—GENERAL STORE MAYOR

Stephen Benedict Grummond (1831-1894) was born on September 18, 1834, in Marine City, Michigan (then called "Newport") which is north of Detroit. His father Stephen Grummond owned a successful general store in Newport.

Marine City was a large ship building area in the 19th Century. At the age of 15 Grummond started sailing on merchant ships and attended local schools in the winter months. He saved his money, and with some invested by his father, bought his own merchant ship and sailed it for several years, until 1855, when he sold it and moved to Detroit.

Marine City, MI. in St. Clair County, about the time of Grummond's time there.

Marine Tycoon

In Detroit he purchased another vessel and was soon engaged in the trade of buying, selling and operating various marine vessels. He established a line of steam ships and named it *Grummond's Mackinac Line.* He came to own the largest tug and wrecking business on the Great Lakes and expanded into barges, lumber, and Detroit real estate. He maintained extensive docks and warehouses on the Detroit River.

In 1861 he married Louisa B. Prouty, daughter of prominent Detroit tavern-owner Col. Nathaniel Prouty. They had eleven children, seven of whom survived Grummond.

Originally a Democrat, he joined the Republican Party to support Abe Lincoln and was elected to the Board of Estimates in 1879. In 1881 he was elected to the Common Council.

In 1883 he was the Republican candidate for Mayor and narrowly defeated the Democratic candidate, Marvin Chamberlain, a prominent liquor dealer and President of the Common Council, by a margin of 9,770 to 9,304.

The Controversial Eagen Bill

Controversy during Grummond's term included his endorsement of the Eagen Bill, which was regarded as a measure to deny foreign-born residents the right to vote. While Grummond was mayor, Detroit annexed the Delray Village, adding considerable acreage to Detroit. Senator Thomas Palmer donated 140 acres to the city. This area, called Palmer Park, grew to 300 acres.   When it came time for reelection in 1885, the reverse of the previous election occurred, as Marvin Chamberlain got 11,992 votes to 10,104 votes for Grummond. Prohibition Party candidate Carleton H. Mills garnered 129 votes.

Grummond remarked that he was glad to be back in private life and wouldn't have to travel so much between Detroit and his company headquarters in Mackinac. He purchased a Detroit hotel he named "The Benedict" and operated it for a few years after his mayoral term.   He died on January 2, 1894 at his home and was buried in Elmwood Cemetery. At the time of his death he was the President of the Police Commission of Detroit. His obituaries described him as a "man of broad and generous impulses, and at all times among the foremost in aiding every good and deserving work."

Although there was at one time a Grummond Avenue named for him, the street name was changed to Woodhall Avenue c1910.

Stephen Grummond gravesite in Elmwood Cemetery

Capitalists, Clowns, and Crooks, Choir-boys, Cops and Clerks: The May-

Marvin Chamberlain, Mayor of Detroit 1886-1887

C HAPTER THIRTY-SIX—MARVIN H. CHAMBERLAIN —LIQUOR AND TOBACCO MAYOR

Marvin H. Chamberlain (1842-1923) was born in Woodstock Township, Lenawee County, Michigan on November 5, 1842. Chamberlain attended local schools and taught before he entered Hillsdale College, a conservative private college in Hillsdale, Michigan. He moved to Detroit to attend business school in 1865 and began working as a bookkeeper and then as a traveling salesman for *F.A. Stokes*, a wholesale liquor business.

Wholesale Liquor and Fearless Tobacco

In 1867 he formed a partnership with his brother. They bought out F.A. Stokes and renamed the business *M. H. Chamberlain & Co.* The firm was immediately popular and became the leading wholesale liquor firm in Detroit. From their distillery they brewed whiskey, bourbon, and rye. In 1873 the

Chamberlain brothers formed the *Fearless Tobacco Co.*

After the business was sold in 1900 and became *C.H. Ritter & Co.*, the company continued to use the Chamberlain brand name.

M.H. Chamberlain & Co. teapot given to taverns to advertise the brand.

In 1874 Chamberlain started the *Commercial Traveler's Association of Michigan* and became its first President. He helped organize the Central Savings Bank and in 1876 he married Ellen Wilson of Niagara, New York.

Chamberlain Whisky label

In 1882 Chamberlain was elected to the Detroit Common Council and in 1885 became its President. In 1883 he ran for Mayor on the Democratic ticket and lost to Stephen Grummond. Grummond was a Temperance, anti-alcohol candidate, which was in direct opposition to Chamberlain's occupation as a liquor dealer.

However, on Chamberlain's next attempt in 1885, he prevailed and became Mayor of Detroit in 1886 and 1887, becoming the third Detroit mayor whose main occupation was alcohol sales (besides Duncan and Langdon). Chamberlain defeated incumbent Grummond 11,972 votes to 10,104.

The Detroit Symphony Orchestra formed during his term and the Detroit Wolverines baseball team won the 1887 baseball championship by coming in first in the National League and then defeating the St. Louis Browns for the championship.

At a reception for the winners at the Russell House, Chamberlain toasted the champions, saying, "Detroit is famed for beauty, culture, intelligence, energy and enterprise. But Detroit's baseball club has carried far and wide, even beyond the bounds of our nation, the renown of our fair city."

The Russell House.

He was not renominated due to a party schism. In 1888 he was a delegate to the Democratic National Convention from Michigan.

In 1898 Chamberlain patented a "liquid separating process" for reduction of garbage. Forming a company called *Detroit Liquid Separating Company,* he received the contract to collect garbage in Detroit and successfully started similar plants in other cities.

He died on February 5, 1923 at the age of 80 and was interred in Woodlawn Cemetery. Chamberlain Street in Detroit was named for him.

Marvin Chamberlain Gravesite.

Alan Naldrett

John Pridgeon, Mayor of Detroit 1888-1889

C HAPTER THIRTY-SEVEN—JOHN PRIDGEON—MARINE MAYOR

John Pridgeon, Jr. (1852-1929) was born August 1, 1852 and was only the second of the first mayors of Detroit actually *born* in Detroit. (John R. Williams was the first Detroit-born mayor.) Most were born elsewhere and moved to Detroit. His father, John Pridgeon, Sr., a sailor in the Mexican War, amassed a fleet of Great Lakes ships, and formed the White Star Line. The family also owned the Detroit & Windsor Ferry.

John, Jr. went to Detroit Public Schools and then attended the *Detroit Business University*. In 1871 he started working in his father's businesses and married Cora Edgar of Pittsburgh, Pennsylvania in 1874. The couple had two sons, but sadly neither of them outlived their parents. Cora received a divorce from John, Jr. in 1911 and John married Blanche Cate in 1915.

In 1876 he relocated to Port Huron, Michigan as an agent of *Chicago and Grand Trunk* line of steamers. When the line was dismantled in 1879 he rejoined his father's businesses.

Pridgeon was a member of the first Detroit Park Commission, serving from 1879-1883. In 1885 he was elected to the Common Council as a Democrat. In 1887 he was elected Mayor of Detroit, serving one term from 1888 to 1890.

One-Term Mayor

During his term, the Detroit Institute of Art opened in 1888, as the Detroit Museum of Art, and was located in a castle-like structure at 7043 E. Jefferson. The Detroit College of Medicine started, later growing into Wayne State University.

The Detroit Museum of Art, which opened in 1888 and was razed in 1960 to make room for Highway I-375.

Detroit's First Skyscraper

Detroit's first skyscraper, the 10-story Hammond Building was built in 1889, during Mayor Pridgeon's tenure. It was demolished in 1956.

The Hammond Building, Courtesy of the Detroit Historical Society

The Detroit International Exposition of 1889

One of the largest events in the history of Detroit was during Pridgeon's term. The Detroit International Fair and Exposition was held September 17 to September 27 in 1889. The city had been planning on something to showcase its diverse industries ever since the popular Philadelphia Exposition of 1876.

This was ten years before the first auto factory but Detroit in the late 1800s Detroit had already become a national leader in the production of soap, varnish, paints, hoopskirts, and shoes, and was well-known for its production of railroad cars, stoves, pharmaceutical medicines, and seeds.

The city purchased 72 acres of vacant land, just outside the Detroit city limits, east of Fort Wayne, by Del Ray. To prepare for the fair, marshes were drained, train tracks were laid, and docks were built.

Detroit International Exhibition Hall of 1889

Architect Louis Camper, later to be the architect for the Book-Cadillac Hotel, designed the 200,000 square foot Exhibition Hall, at the time the world's largest. The tower allowed for panoramic views of the larger Detroit area, including Canada.

The fair offered agricultural and mechanical exhibits, a house made of soap, trained seals, a pig who could play cards, a model of the Statue of Liberty, as well as the usual carnival attractions.

The main boat landing for the fair was at the intersection

of the Detroit River and the Rouge River. Ferryboats ran daily from Canada and Port Huron. The fair was successful, providing a tidy profit for its investors.

The exposition hall was used for two more expositions after the 1889 event and sporting events after the fair was over, until 1895, when the Solvay Process Company purchased the land. They tore down all the buildings and began mining for salt.

Near the end of the 19th Century housing began to greatly improve for the average Detroit homeowner. Houses began to be built with indoor bathrooms, sinks and built-in bathtubs, more modern stoves and kitchen appliances, backyards, and electricity throughout.

From 1886 to 1892 Detroit had a housing boom. The housing in Detroit was said to be superior to most major cities of the time. It was promoted as "one of the most beautiful cities of the West" due to its many trees and wide streets, allowing for lack of congestion. The city that later came to be known as "Murder City" in 1990 had one of the lowest "death rates" in the U.S. in 1890 when Detroit's population was 205,000.

Detroit real estate increased by five times from 1892 to 1910, as the surge of auto workers moving to Detroit to work in the auto factories increased the demand for housing. It increased by five times more in 1920, so a property worth $3,000 in 1892 was worth $15,000 in 1910 and $75,000 in 1920! Detroit continually ranked among the top cities in home ownership, even before the auto factory boom in 1910.

Before 1910, Detroit had a stable industrial economy, with a diverse number of products produced in Detroit before the auto boom with its up-and-down cycles. Before 1910, Detroit was a leader in producing malleable iron, disinfectant, gas engines, paint, aluminum castings, and varnish. Detroit had large pharmaceutical businesses like Parke-Davis and was a leader in ship-building and seed production. Over 95 percent of the country's stoves and furnaces were manufactured in Detroit. Detroit ranked second in the nation (behind New York City's garment district) in dress-making, and fourth in print production.

Detroit was also a leader in the production of railroad cars, jewelry, picture frames, corsets, furniture, fountain pens, corsets, perfume, yarn, milk cans, and pickles.

In the 1890s the wealthy still lived in the city's center on Woodward and on Jefferson, and in the Brush Park neighborhood, but they would soon migrate to new enclaves in the city, including Palmer Park, Arden Park, Indian Village and the Boston-Edison neighborhood.

John Pridgeon's home at 456 Woodward in Detroit. The house was built in 1868.

After his term as Mayor ended in 1889, Pridgeon became

the Police Commissioner of Detroit from 1891-1892.

After 1890 he concentrated on his business interests and became Vice-President of the White Star Line, and VP of the Red Star Line, the President of the State Transportation Co., Vice-President of the River Savings Bank, and President of the Pridgeon Transportation Company.

He died in 1929 at the age of 77 and was buried in Wood-mere Cemetery.

John Pridgeon tombstone in Woodmere Cemetery

Alan Naldrett

Hazen Pingree, Mayor of Detroit, 1890-1897

CHAPTER THIRTY-EIGHT—HAZEN PINGREE—POTATO PATCH PINGREE

Hazen S. Pingree (1840-1901) was one of the most famous big-city mayors in Detroit and the nation. He was one of the first Progressives, fighting corporations and big business.

Pingree was born in Denmark, Maine on August 30, 1840, and went to public schools until he was 14, when he moved to Saco, Maine and worked in a cotton factory. His father Thomas, a Revolutionary War veteran, was a farmer in the warm months, and a cobbler in the winter months, traveling around repairing shoes and boots.

Cutter in a Shoe Factory

In 1856 Hazen moved to Hopkinton, Massachusetts where he secured employment for several years as a cutter in a shoe factory.

In 1862 he enlisted in the Union Army in the 1st Massachusetts Heavy Artillery Regiment (Company F). He fought on the front lines during the Battle of the Second Bull Run and during

General Pope's Northern Virginia Campaign. His regiment defended Washington, D.C. until 1884, when he fought with the Second Brigade of Tyler's Division in battles at Fredericksburg Road, Spotsylvania Court House, and Harris Farm.

Pingree was then assigned to the Second Corp, Third Division, in the Army of the Potomac. He was taken prisoner at North Anna and sent first to prisons in Virginia and North Carolina and was then transferred to Andersonville in Georgia. He escaped, made his way back to his regiment where he fought at a few more battles, and then was present during the surrender of the Southern forces at Appomattox Courthouse in 1865.

Imprisoned at Andersonville

While he was imprisoned at Andersonville, Pingree met some soldiers from Detroit. He was impressed with the stories they told him about the economic opportunities there. After the war he moved to Detroit and got work as a cobbler at H. P. Baldwin's shoe company. In 1866 Pingree and accountant Charles Smith bought out the business, including the shoe-making machinery, and named it The Pingree and Smith Company. Smith retired from the firm in 1883 and Pingree's son joined the firm.

In 1872 Pingree married Frances A. Gilbert, a school-teacher from Mt. Clemens, Michigan. Two of their three children lived to adulthood—Hazel and Hazen, Jr.

Second-Largest Shoe Manufacturer in the U.S.

By 1886 Pingree's shoe factory was the second-largest shoe manufacturing factory in the United States. Pingree's company employed over 700 employees, manufacturing over a half-million boots and shoes each year. The company was worth over a million dollars in the 1880s, which would be worth about $28 million dollars today. Even though in 1887 the shoe plant burned down, the company soon recovered.

Detroit government in the 1880s was known to be corrupt,

political-machine controlled, and in need of reform. It was a reform platform that Pingree ran on for mayor in 1890. He promised to expose and end corruption in the school board, city paving projects, and sewer construction. One of the entities he focused on were privately-owned utility companies.

Pingree Becomes Mayor on Reform Platform

Pingree won the election over his Democratic opponent, John Pridgeon, 13,954 to 11,616. In his reelection in 1891, he beat his two opponents with 15,335 votes to Democrat William Thompson's 9,015 and "Regular Democratic Party" John Miner with 5,263. In his next election in 1893 he beat Democrat Marshall H. Godfrey 24,924 to 19,124. In his last Mayoral election in 1895 he beat Samuel Goldwater 21,024 to 10,432.

Inside Pingree's Mayoral Office

Pingree started municipally-owned gas and electric companies, challenging the privately-owned utility companies. He was thwarted by the courts on starting a municipal street car company but was successful in most of his other endeavors.

Potato Patches for the People

During the Depression of 1893, Pingree performed the act that got him the nickname "Potato Patch Pingree." He set aside 430 acres for the poor people of Detroit to use for personal gardens. He also created more municipal jobs to help ease unemployment.

Many immigrants were starving and burning furniture for heat. Pingree thought that some of them might be able to take unused urban land and use it for farming. To get his idea going, he went to the large churches of Detroit for donations of tools and seed. The churches treated Pingree with contempt and the Democratic newspapers made fun of the idea.

Pingree in one of his potato patches in Detroit.

This didn't stop Pingree, who sold his prize race-horse at a third of its worth to kick off the project. On June 6, 1893 he got the 430 acres and 945 families grew $14,000 worth of food, so much that there was a surplus. The next year 1,500 families had garden plots and in 1896 the value of the produce exceeded $30,000, more than the total outlay of the City Poverty Commission. The Potato Patch Program saved many families from starving. When news of his success began to be known, Pingree became a national hero.

Hazen Pingree statue in Grand Circus Court, Downtown Detroit.

Plaque on Hazen Pingree statue

Corrupt School Board Busted

At an 1890 Detroit School Board meeting, shortly after Pingree took office, he strode in and announced, "There are quite a number of the members of this board who are going to jail tonight."

Pingree then called on the School Board officials, without naming the guilty ones, to "resign and save the city from disgrace." When no one moved, Pingree began to read the names and charges of the four board members to be placed under arrest. He called on policemen present to arrest them and take them to jail. Many charges were read, chief among them was taking payoffs from building contractors.

Pingree had used a school furniture salesperson to gather proof to ensnare the corrupt members. A meeting had been held with the officials in which each one outlined their bribe requirements. Unbeknownst to them, Pingree had installed a stenographer next door where she could hear and take notes. At trial, two were convicted, one acquitted, and one jumped bail and was never seen again.

Battling Corporate Corruption

Pingree spent his first term trying to eliminate government inefficiency and graft. His battle with the utilities over excessively high rates started with the gas company, forcing down their prices with municipal competition. The Bell Telephone Company had to cut their rates in half once Pingree introduced a competitive phone company.

Another of Pingree's successful campaigns was to eliminate waste. He cut out redundant jobs and departments. He made garbage inspectors and other departments work more efficiently. He required janitors and other municipal employees to work their entire 8-hour shift, instead of going home after 6 hours. He refused raises for municipal clerks and election inspectors, telling them their unsatisfactory work didn't merit higher paychecks.

Battling the Streetcar Companies

Pingree had numerous battles with the *Citizens Company*, which ran the antiquated, horse-drawn, street-car system. They abrogated their agreements they made with the city as far as upgrading the system and maintaining the roads. After a long battle to view the company's books, it was found they were not meeting their tax requirements and that their stock was "watered down." This caused the oppressive-for-the-times rate of 5 cents, to make up for the overvalued, watered down stock.

Pingree and the first run of the 3-cent trolley.

In retaliation, Pingree invited another company into town to operate a more modern system with a lower fare. On July 8, 1895, the new rail line, *Detroit Railway Company,* was completed and charged only three cents for fares.

On the inaugural run, Pingree drove the train with the City Aldermen in the second car. They were met with wild jubilation and instant success. Hundreds of people gathered by the tracks, many of them throwing bouquets of flowers into the train. Pingree reveled in the attention, to the point that he almost ran into a herd of cows on Riopelle Street.

"Free Music in City Parks" started in 1890; in 1891 *the Detroit College of Law* opens. Palmer Park is established in 1893, and in 1895 public lighting is installed in Detroit.

Charles King is Detroit's First Motorist

While Pingree was Mayor, Detroit took its first steps toward becoming the Motor City. March 6 1896, Charles B. King, inventor of the pneumatic hammer, with his assistant Oliver Barthel, drove Detroit's first vehicle down Woodward. Henry Ford drove his Quadricycle down Woodward Avenue 3 months later on June 4, 1896. In 1897, Barton Peck, who owned the machine shop/bicycle shop at 81 Park Place in Detroit where King and Ford worked on cars, was the third man to drive a car he built himself (with a little help from his friends Henry Ford and Charles King) in Detroit.

In 1896 Bennett Park, hosting Detroit Tigers ball games, became the first of many stadiums at Michigan and Trumbull Streets in Detroit.

Progressive and Productive Four Terms as Mayor

Pingree served four terms as Detroit's Mayor, and during that time he had revolutionized the Detroit road situation, added more paved roads, and eliminated the toll roads. Roads paved with asphalt in Detroit included Jefferson, Lafayette, Second, and Cass Streets. The other roads were cobblestone, cedar block, brick or unpaved.

Pingree took care to move unsightly wires out of the way, had new parks built, instituted new schools, and had a free public bath constructed. He updated the sewer system and expanded public welfare. Because of his work, the office of Mayor of Detroit began to hold great prestige.

The first policewoman in the U.S. was Marie Owen in Detroit in 1893. In 1895 Detroit Public Schools established Kindergartens and the Detroit Power Station began providing power for Detroit's public buildings and streetlights. In 1896 the Central High School building opened at Cass and Warren Avenues. It is later one of the central buildings for Wayne State University, now known as Old Main.

Old Main building of Wayne State, formerly Detroit Central High School

Mayor and Governor

Pingree's fame grew throughout the U.S., with talk of him running for President in 1900. He was nominated as the Republican candidate for Governor of Michigan in 1896. He succeeded in winning the election while helping to carry Michigan for Presidential winning candidate William McKinley.

Pingree expected to finish out his last year as Detroit Mayor simultaneously with his term as Governor. But the Michigan Supreme Court ruled that he couldn't serve in both offices at the same time, so Pingree chose to remain Governor, resigning as Mayor.

Pingree served two two-year terms as Governor, during which he promoted the regulation of railroad rates, municipal ownership of utilities, and equal taxation for all. He supported fair income tax rates, and compulsory arbitration for labor disputes. He worked to abolish child labor and succeeded in ending the most flagrant tax violations by large corporations.

Although many of his reforms were blocked at the time, most have since been implemented. He said, "I do not condemn corporations and rich men, but I would keep them within their proper spheres. It is not safe to entrust the government of the country to the influence of Wall Street."

Contempt of Court

He chose not to run for reelection in 1900. In fact, he had just received a contempt of court citation for insulting an Ingham County judge. In a farewell address he said, by way of explanation, "If this young man thinks he has a monopoly on my contempt and that I have contempt for just his court alone, he is mistaken. For I have contempt for dozens of courts in this state, knowing their methods of procedure."

Pingree's last statement was "To hell with you and your contempt!" Instead of going to court, he went on an African safari. Unfortuneatly, he took ill on his way to London. Ironically, his "twin," Edward VII, King of England, who bore an uncanny resemblance to Pingree, sent his personal doctors to attend Pingree where he lay in London's Grand Hotel. But sadly, Pingree succumbed to peritonitis at the age of 60 on June 18, 1901.

His body was returned to the U.S. where it was at first interred in Elmwood. It was moved to Woodlawn Cemetery upon construction of a large mausoleum there.

There is a large statue of a seated Hazen Pingree in Grand Circus Park, which denotes him as "The Idol of the People." There was a mass outpouring of Detroiters contributing to the erection of the statue. Detroit also has a Pingree Street and Pingree Square named for Hazen Pingree.

Pingree and look-a-like King Edward VII of England

Pingree Mausoleum in Woodlawn Cemetery

William Richert, Mayor for 16 days in 1887

C HAPTER 39— WILLIAM RICHERT—FILL- IN MAYOR

When Hazen Pingree was ordered by the Michigan Supreme Court to resign as Mayor (since the Supreme Court ruled that he couldn't be both Mayor of Detroit and Governor), there was still a month left on his term. So, William Richert (1858-1912), Alderman and President of the Common Council, was appointed to fill in from March 22 until the election on April 5, 1887, about 16 days.

Richert was born in Germany on October 8, 1858 and moved with his family to the U.S. when he was a teenager. He became a grocer and a wholesale liquor distributor. He was elected to the Detroit Common Council four times and was President when Pingree resigned as Mayor.

Richert signed his few documents as "Acting Mayor." During his short term he filled vacancies on the fire and the lighting commissions. He was Mayor of Detroit for 16 days, March 22, until April 5, 1887.

In later years Richert worked as a foreman for the Detroit Board of Public Works. He died June 16, 1912 and was buried in Elmwood Cemetery.

William C. Maybury, Mayor of Detroit 1897-1904

C HAPTER FORTY —WILLIAM C. MAYBURY—DETROIT BICENTENNIAL MAYOR

William Cotter Maybury (1848-1909) was Mayor of Detroit after Pingree—and during the rise of the automobile in Detroit.

Maybury was the third mayor born in Detroit, born on November 20, 1848. He attended Detroit's Old Capitol Public School, graduating in 1866. He then attended the University of Michigan and graduated in 1870 with a Bachelor of Arts. In 1871 he attained a Bachelor of Law from U. of M. He was admitted to the bar in 1872 and opened a law practice in Detroit with partner Edward F. Conely. From 1876 to 1880 he was the City Attorney for Detroit.

Michigan Congressional Representative

In 1882 and 1884 Maybury was elected to the U.S. House of Representatives from Michigan's 1st Congressional District, after trying for the position but losing in 1880. He didn't run for reelection in 1886 but instead returned to private practice. Maybury was nominated by the Democrats for Detroit Mayor in 1897. Maybury won the election, which was to complete Pingree's last year as Mayor when he resigned to become Michigan's Governor.

In 1897, Bob-Lo Island was established as an entertainment destination, with two boats used to transport people to the island carnival area. Ford started his first auto company, the Detroit Automobile Company, in 1899 with Maybury as one of the investors. In 1901 the Detroit Tigers baseball team started playing.

The First Auto Show in 1899

In 1899, William Metzger held the nation's first auto show, a year before New York and Chicago. He held it in conjunction with sports manufacturer Seneca Lewis and Fletcher Hardware, at the Light Guard Armory in Detroit. Metzger had started off selling bicycles and began selling autos from his bicycle shop. He brought two electric *Waverly* cars and two steam *Mobile* cars to the show. The cars were an immediate sensation, and undoubtably inspired many of Detroit's future auto builders.

The auto show was so successful for Metzger that, despite spending all his profits celebrating and buying drinks for everyone at the Russell House, the next year he was confident enough to hold the second auto show, solo, without Fletcher Hardware or any sporting goods manufacturers. By the second show autos were catching on more in Detroit and there were more auto exhibitors besides Metzger.

Metzger went on to organize car dealers to sell the cars of the Cadillac Motor Company. Because of this dealer system, Cadillac came from nowhere to be the second-highest selling car in the U.S. (Ford was first). He went on to become affiliated with the Northern Motor (Manufacturing) Company to oversee sales and was the "M" as part of the E-M-F Motor Company.

Mayor Maybury was an early investor in Henry Ford's auto companies.

In 1899 Sebastian Spering Kresge opened the first S.S. Kresge "Five and Dime" store on Woodward. The Kresge stores were very successful and a large chain of Kresges opened, growing into a business empire. The culmination of Kresge's work was the K-Mart chain. S.S. Kresges' name appeared on many libraries and other buildings throughout the Detroit area due to Kresge's philanthropy.

An early Kresge's "Five and Dime" store.

A RISE IN CRIME

Unfortunately, during Mayor Maybury's term was when the proliferation of organized crime first became widely known, as Filippo Tocco is sentenced to fifteen years for murder and extortion. The emergence of an Italian area in Detroit called Little Sicily or Little Italy (east of Woodward between Brush and Beaubien) caused alarm, as the inhabitants, familiar with the Mafia and Cosa Nostra from their previous homes, grew paranoid. Accusations of extortion and human trafficking were rampant.

Where Woodward Avenue met the Detroit River c1910

In 1900, the turn of the century, a time capsule called the "Detroit Century Box," with documents by Mayor Maybury from 1900 was buried and opened in 2000.

In 1900 the Detroit Tigers joined the American League, becoming a "major league" baseball team, the first in Detroit since 1888, when Mayor William G. Thompson's Detroit Wolverines were in the major league of their day. Detroit's population was 285,704 people, making it the 13th largest city in the U.S. Of the large number of immigrants, nearly 12% of Detroit residents didn't speak English.

Detroit, the Stove Capital of the World

In 1900 Detroit was called the "stove capital" of the world because the city was the largest manufacturer of heating and cooking stoves. Other major industries in the growing city included pharmaceuticals, cigar, tobacco and beer manufacturing, ship-building, and foundry and machine shop products.

The latter products helped set Detroit up to become the Motor City, the nexus of auto manufacturing in the United States. A lot of auto history occurred during Maybury's tenure. In 1898 Henry Ford organized his first auto company, the *Detroit Automobile Company*, which failed after producing only two vehicles, neither of which were satisfactory. During Maybury's tenure Ford also begins his second company, the *Henry Ford Company*, in 1901. This company became the *Cadillac Motor Company*.

Detroit's First Car Factory

Ransom E. Olds founded the factory for Detroit's first successful auto company, the *Olds Motor Works*, near the Belle Isle Bridge, during Maybury's term. When the factory burnt down, Olds moved back to his hometown, Lansing, Michigan and set up a factory there to build America's first successful gasoline vehicle, the Curved-Dash Oldsmobile. Lansing had offered Olds tax concessions to rebuild his factory there.

While Maybury was Mayor, the city annexed the Village of Beech in 1900. This municipality had been first settled in 1827.

*William C. Maybury, Mayor of Detroit, statue
in Grand Circus Park*

Maybury went on to win two more mayoral terms, ending in 1904. Maybury ran for Governor of Michigan in 1900 but was defeated by Republican Aaron T. Bliss.

In 1903 the Century Theatre opened, ushering in Detroit's "theatre era." It was originally built for a local women's civic group to meet in. In 1928 the civic group built a two-story theatre, named the Gem, next door. The theatre was used for vaudeville performances and film screenings. In 1997 the theatre was moved five blocks away, setting the world's record, at 5.5 million tons, as the heaviest structure ever moved on wheels.

In 1904 it was decided by J.L. Hudson and other city dignitaries to give the Michigan State Fair, the oldest in the nation, a permanent home. It had been at different venues since its inception in 1849.

An area of 135 acres was purchased between 71/2 Mile Road (later renamed State Fair Road) and 8 Mile, east of Woodward. The fair was there until 2009, when it was discontinued by Governor Jennifer Granholm.

Detroit Bi-Centennial

Maybury also officiated during the ceremonies marking Detroit's 200th Anniversary in 1901. Maybury, who was later sculpted sitting in a chair across from Mayor Pingree, ironically presided over the unveiling of Detroit's gift to itself, the Cadillac Chair. Unveiled in Cadillac square, east of Campus Martius, on July 24, 1901, it was a large sandstone chair.

Inscribed on the chair was "This chair, erected July 24, 1901, is located on the site of the City Hall built in 1835 and occupied until 1871 as the seat of Civic Authority. "It is symbolic of the Seigneurial Rule of Antoine de la Mothe Cadillac,

Knight of St. Louis, who, with his company of colonists, arrived at Detroit, July 24, 1701. "On that day, under the patronage of Louis XIV, and protected by the Flag of France, the City of Detroit, then called Fort Ponchartrain, was founded."

The chair unveiling was accompanied by speeches proclaiming the chair as "a true testament to how grand Detroit was, and that it would be something that would stand for ages and tell future generations of the city's heritage." But it barely lasted 40 years. When the chair became a popular seat for vagrants, the city decided to remove it, but probably not to some historical warehouse, in 1941. The use of sledgehammers to remove the chair didn't bode well for its future.

The removal of the Cadillac Chair in November 1941.

After his mayoral term, Maybury retired from public life.

He joined the law firm *Conely, Maybury, and Lucking* and worked as an attorney for the *Standard Life & Accident Insurance Company*. He died in Detroit and was buried in Elmwood Cemetery in 1909.

In 1912 a statue of Maybury was unveiled in Grand Circus Park, across from Hazen Pingree's statue. Both of the statues show their respective mayors seated. Maybury Grand Avenue in Detroit was named for Mayor Maybury.

Wil-liam Maybury gravesite in Elmwood Cemetery.

Alan Naldrett

George P. Codd, Mayor of Detroit, 1905-1906

C HAPTER FORTY-ONE—GEORGE P. CODD—BASEBALL PITCHER AND MAYOR

George Pierre Codd (1869-1927) was born in Detroit on December 7, 1869. His father, George C. Codd, was active in civic matters, serving as Detroit Postmaster, a member of the Common Council, and Sheriff of Wayne County.

George P. Codd went to Detroit Public Schools and graduated, entering the University of Michigan and graduating in 1891 with a Bachelor of Arts. While in college he was a pitcher for the Michigan Wolverines college baseball team from 1888 to 1892 (not to be confused with the Detroit Wolverines, who won the NL championship in 1888).

Codd studied law after graduation and was admitted to the bar in 1892. He joined a law office, *Griffin, Warner, and Hunt*, in Detroit in 1893. In 1894 Dodd married Kathleen Warner and they had three children, John, George C., and Kathleen.

Assistant City Attorney for Detroit

From 1894 to 1897 Codd was the Assistant City Attorney for Detroit. He became a partner in the firm of *Warner, Codd, and Warner* in 1898 and in 1901 started his own law firm.

In 1902 and 1903 Codd was a city alderman and in 1904 was elected Mayor of Detroit. He was mayor in 1905 and 1906 but was defeated for reelection. When he supported a compromise with the Detroit United Railway, he lost a lot of public support.

While Codd was Mayor, the city annexed the part of the Village of Del Ray not previously annexed, as well as more acreage from Springwell Township. Detroit also annexed the Woodmere Village, which had grown around the Woodmere Cemetery and was essentially a bedroom community for workers at Ford's Rouge River Plant. The Village of Bell Branch, formerly part of Redford Township, was annexed in 1907.

In 1908 Codd was a delegate to the Republican National Convention from Michigan and served as a Regent for the University of Michigan in 1910 and 1911. From 1911 to 1921 he was Circuit Judge of Wayne County for the 3rd District.

Elected to House of Representatives

In 1921 Codd was elected from the 1st Congressional District to the U.S. House of Representatives and served one two-year term, from 1921 to 1923. He declined to run for reelection and returned to private law practice.

He was again elected Circuit Judge for Wayne County in 1924 and served until his death in Detroit on February 26, 1927, at the age of 57. He was interred in Elmwood Cemetery.

William B. Thompson, Mayor of Detroit 1907-1908, 1911-1912

C HAPTER 42 —WILLIAM B. THOMPSON—MEAT MARKET MAYOR

William Barlum Thompson (1860-1941) was born on March 10, 1860, in Detroit and went to Detroit Public Schools, graduating from Detroit Central High School. In 1876 he graduated from Goldsmith's Detroit Business University in Detroit.

After graduation Thompson went into the meat-market business with his Uncle Thomas Barlum and became a partner in 1880. In 1882 he ventured off on his own, opening a store in Cadillac Square called Thompson and Brothers. Other businesses followed, including Robinson's Beef Company and the Cadillac Square Improvement Company. He became the Treasurer of the Detroit Furnace Repair Company and was Secretary-Treasurer of the Michigan Salt Pickle and Supply Company of Saginaw, Michigan.

The Cadillac Improvement Co. constructed the Barlow Tower (now the Cadillac Tower), the Lawyer's Trust Building, and the Barlum Hotel.

The Lawyer's Trust Building, now known as the Lawyer Building

In 1887 he married Nellie Hymes and they had nine children together: Mary, Kathleen, Irene, William, Francis, Helen, Edna, Edith and Virginia.

Detroit City Treasurer

Thompson, a Democrat, served as an alderman for two terms, from 1891 to 1894, and then again in 1896. He resigned his seat as an alderman when he was elected to the City Treasurer position in 1897. He served as Treasurer for nine years.

In 1906 Thompson was elected Mayor of Detroit for the 1907-1908 term. He beat Republican incumbent George Codd, 30,042 to 27,241.

Mayor Thompson is at the head of the table.

Detroit Becomes the Motor City

During Thompson's first term, Detroit's ascent to become the Motor City was cemented as Ford Motor Company released the Model T. The "Tin Lizzie" was a dependable, and most importantly, affordable auto that put the nation on wheels. Detroit began to grow beyond being the stove capital of the world.

People began to rush to Detroit to work in the new auto factories. Besides Ford, other major auto factories in Detroit included Packard, Fisher Auto Body, Budd, Hudson, Chalmers, Hupp, Paige, Studebaker, Wayne, and Northern, to name just a few. Many of these were in the Milwaukee Junction section of Detroit, at the nexus of two railroad lines.

While William B. Thompson was Mayor, the Detroit Tigers were in the World Series for three years in a row, 1907, 1908, and 1909, winning the pennant for the American League. They didn't win the Series in any of those years, even though the all-time-great baseball player Ty Cobb was on the team then.

Ty Cobb was considered by many the greatest baseball player of all and held many records for decades, spending all his years with Detroit. He was also known for having a devil-may-care attitude about the game also. One time he cut across the field from first to third base when the umpire wasn't looking. This was in the days when there was only one umpire.

Coincidentally enough, Mayor William B. Thompson was not to be confused with Mayor William G. Thompson, the man who brought the Detroit Wolverines to Detroit and won the Baseball Championship in 1888.

Thompson was reelected in 1910 for the 1911-1912 term, besting Republican Proctor K. Owens 22,461. In his second term he tried coming up with a solution to the streetcar problem, but it was voted down. Thompson ordered the arrest of several city Councilmen on charges of corruption but was unable to make any charges stick.

In 1907, when Thompson was Mayor, Detroit annexed the Village of Fairview, which contained a big racetrack. Detroit wanted the area to better compete in the streetcar business. The people of Fairview voted to be annexed because they wanted to hook up to the superior Detroit Sewer System.

In 1910 the Detroit Housing Commission was formed and in the same year, the city established a building code. More stringent zoning laws were enacted to prevent taverns, factories, and other inappropriate businesses from encroaching on residential neighborhoods.

After 1912 he returned to operating his business enterprises. On February 12, 1941, Thompson died at home in Detroit at the age of 80. He was interred in Detroit's Catholic cemetery, Mt. Olivet. There is a Thompson Street in Detroit, possibly named for either William Thompson that was mayor.

Breitmeyer, Mayor of Detroit, 1909-1910

C HAPTER FORTY-THREE—PHILIP BREITMEYER— FLORIST MAYOR

Philip Breitmeyer (1864-1941) was a famous horticulturist, the son of John and Fredericka Breitmeyer. He was born in Detroit on May 3, 1864 and attended Detroit Public Schools until he was eleven, when he quit to work in his father's florist shop, John Breitmeyer and Sons. When his father died Philip bought out his brothers and became sole owner of the firm.

He was President of Breitmeyer's Nursery and the Broadway Market Company. However, his greatest fame came from being one of the founders and President of the Florist Telegraph Delivery Co., also known as FTD Florists. The firm was founded to enable customers to send same-day flowers to someone, using the FTD network of florists all over the United States. The Breitmeyer-Tobin Building was built in Detroit to house the firm.

Breitmeyer was also President of the American Society of Florists, President of the Michigan Cut Flower Exchange, Vice-President of the German-American Bank, Director of the Detroit National Fire Insurance Company, and Director of the Lohrman Seed Company.

The Breitmeyer-Tobin Building, now known as the Harmonie Center, on Broadway Avenue in the Downtown Broadway Historic District of Detroit.

Breitmeyer married Katherine Grass of Philadelphia, Pennsylvania on March 9, 1886 and they had two children, Harry and Katherine. The family were Christian Scientists.

Breitmeyer was appointed by Mayor George Codd to a two-year term as Commissioner of the city's Parks and Boulevards Department in 1907 and 1908. Breitmeyer was elected Mayor of Detroit as a Republican in 1909. Detroit's population was over 465,000 during Breitmeyer's term.

The Detroit Salt Company began mining the salt deposits underneath Detroit in during Breitmeyer's term in 1910. Beneath the city is over 100 miles worth of tunnels. By 1914 the mine was producing over 8,000 tons of salt each year. While originally selling to the leather and food industries, today the salt is mostly used on highways in the wintertime to melt ice.

The Detroit Salt Mines opened in 1910 and consists of a network of tunnels below the city of Detroit.

Auto Businesses Continue to Grow

During Breitmeyer's term, Detroit continued to expand its auto businesses, as Ford built a large plant at 7 Mile Road and Woodward. The first mile of cement road in the U.S. was poured between 6 and 7 Mile on Woodward in 1909. The actual municipality of that location is Highland Park, a city within Detroit.

Like the mayors before him, Breitmeyer's biggest problem as mayor was the disagreements with the city trolley system, the DUR.

The Dime Savings Bank Building is a 23-story white terra-cotta skyscraper started in 1910 and completed during Brietmeyer's term in 1912. The Dime Savings Bank started in Detroit in 1884 with only $60,000 in capital. Since they had so little, they made a big effort to recruit new customers. Anyone could open a savings account for as little as a dime, hence the name of the bank. The bank merged with the Merchant's National Bank, but the building continued to be called the "Dime Building" until purchased by developer Dan Gilbert in 2011. He renamed it the "Chrysler House" in 2012.

Dime Savings Bank, Detroit.

The Dime Bank Building, now the Chrysler House

After his mayoral term, Breitmeyer concentrated on his successful businesses until 1933, when he made a failed attempt to again be elected Mayor of Detroit. In 1937 he was elected to a seat on the Detroit Common Council.

He died on November 9, 1941 in Detroit and was interred in Roseland Park Cemetery in Berkley, Michigan.

Roseland Park Cemetery Mausoleum in Berkley, MI.

Oscar Marx, Mayor of Detroit, 1913-1918

C HAPTER FORTY-FOUR—OSCAR MARX—OPTICAL MAYOR

Oscar Bruno Marx (1866-1923) was born on July 4, 1866 in Wayne County, Michigan—the son of German immigrants Stephen and Eleanor. He attended Detroit public schools and then went to the German-American Seminary. He spent much of his youth farming, until Detroit and Hamtramck city limits swallowed up the family farm. His father sold the land, giving each of his sons several thousand dollars apiece to start a business with.

Oscar used his money to buy controlling interest in the Michigan Optical Company in 1891 and turned it into the largest optical company in the Midwest. He diversified into being Vice-President of the Robert Oakman Land Company and a member of the Board of Directors of the Standard Computing Scale Company.

One of the Standard Computing Scale Company's scales

In 1897 Marx married Lydia Darmstaetter and had no trouble remembering their children's names as they gave their son and daughter the names of Oscar and Lydia, after themselves.

In 1894 Marx became the Estimator for Detroit until 1895, when he was elected an Alderman and held that office until 1903. In 1904 he ran for City Treasurer but was defeated. He was the delegate to the Republican National Convention from Michigan in 1908 and 1916 and was appointed the City Assessor in 1910.

Oscar Marx (in auto) on the campaign trail

Mayor of a Growing City

In 1912 Marx was elected to the first of his three terms as Mayor of Detroit. In 1912, he received 36,067 votes, while the incumbent Democratic candidate William B. Thompson polled 25,268. The Progressive Party candidate received 7,985 votes. The next term he won was in 1914 and he got 36,845 to Democrat Frederick F. Ingram's 25,268. His best showing was in 1916 when he beat Democrat William F. Connolly 63,305 to 49,702.

Marx presided over the first time auto factories transformed into the Arsenal of Democracy, building much-needed planes, torpedoes, munitions and other military equipment for the U.S. troops and their allies.

Horace and John Dodge

Horace and John Dodge, the Dodge Brothers.

John Dodge Funds the Marx Campaign

During the 1910s, the Michigan Republican Party was mainly run by three people: Oscar Marx, Robert Oakman, realtor and land developer whom Oakman Boulevard was named for, and auto mogul John Dodge of the *Dodge Brothers Motor Company.*

John and Horace Dodge poured a lot of money into the Republican Party, to the benefit of Marx. The money was used for promotions and campaigns for Republicans. John and his brother Horace were mainly looking for influence and liked Marx.

Although the Dodge Brothers were known for their bar carousing as well as astute leadership of their company. At the party in the Book-Cadillac Hotel to celebrate their 1914 Dodge automobile, to end the party John Dodge jumped on the table and smashed out all the bulbs in the chandelier with his cane.

The same John Dodge received the Distinguished Service Medal from France for his expert design of parts that helped the French win World War I.

The Dodge Brothers were very close. When Horace contracted pneumonia, John sat at his bedside until Horace recovered. However, this left him so weak that when he contracted the disease himself, he couldn't fight it off. Horace was so upset at John's death that he died just months after. They are both buried in an Egyptian-style mausoleum in Woodlawn Cemetery.

The Dodge Mausoleum in Detroit's Woodlawn Cemetery

Although John and Horace Dodge were close, they still had their disagreements. One time they had purchased a yacht together (the *Delphine*) and were going to take a cruise with their families. Only they couldn't agree on where to go. John wanted the Chicago area and Horace wanted the Thousand Islands. This led to an argument over who owned the yacht. They agreed to decide it with a coin toss. John won, and then decided they would go the Horace's choice, the Thousand Islands.

The Dodge Brothers would go to workingman's bars, have fights, break mirrors and more, and even make the bartender dance on the bar to the tune of gunshots. After the night was over and the damage was done, the chauffer would be sent in to pay for the damage.

Mayor Marx and his supporters, including John Dodge.

Immigrants Move to Detroit for Auto Jobs

While Marx was Mayor the city's population doubled, from about 450,000 to about 900,00. As Detroit began building automobiles, workers flocked in from all over the country and Canada to take advantage of Ford Motor Company's $5 a day wage. From 1916 to 1929 a major migration of African-Americans moved to Detroit to capture some of the auto factory jobs.

Other large auto concerns hiring immigrants included the Packard Motor Company, Hudson Motor Company, Chalmers Motor Company, Studebaker Motor Company, and the body and frame builders Budd, Briggs, and the Fisher Brothers. Also, Paige, Scripps-Booth, Maxwell, Oak, and Saxon.

Besides these companies, many other companies taking advantage of the newly developing auto industry came to or began in Detroit, such as Champion Spark Plugs and Delco Starters. The many employment opportunities became a reason for immigrants to settle in Detroit.

The municipal ownership issue of the streetcar system was still not settled. Marx formed the Streetcar Railway Commission and the system was able to immediately start charging only 3 cents per ride. It would eventually pay off the Detroit United Railway and the streetcar system would fall under city control. After all the streetcar battles were over and won by the city, they were eventually removed, a casualty of the auto age.

Detroit Building Surge

During Marx's term Detroit had a building surge, adding a new Detroit Public Library in midtown on Woodward, a new Municipal Court building, and the Receiving Hospital. Marx appointed James Couzens as Police Commissioner and started a committee for building the Outer Drive overpass in the city.

Detroit annexed more land during Marx's term, including the Villages of St. Clair Heights and Leesville. This caused Highland Park to incorporate as a city in 1918 to protect its tax base by preventing annexation by Detroit. Hamtramck would later do the same in 1922. Detroit is the only major city with separate, independent cities within its boundaries.

Detroit Public Library, Main Building, on Woodward Avenue

The Detroit Public Library, exterior and interior, opened during Marx's mayoral term.

One big factor adding to the growth of Detroit, especially skyward, was the Book Brothers. They were the grandsons and heirs of one of Detroit's largest landowners, Francis Palms. Palms started off buying the Indian Reserves lands when they became available in the early 1800s. He divided them and sold them to settlers. He then used the profits to purchase Upper Peninsula timberland and land with iron deposits. He eventually owned banks and insurance companies and was President of the Michigan Stove Company.

Palms' heirs were his grandsons Charles Palms, a banker who helped form Northern Motor Car Company, and James Burgess, Jr. (1843-1916), Herbert (1895-1963) and Frank (1893-1961) Books, known collectively as the Book Brothers. Francis Palms had started buying whole business blocks in Detroit and the Book Brothers put buildings on them.

One of the most well-known buildings they built was when they tore down the building, the Cadillac Hotel, that they had grown up in (so much for sentiment). They built a brand-new hotel, the Book-Cadillac, keeping the old name and adding theirs. The Romanesque, Italianate styled Cadillac Hotel, had grown to encompass the whole block at Washington Boulevard and Michigan Avenue, and stood from 1888 until 1923. Presidents of the U.S. Benjamin Harrison, William McKinley, Teddy Roosevelt, Grover Cleveland, and William Howard Taft all stayed there.

The original Cadillac Hotel (Courtesy of Library of Congress)

The Book-Cadillac Hotel

The Book Brothers inherited a large parcel along Washington Boulevard. To add to this parcel, they purchased more land along the street, hoping to achieve their dream of transforming the "ragged and rundown" Washington Boulevard into a fashionable shopping district.

Other well-known Book Brothers buildings are the Book Building, the Book Towers, and the Francis Palms Building, named for their grandfather. The Francis Palms building contains the Fox Theatre and the State Theater and is across from Comerica Park, on Woodward Avenue in Detroit. The heyday of this building boom in Detroit started during the mayoral term of Oscar Marx and continued into the term of James Couzens.

During Marx's mayoral tenure Michigan passed a law prohibiting alcohol in the state. Most of the rural communities voted for it and Wayne County and Detroit voted against it. This would give Michigan a 2-year head start on coming up with ways to smuggle alcohol into Detroit.

Pre-World War I, Detroit was one of the principal centers of German spy activities in 1914, with buildings burned, factories dynamited and a railway bridge to Canada blown up. A plot to blow up the Michigan Central Railroad was foiled.

In 1915 a plan was unveiled for a Detroit subway system, with the Detroit Urban Railway (DUR) included in the plans. The DUR was purchased by the city in 1922 for almost $20,000,000 and after that cash outlay, the subway was rarely discussed.

During the Marx term, Woodward Avenue was paved all the way to Pontiac, and Ford's Highland Park plant became outmoded. Ford made plans to move to the River Rouge Plant, completed in 1919.

Marx had some problems when he appointed his friend, John Gillespie as police commissioner. Undesirable characters started going in and out of the police headquarters, causing ugly rumors. Gillespie was convinced to resign, and Marx appointed James Couzens as Police Commissioner. Couzens would go on to be Marx's successor as Mayor.

Marx retired from public life after his third mayoral term in 1918. He kept himself busy with his optical business and real estate interests and died on November 23, 1923. He was the first Mayor of Detroit to be cremated. His ashes were given to his son, Oscar B. Marx, Jr. There is a Marx Street named for him in Detroit.

James Couzens, Mayor of Detroit, 1919-1922

C HAPTER FORTY-FIVE—JAMES J. COUZENS—FORD PIONEER, MAYOR AND SENATOR

James Joseph Couzens (1872-1936) was born in Chatham, Ontario, to English parents James and Emma. His father operated a soapmaking operation. Young James went to the local Chatham schools and spent two years in high school, and two years in business college.

He once described to friends at the Detroit Athletic Club how poor his beginnings were. "We were so poor in Chatham that we could not have a hanging kerosene lamp in our parlor, like the neighbors. I organized the rest of the kids in the family and we went into the alleys and collected old iron and scraps to get pennies for a lamp fund" reminisced Couzens.

Couzens took a job as a "newsbutcher" for the Erie and Huron Railroad when he was 16. A newsbutcher hawked or sold newspapers on the train. Inventor Tom Edison had a similar job when he was younger. When Couzens turned 18 in 1890, a friend encouraged him to come to Detroit, where he found a job as a car checker in the Michigan Central Railroad yard.

Couzens Becomes Associated with Alexander Malcomson and Henry Ford

In 1895, Couzens was hired by coal merchant Alexander Malcomson as a bookkeeper. When Malcomson decided to invest in Henry Ford's new auto company in 1903, he brought Couzens along to help with the new car company's bookkeeping. Before long, Couzens was working exclusively for the Ford Motor Company.

Couzens worked hard and was a harsh taskmaster and tough horse trader, insisting the first batch of Ford autos go out to be sold to the public. This was to maintain cash flow, even though perfectionist Ford wasn't happy with the autos yet. Through Couzens' precise accounting, insistence on cash for advance orders, and other mercantile practices, Ford Motor Co. made a profit, and stayed profitable. This was contrary to the myriad of other auto companies in the early 1900s.

Investing in the Ford Motor Company

In 1900 Couzens married Margaret Manning and had six children, including Frank Couzens, future mayor of Detroit. James assured their future when he invested in the new Ford Motor Company. He took $1,000 of his and his sister Rosetta's money, and borrowed $1,500 to invest in the company. When he sold the stock in 1919, he received $30 million dollars.

By 1906 Couzens was General Manager and Vice-President of Ford Motor Company. He branched out and was also the director of a Detroit bank and the President of the Highland Park Bank. He was the founder of the Highland Park Land Company.

James Couzens and Henry Ford

As the Model T became the most famous car ever, there were lots of jokes about the venerable auto at its center. In 1915 a best-selling book called *Funny Tales of the Ford* collected many of them. Jokes such as, "A guy was riding in a Ford cab and said to the driver, 'Can't you go any faster?' The driver said, 'Sure, but I have to stay with the car.'"

Another joke was: A Model T owner didn't have a speedometer in his car. He explained, "I don't need one at all. At ten miles an hour the hood rattles, at fifteen the radiator rattles, at twenty the bottom rattles and at twenty-five miles an hour the engine catches on fire."

As an officer of the Ford Motor Company, Couzens didn't care for any "negative publicity." One time the *Detroit News* printed several of the jokes and Couzens sent the newspaper a letter saying that he forbade the newspaper from ever mentioning the Ford Motor Company name again. And then he cancelled all the Ford advertising in the *Detroit News*.

The *Detroit News* sent a reporter to talk to Henry Ford who laughed and explained that Couzens had no sense of humor. Ford thought the jokes were good advertising. Ford restored the advertising and told the reporter a few of the Model T jokes that HE had heard.

When Ford and Couzens decided to fight the Selden Patent,

an 1870s patent on the automobile by attorney James Selden, they formed an organization, "The American Motor Car Manufacturers' Association." Couzens was chosen to be the first President. Ford went on to win the patent fight with Couzens' assistance.

In 1913 he started becoming involved in civic affairs when he became chairman of the Detroit Street Railway Commission. This job was a stepping stone to mayor that many past mayors had used.

Resignation at Ford

In 1915 Couzens resigned his positions at Ford Motor Company because of disagreements with Henry Ford over company policies and political views. Henry Ford was a pacifist during World War I and Couzens refused to let Ford's personal views creep into the company newsletter and literature. When he confronted Ford on it, the two men argued, leading to Couzens' resignation.

In 1916 Couzens was appointed Police Commissioner by Mayor Oscar Marx, a position he held until 1918 when he was elected Mayor. As Police Commissioner he went undercover in the city and found that "hundreds of houses of prostitution were scattered around, and 1,400 (illegal) saloons ran all day and all night and on Sundays." He announced a crackdown on crime, and then had his own car stolen the first month he was commissioner.

When he first became Police Commissioner, he caused laughs at his ignorance of crime jargon of the day. When he was asked by the press if he was going to put the bookmakers out of business, he replied, "I don't see why, people ought to read books."

Detroit had no official traffic laws, or even parking laws. Couzens initiated the city's first modern traffic code. It was only a year before Couzens started as Police Commissioner, in 1915, that stop signs were first put at major intersections. By

1923 most Detroit corners had stop signs. The first three-way signal, with red, yellow, and green lights, were installed at Woodward and Monroe Streets on New Year's Eve, December 31, 1918, during Couzens' tenure as Police Commissioner.

Couzens was against judges "giving blanket releases to professional bondsmen with the names of prisoners to be written in as the occasion arises." Judge Albert Sellers issued a contempt of court charge to Police Commissioner Couzens when he told the police department to ignore Judge Seller's releases unless they had been issued in a courtroom.

Couzens was arrested and spent the night in jail. This caused the previously unpopular Police Commissioner to rise in popularity, especially as he led the fight to the Michigan Supreme Court and was victorious in outlawing the practice of giving blanket releases and pardons.

Organized Crime Comes to Detroit Via Prohibition

Michigan got an early start on declaring alcohol illegal in 1917, more than a year before the nation's Prohibition began. This gave Detroit gangsters a year head start on perfecting the smuggling of liquor over the border. The Purple Gang started with the four Jewish Burnstein brothers. They all grew up at the family home at 404 Gratiot in Detroit. They began illegal operations, including smuggling, murder, and protection rackets, and continued through the 1920s.

In 1918, Couzens was nominated by the Democrats to run for Mayor. He was depressed due to his son Homer dying in an auto accident. (His other son was Frank Couzens, later Mayor.) The offer to run for Mayor came at the right time to take his mind off the tragedy.

The new charter for Detroit specified that mayoral elections would be non-partisan, so in a run-off primary leading up to the election, the top two candidates would run in the main election. This was Couzens and, in second place, William F. Connally, technically another Democrat.

Four generations of Couzens, l. to r.: Senator James J. Couzens, Mayor Frank Couzens, Frank Couzens, Jr., and James Couzens (child on lap)

Couzens Ejected from Streetcar

Three weeks before the election, Couzens once again found a way to court public opinion and favorable press. He had earlier objected to the Detroit Urban Railroad raising their rates to six cents from a nickel. When they did, candidate and still-Police Commissioner got on the railway car, paid a nickel, and sat down. The conductors came and warned him about the additional penny, which Couzens refused to pay. As he was ejected from the train car, the press, previously alerted, recorded it all. (In retrospect, Couzens had also participated in the 1891 Trolley Riot.)

Couzens won the election, besting candidate William F. Connally, 38, 516 votes to 30,618. By 1920 Detroit had

990,000 people and had doubled in size, annexing much of the area around it. This included the former communities of Redford, Bell Branch, Del Ray, Norris, Connor Creek, and Springwells.

In 1920 the streetcars were still a political issue. Couzens successfully fought for municipal ownership of the streetcar lines in the city. In 1922, after years of wrangling that began in 1895 with Hazen Pingree, the *Detroit United Railway (DUR)* sold its property to the city for $19,850,000.

Detroit in the 1920s

The Ambassador Bridge was started in 1920, and when completed in 1922, the bridge from the U.S. to Canada was the world's longest suspension bridge.

Also, in 1920, one of the first U.S. radio stations, WWJ, or 8MK as it was first called, began broadcasting. It was at first called "wireless telephone." The station was owned by the Scripps family, who founded the Detroit News. On August 20, 1920, the first radio commercial broadcast originated from Detroit. The program was called "Tonight's Dinner." On August 30, 1920, they broadcast primary election returns.

The ground-breaking radio station broadcast out of the Detroit News building, which was designed by architect Albert Kahn. Kahn was also responsible for the Fisher Building, Ford's factories, the Packard factory, and much more.

The General Motors Building was started in 1919, with one tower of four occupied in 1920 and the rest of them completed in 1920. Billy Durant, the founder of GM, sunk over 20 million dollars into the building which was going to be called the Durant Building. There are still ornamental "D's" on building columns even though it was never officially named for Durant once he was ousted from the company in 1920.

When Durant was ousted the building was renamed the General Motors Building. Nowadays, GM has moved its headquarters into Detroit's Renaissance Center (in 2002) and the Detroit City Government has moved into the building and renamed it Cadillac Center.

The General Motors Building in 1922, now called the Cadillac Center.

While the Albert Kahn-designed building was being erected and was taking years to finish, Mayor Couzens offered to buy it off General Motors to use for city offices but was refused. Ironically, that's what the building is used for now.

There are over 1,800 offices in the Cadillac Center complex. At the time it was built it was the second-largest office building in the United States, second only to the Equitable Life Assurance Building in New York City.

From Mayor to Senate

In 1921 Couzens was reelected Mayor, beating Republican Daniel Smith 70,719 to 38,905. He cut his term short however —in 1922 Governor Alex Groesbeck appointed Couzens to fill the rest of the U.S. Senate term of Truman Newberry, who was retiring early due to being tried and convicted under the Federal Corrupt Practices Act for election "irregularities."

Continuing during Couzens' term, the 1920's, or the "Roaring Twenties," saw Detroit become the Rum Runner Capital of the United States. The Purple Gang, and Italian gangs like the "Green Pepper Gang," who would hide their liquor in green peppers, soon ruled the Underworld of Detroit. The gangs had no trouble smuggling alcohol from nearby Canada, using fast boats, or in the winter, driving fast cars over the ice.

In 1922, Detroit annexed the Oakwood Heights settlement, almost completing the annexations that would make Detroit one of the largest U.S. cities in area. The cities of Boston, San Francisco, and the borough of Manhattan could all fit within the boundaries of Detroit.

Building the Automobile Infrastructure

As Detroit continued to be the Motor City, it was evident that the roads had to be improved and traffic laws instilled. In the 1920s Detroit was the fourth largest city and had the second worst traffic jams (Los Angeles was first, even then). Detroit and the state of Michigan added many cement roads. Grand River Avenue was paved for 75 miles, from Detroit to Lansing, mostly using convict labor.

Detroit had no official traffic laws, or even parking laws. Couzens initiated the city's first modern traffic code. He was against judges "giving blanket releases to professional bondsmen with the names of prisoners to be written in as the occasion arises."

Judge Albert Sellers issued a contempt of court charge to Police Commissioner Couzens when he told the police department to ignore Judge Seller's releases unless they had been issued in a courtroom. Couzens was arrested and spent the night in jail. This caused the previously unpopular Police Commissioner to rise in popularity, especially as he led the fight to the Michigan Supreme Court and was victorious in outlawing the practice of giving blanket releases and pardons.

Booze smuggling on the Detroit River, off Riopelle Street

Couzens remained in the Senate until he died on October 22, 1936. He was interred in the family mausoleum in Woodlawn Cemetery. Among other honors, James Couzens was inducted into the Automotive Hall of Fame in 2012. James Couzens Highway in Detroit is named for him.

Couzens' Mauseleum, final resting place for father and son Mayors of Detroit, James and Frank Couzens.

C HAPTER FORTY-SIX— JOHN C. LODGE— MORE THAN JUST A FREEWAY

*John C. Lodge, old and older, Mayor of Detroit,
1922 and 1923, 1928-1930*

John Christian Lodge (1861-1950) was born on August 12, 1862, in Detroit to homeopathic physician Edwin Albert Lodge, an abolitionist who contributed to the Underground Railroad. His mother was Christine Hanson Lodge. One of his great-nephews was Charles Lindbergh. The sixth of eleven children, he grew up in a mansion on Jefferson Street.

Lodge went to Philo M. Patterson's Private School for Boys and then on to high school at Detroit Public Schools. He then attended Michigan Military Academy in Orchard Lake, Michigan.

Working at the Detroit Free Press

In 1886, at the age of 24, Lodge started working as a copy boy for the *Detroit Free Press*. By 1893 he had worked his way up to City Editor. In 1897 he resigned to become Chief Clerk to the Board of County Auditors.

Lodge began his political career in 1907 when he was elected to the State Legislature as a Republican. He became a Detroit City Alderman in 1909 and in 1918, when Detroit introduced the new City Charter for the Common Council/Mayor system. Lodge was elected President of the Common Council, a position he held for 13 years. He was elected to the Common Council *ten* times and was considered the "elder statesman" of Detroit politics.

Lodge served twice as Acting Mayor before being elected Mayor in his own right. The first time he was Acting Mayor was in 1923-1924 when James Couzens was appointed to the Senate and Lodge finished out his mayoral term. The next time was in 1924 when Acting Mayor Joseph A. Martin resigned to—run for mayor! Lodge filled in from August to November. Martin lost to John W. Smith.

In 1927 Lodge ran for Mayor in his own right (without campaigning) and defeated Democrat John W. Smith. During his single term as mayor, Lodge unsuccessfully lobbied for an $8 million-dollar bond issue to erect a new administration building at the corner of Woodward and Jefferson Avenues.

In 1927, the Gordon Bennett Balloon Races were held in Detroit. This was for hot-air balloons and for a while Detroit was very interested in aviation. In 1928, the masterpiece of Albert Kahn, the 30-story Fisher Building, was completed.

Built by the Fisher Brothers, Frederick, Charles, William, Lawrence, Edward, Alfred and Howard, it was the culmination of their Fisher Body plants throughout the city. Meant to be offices, the Art Deco-designed skyscraper was built of limestone, granite, and marble. It is decorated throughout with statues, frescoes, and artwork. It has three art galleries and boasts a theatre and retail space.

The Fisher Building, named for the Fisher Brothers

The Fisher Building was just the beginning of a planned three-tower complex, but the Depression interrupted those plans. There is a tunnel linking the Fisher Building with the Cadillac Square Building and New Center. There are retail stores and storefronts located in the tunnels.

Original planned design of the Fisher Building. The one on the right was the one built.

The Fisher Brothers came from Ohio originally and made a fortune building auto bodies. "Body by Fisher" is a well-known trademark. The company was purchased by General Motors in 1928.

In 1929, The Golden Jubilee of Light was held in Greenfield Village, commemorating the 50th Anniversary of the invention of the light bulb by Thomas Edison, who attended and presented one of his first light bulbs to the museum. Also attending were President and Mrs. Herbert Hoover, Marie Curie, George Eastman, Orville Wright, Will Rogers, and Lodge.

The Fox Building joined Detroit's theatre district in 1928. Part of the Francis Palms Building, the theatre would go on to be refurbished in 1998 by Mike Ilitch, owner of Little Caesar's Pizza, the Detroit Tigers, and the Detroit Red Wings.

Lodge was defeated for reelection by Charles H. Bowles, who would be deposed as Mayor after only seven months. Re-elected to the Common Council, Lodge served until his death, from 1932 to 1950, except for a brief period of ill health from 1947 to 1948. Lodge was still a member of the Common Council on February 6, 1950, when he died at the age of 87. He was buried in Elmwood Cemetery. Following his death, the John C. Lodge Freeway (M-10) and Lodge Drive in Detroit was named for him.

John C. Lodge gravesite

Frank

E. Doremus, Mayor of Detroit, 1923-1924

CHAPTER FORTY-SEVEN—FRANK E. DOREMUS—BAREFOOTED MAYOR

Frank Ellsworth Doremus (1865-1947) was born on August 13, 1865 in Venango County in Pennsylvania. His parents were Sylvester and Sarah Doremus. The family moved to Ovid, Michigan in 1866, and then to Portland, Michigan in 1872. Frank went to Portland public schools and then he moved to Detroit and attended and graduated from the Detroit College of Law.

In 1882 Doremus worked for the newspaper the *Portland Observer.* He moved on to the Pewamo *Plain Dealer* and then started the *Portland Review* in 1885, which he edited until 1899.

Michigan House of Representatives

In 1890 Doremus married Libby Hatley and the couple had a son, Robert. He was the Postmaster for Portland from 1895 to 1899. He was elected township clerk in 1888 and 1889. In 1890 he was elected to the Michigan House of Representatives from Ionia County's 1st District, serving one term until 1892.

Relocating to Detroit, he was admitted to the bar and started practicing law in 1899. He was Assistant Corporation Counsel of Detroit from 1903 to 1907 and City Comptroller from 1907 until 1910. He was later referred to as "the barefooted country boy who came to town" due to his rural beginnings.

Elected to U.S. House of Representatives

In 1910 he was elected to the U.S. House of Representatives from Detroit as a Democrat, besting Republican Edwin C. Denby. He served from 1911 to 1921, and in 1913 was elected the Chairman of the Democratic Congressional Campaign Committee. In 1916 and 1920 he was the delegate from Michigan to the Democratic National Convention.

In 1923 Doremus ran for Mayor in a special election after James Couzens was appointed to the U.S. Senate. In the election he defeated Dr. James Inches 83,391 to 34,649. Running for reelection he overwhelmingly beat his Democratic opponent, Thomas C. O'Brien, 84,468 to 8,610. Detroit's population at this time topped one million people.

While he was Mayor, the city annexed part of Greenfield Township and the community of Rosedale Park. Detroit wanted the territory for more employee housing for the many workers coming to the Motor City. Rosedale Park citizens voted in favor of annexation due to the fire protection being part of Detroit offered. However, they were disappointed in the higher taxes.

Doremus's mayoral term didn't last long. In poor health, he resigned in 1924. Recuperating, he moved to Fowlerville, Michigan and resumed his law practice. He lived to be 83, dying in Howell, Michigan in 1947 and interred in Berkley, Michigan.

Alan Naldrett

Doremus in Roseland Park Cemetery Berkley, MI.

C HAPTER FORTY-EIGHT— JOSEPH A. MARTIN— SUBSTITUTE MAYOR

Joseph A. Martin (1888-1928) was Mayor of Detroit from June 10, 1924, to August 2, 1924, a little less than two months. He was stepping in until a special election could be held to fill Frank Doremus' term when he resigned. Martin was chosen because he was the President of the Common Council.

Martin was born in Detroit on June 26, 1888 and was educated in Detroit Public Schools. He then attended the University of Detroit, graduating in 1905. He joined *Union Trust Company*, starting as an office-boy and graduating to bookkeeper and then head of the real estate department. In 1915 he developed a cost-accounting system for Gray-Dort Motors in Chatham, Ontario.

Advertisements for the Gray-Dort auto

He then became chief auditor for the People's Outfitting Co. in Detroit, and then in 1819 returned to the automotive field by joining the central accounting department of Studebaker Motor Co. in their Chicago office. In 1920 Mayor James Couzens appointed Martin to be the Commissioner of Public Works, a post he held until 1923. He was then elected to the Common Council in 1924.

Joseph Martin and ads for his clothing business

On June 10, 1924, upon Mayor Doremus' resignation, Martin became Acting Mayor of Detroit, until August 2, 1924, when he resigned to run for Mayor. From August 2 to November 21 John C. Lodge became Acting Mayor.

James Martin ran as the Democratic candidate in the Special Election but lost to John W. Smith. It was reported that Charles Bowles, reportedly corrupt candidate with ties to the

311

KKK, had enough write-in votes to come in first, but over 15,000 of his ballots had his name spelled wrong or were otherwise incorrect. After these were thrown out, Smith was declared the winner.

Martin's life came to an untimely end when he was killed in a traffic accident on October 17, 1928 at the age of 40. The car he was riding in hit a tree after the driver hit a hole on Woodward Avenue. Martin was interred in Mt. Olivet Cemetery in Detroit.

Mausoleum of Joseph Martin, Mayor of Detroit for about two months.

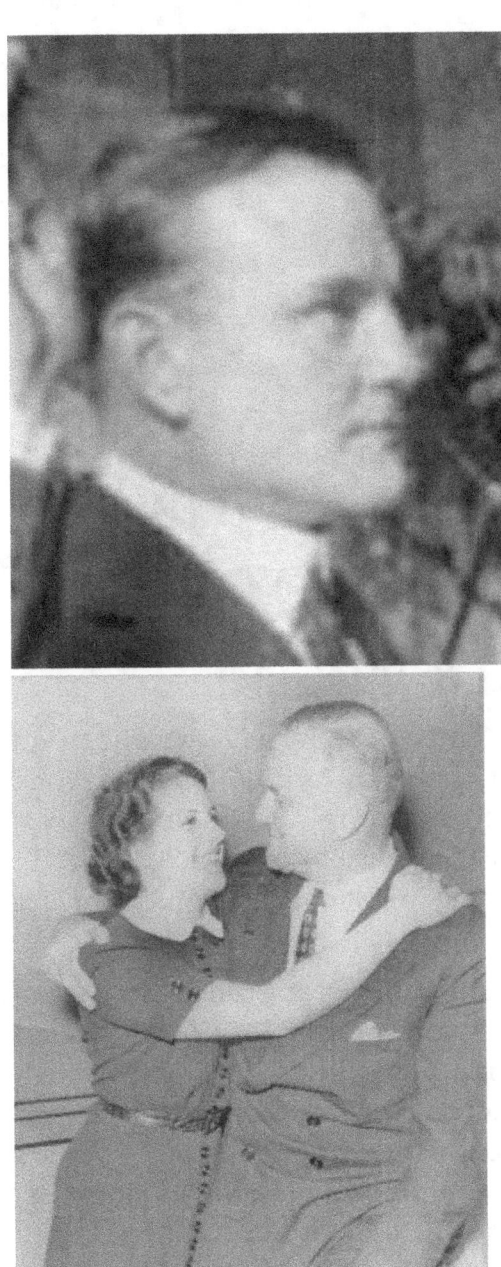

John W. Smith, Mayor of Detroit 1924-1928, September 8,1933-January 2, 1934

C HAPTER FORTY-NINE—JOHN W. SMITH—NOT A PSEUDONYM

John "Johnny" William Smith (1883-1942) was born on April 12, 1882 in Detroit, the son of John W. and Gertrude Smith. The family emigrated from the Austria-Poland area, where the original family name was Jednoralski. The family was poor, due to the elder John Smith dying when the future mayor was only five.

Helping to support the family, Smith started selling newspapers in Detroit at the age of six. His spot was at the Russell House, a popular hotel across from the old City Hall. Smith first became interested in politics from seeing and hearing all the politicians. He quit school in the fifth grade and kept his job as a newsboy, as well as becoming a pin-setter in a bowling alley (Detroit at one time had the most bowling alleys in the United States). Smith continued his education at the Detroit Public Library, reading books whenever he had the free time.

The Russell House, John W. Smith's newspaper spot

Boxing as Kid Smith

Smith started boxing when he was young as "Kid Smith," learning to box from warding off bullies on his news corner. He joined the Army at age 15 to fight in the Spanish-American War, going to the Philippines. He was deafened by an artillery shell and didn't regain his hearing until years later.

When Smith returned to the U.S. in 1901, he went to the University of Detroit for a year, while also becoming a journeyman pipefitter. He then joined the Detroit Shipbuilding Company as a plumber's assistant, pipefitter, and steamfitter. He married Marie General, and they had two children, Dorothy and John W. Smith.

In 1908 Smith entered the public life as a campaign worker for the Republicans. Veteran politician John C. Lodge took Smith under his wing, mentoring him to become Deputy U.S. Marshall in 1911, Deputy State Labor Commissioner in 1912, Deputy Sheriff of Wayne County in 1913, and Deputy County Clerk from 1918 to 1920. Smith served in the Michigan State Senate, and from 1920 to 1924 was the Postmaster of Detroit.

The Union Trust, later the Guardian Building, was built in 1926 during John W. Smith's mayoral term.

Substitute Mayor

Smith was elected to fill Mayor Doremus' term when he resigned in 1925. Smith then went on to win the 1926 election with 115,722 votes, with Independent candidate Charles Bowles garnering 105,902 votes, and Democratic candidate Joseph Martin getting only 83,769.

In 1925 the Five Points neighborhood was annexed. The city annexed the 4-square mile Brightmoor neighborhood. Brightmoor was one of the first planned communities of the Detroit area, opening as a subdivision in 1922. When it opened, it was a mile from the city limits of Detroit. In 1926 Detroit made its last annexation due to the State Legislature passing a law making it more difficult for cities to annex nearby property.

Brightmoor was at the nexus of "worker housing," more primitive, and more modern homes built just a few years later. Brightmoor homes had outdoor toilets, outhouses, for most of the homes. The outhouse was usually located on a platform outside of the kitchen door. The few that did have an indoor bathroom were not necessarily hooked up to a sewage system. Water was delivered twice a week by a horse-drawn tank wagon. While other housing blocks were being built with all the modern necessities, Brightmoor houses were heated by coal stoves and illuminated by kerosene lamps when the rest of the city enjoyed electricity. Some of the houses were built with old lumber with sheets of tin for the roof, causing the area to be called "kitchen town."

During his term the iconic Union Trust Building (now the Guardian Building) opened in 1926. An art deco structure, it has long been considered one of the most beautiful skyscrapers in the U.S. The Union Trust Bank was organized so Detroit automakers wouldn't have to go to New York for loans and banking.

Also built in 1926 was the Masonic Temple, with many features, including a 4,400-seat auditorium. In 1927 the new Detroit Institute of Arts opened in mid-town on Woodward Avenue. It replaced the Detroit Museum of Art on Jefferson, which was leveled in 1960 to build Highway I-375.

In 1925 the city's second radio station started broadcasting as WGHP, after George Harrison Phelps, its owner. It became part of the CBS network in 1927. In 1930 the station was purchased by George W. Trendle, and the call letters changed to WXYZ, which Trendle acquired from a U.S. Army Radio Station. As WXYZ the station was famous for its nationwide radio serials, the Lone Ranger and the Green Hornet. In 1946 the station was purchased by the American Broadcasting Company (ABC) and in 1982 they began using the call letters WXYZ for their Detroit TV station, and the radio's name was changed to WXYT.

The 1934 Tigers won the World Series while Smith was Mayor.

Tigers banner on the Hudson's Department Store celebrating the Tigers' victory in 1935.

After his first mayoral term Smith went back to a seat on the Common Council, until 1933, when he became Acting Mayor for three months from September 8 to January 2. After this term he again went back to the Common Council.

The Art Museum of Detroit on Jefferson, c1898. Replaced by the DIA and razed in 1960. (From LOC)

The Detroit Institute of Arts in 1927.

Smith was known as pro-labor, a strong supporter of fiscal integrity, and a staunch opponent of the Ku Klux Klan, which was getting strong in Michigan at the time. He unsuccessfully ran for Mayor again in 1930 and 1936, and Governor of Michigan in 1934.

Many of Detroit's notable downtown skyscrapers were built during Smith's term. The Book-Cadillac was built by the Book Brothers in 1924. The Book Building was built in 1917 and the Book Tower added in 1926. Book Tower courtesy of LOC.

While Smith was mayor B.E. Taylor subdivisions were being built. Taylor subdivisions sprouted up all over the city, beginning in 1926, with the Strathmoor, Belmont, Hollywood, Sunset Glen, and Commodore enclaves of new homes.

John W. Smith died in the Detroit Tuberculosis Sanitarium of TB and other maladies on June 17, 1942, at the age of 60.

He was buried in Mt. Olivet Cemetery in Detroit. The John W. Smith Old-Timers Club was named in his honor and is involved in Philanthropy, Voluntarism, and Grantmaking Foundations. Smith Street in Detroit was also named for him.

Charles E. Bowles, Mayor of Detroit, January to July 1930

C HAPTER FIFTY— CHARLES E. BOWLES —FIRST MAYOR EVER TO BE RECALLED

Charles E. Bowles (1884-1957) was recalled after only seven months in office—he was Mayor from January 14 until September 22, 1930.

Bowles was born in Yale, Michigan in St. Clair County on March 24, 1884. His father Alfred died when Charles was young, so he helped his mother Mary by peddling newspapers and performing other jobs. He attended Yale Public Schools and then attended Ferris Institute in Big Rapids, Michigan, now Ferris State University. He transferred to the University of Michigan, where he graduated with a law degree in 1909. He practiced law in Detroit from 1909 until he died in 1957. He had his post-mayor office in the 40-story Barlum Building, now called the Cadillac Tower.

Charles Bowles had his office on the 25ᵗʰ floor of the Barlum Tower, now the Cadillac Tower, known for its murals on the outside. Before he was mayor he was in the Dime Building.

Bowles had his first law offices in the Dime Building. He held high office in several Masonic lodges and was the first President of the Detroit branch of DeMolay International, a masonic order for boys that raises scholarship money and other philanthropies.

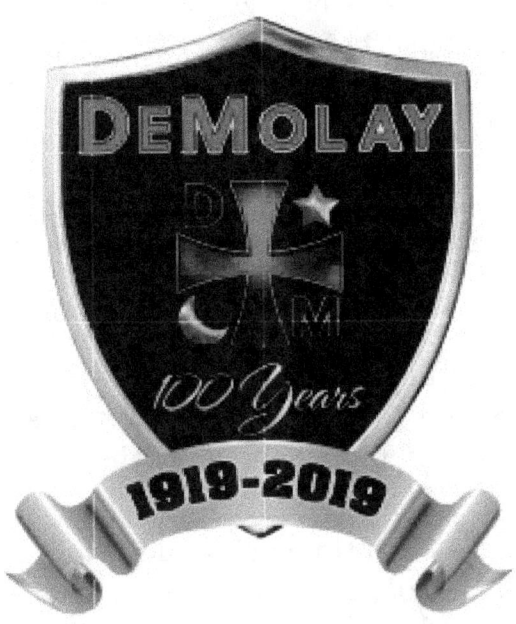

DeMolay International logo, the first President of the Detroit branch was Charles Bowles

Prohibition and the Purple Gang

As his law practice became more successful, Bowles turned his attention to politics. The "Roaring Twenties" were a time of lawlessness for Detroit. With the Purple Gang and the Detroit area becoming one of the main entry ports for illegal alcohol into the country, the city had a bad reputation which rivaled Chicago and New York.

In fact, on July 12, 1926, the *New York Times* ran a story about a report from the ASHA, the *American Social Hygiene Association,* funded by the Rockefeller Institute. The study found Detroit to be the "most vile city" in America. The study was designed to study the social morality of cities and said, "Detroit is the worst city in the United States in the matter of social evil."

The study found 570 "disorderly houses" (brothels), and in a one-square mile area around Warren Avenue counted over

500 street prostitutes. There was also an estimation of over 10,000 "dope fiends" (heroin addicts) in the city. But the two main areas of Detroit vice continued to be booze and gambling for the 1,568,000 people who lived in Detroit in 1930. The booze and gambling helped cause the high level of crime and gang killings. Blind pigs and illegal gambling joints were mostly ignored by police, and many took bribes to look the other way.

In 1923 the Ku Klux Klan had reformed in Detroit, Indianapolis, and other areas, after the movie *Birth of a Nation* glorified their post-Civil War crimes. Racial incidents such as the Dr. Ossian Sweet attempt to integrate the Garland Street area fueled the fire.

In Detroit the Klan threw several rallies in fields around metro Detroit. Thousands of Klansmen attended these meetings at Snyder and 7 Mile in Detroit, John R and 15 Mile, a vacant lot in Royal Oak, and other secret locations. On Christmas Eve in 1923, they held a large rally at the county building where they burned a six-foot cross. It was climaxed by the appearance of a Klan-robed Santa Claus!

As the KKK gathered in strength across the Midwest, they attempted to get Klan sympathizers elected to office. Attempts to get KKK governors and legislatures elected met with varying degrees of success throughout the nation.

Mayoral Write-In Campaign

The Klan began to make its presence known in Detroit local politics in 1924, when Bowles declared his intention to run for Mayor of Detroit. Bowles ran on a platform that included building a Detroit subway and "strict law enforcement." The Klan announced their support for him. The local newspapers noted how his biggest campaign contributors were many of the city's most well-known gangsters.

When the Klan endorsed Bowles, they plastered alternating posters of the Klan and Bowles all the way down Woodward Avenue. On October 23, 1923, an anti-Klan rally was held with Aldrich Blake of Oklahoma talking about the secrets of the KKK. It was held at the Arena Gardens on Woodward Avenue in mid-town, used for boxing matches and later roller-skating.

The Klan gathered at the event, a "menacing crowd" of 6,000 men and boys. They blocked entrance to the anti-Klan rally by forming a wedge around the box office. While doing so, they chanted "Bowles, Bowles, Bowles!" Cars that stopped to observe were plastered with a Bowles campaign sticker on its windows. Police were unable to disperse the mob until morning.

The Arena Gardens, where an Anti-Klan rally in 1923 led to the Klan denying admission to people by blocking the box office. It was torn down in the mid-1960s to make room for the I-94 freeway

In the Democratic primary, Bowles came in third but decided to run as a write-in candidate. He was called the "sticker candidate" and directions were given on how to write Bowles in. On the evening before the election, a large KKK rally was held at a field in Dearborn Township where Bowles was endorsed. Attendance was estimated at 25,000 to 50,000.

Once all the votes, including the write-ins, were counted, Bowles had the most votes, but there were over 15,000 Bowles write-in votes disqualified, mostly due to misspelling Bowles' name. Charles Bowles was given 105,902 votes, and Democratic candidate Joseph Martin got 83,769. Republican John W. Smith was declared the winner with 115,772 votes.

With dismay, the *Christian Century* magazine wrote, "In Detroit, a Klan write-in candidate, almost unknown in the city, whose name was not even printed on the ballot, came within a few thousand votes of being elected Mayor of the fourth largest city in the United States."

In 1925 Bowles once again unsuccessfully ran for Mayor but again was very close to winning. A Klan candidate was elected to the Common Council. In 1927, Bowles ran for Recorder's Court Judge and won, getting reelected and serving until 1929, when he resigned as Judge to run for Mayor of Detroit again. This was a significant time in Detroit's history, since the stock market crash had recently occurred in October 1929. Unemployment was rising, fortunes were lost, and banks were failing.

One of the cases Bowles presided over as Judge was the Purple Gang "Cleaners and Dryers War" in September 1928. The Purple Gang controlled a "union" of the professional laundry businesses in Detroit. Stores that didn't join would be bombed or set afire. The Purples would often leave a half-burned stick of dynamite by a store as a warning. Incredibly, the Purple Gang members were all acquitted.

Mayor at Last

So, in the 1929 race to be mayor, Judge Bowles beat John C. Lodge in the primary to become the Democratic candidate and then defeated Republican John W. Smith in the general election. Bowles was sworn in as Mayor on January 12, 1930.

He had campaigned on an anti-crime platform, but Bowles had ties to both the Purple Gang and the Ku Klux Klan. He even received an endorsement from the Klan.

Bowles did little to stop the gang warfare that had taken over the streets of Detroit. Once, when asked what he thought about all the murders in the city, he said that "as long as gangsters shoot each other, they perform a public service."

Several "secret" new gambling establishments opened downtown as soon as Bowles took the oath of office. Newspapers soon noted that crime and vice were already worse than when "anti-crime" mayor Bowles took office. Break-ins and all other petty crimes were up.

Recall Campaign Starts

Two months after Bowles took office, a recall campaign had already begun. Bowles was vilified by both the *Detroit Free Press and Detroit News* newspapers. Radio commentator Jerry Buckley, broadcasting for WMBC from the top of the La Salle Hotel (now the Detroiter Hotel), talked about Bowles and his crime-ridden administration on his radio show every night.

The La Salle Hotel at Woodward and Adelaide Street in Detroit was where Jerry Buckley's radio station was located. Buckley lived there and was shot to death in the lobby the evening it was announced that Bowles had been deposed.

One of the reasons given to recall the Mayor included his selective enforcement of the vice laws. Bowles took the enforcement of vice crimes out of the control of the precincts and established a separate vice unit, instructing the unit which places to bust and which ones to leave alone. The ones the Vice Squad were told to ignore were coincidently enough, the establishments of Bowles' largest political contributors.

Bowles also made some very questionable appointments to many unqualified job candidates. His friend Wesley Stephens from the Odd Fellows, that he appointed to the DSR (Detroit Street Railways), wasted no time in telling his lodge brothers that his first priority would be to find *them* jobs too!

Bowles appointed a man whose law firm represented many people with claims against the DSR to the Street Railway Commission, a clear conflict of interest. He rewarded campaign workers with jobs, including one that became the head of the Detroit Civil Service Commission. Bowles' crony John Gillespie was appointed to be the Commissioner of Public Works and immediately began making decisions that enriched his personal businesses.

Banning the Press

Bowles retaliated against the bad press given to him by the *Detroit News* and *Detroit Free Press* reporters that were against him. He broke all relations with those newspapers and City Hall. (The *Detroit Times* had managed to remain neutral and wasn't outright banned.) Bowles refused to answer any questions and denied the major newspapers access to public and relevant records.

A public outcry went up when Mayor Bowles agreed to let the DSR raise rates from six cents to eight cents. When Councilman Frank Couzens, who was also against the fare increase, protested, the Mayor asked Couzens to resign (which he didn't). Bowles then switched the city insurance to a carrier owned by a crony.

Bowles and his aforementioned crony John Gillespie went to the Kentucky Derby together in Louisville, Kentucky, on May 20, 1930. While the Mayor was out of town, Police Commissioner Emmons, with the press in tow, raided several gambling establishments, blind pigs, and brothels. Many places were closed, and many Bowles cronies arrested.

Upon his return the next day, May 21, Mayor Bowles requested that Emmons resign; when he refused to do so, Bowles fired him. This increased the public outcry, and soon different locations were established throughout the city where people could go to sign petitions for Bowles' recall.

Blind Pig Raid

Bowles Recalled

From July 4 to July 20 there were ten homicides in Detroit —ten murders in fourteen days. With the gangland murders happening at the time, citizens were getting sick and tired of all the corruption. This was bad timing for Bowles as the recall was successful, with 57% of the Detroiters (120,863) voting to oust Bowles, the first time a big-city mayor in the United States was recalled.

Radio commentator for WMBC Detroit, Jerry Buckley

Buckley Murdered

Jerry Buckley had just announced the results of the recall live from City Hall on his radio show on July 22, 1930 that evening. He was relaxing in the lobby of Hotel LaSalle, where he lived and where WMBC was located after his radio broadcast. All of a sudden, three gunmen entered at 1 a.m. and fired eleven bullets into Buckley, killing him instantly. Buckley's brother, Assistant Prosecutor Paul Buckley, said his brother Jerry was executed due to his part in Bowles' recall. Over 100,000 people attended the funeral. No one was ever arrested for the murder, but the gunmen were identified years later as Russell Syracuse, Joseph English, and John Mirabella.

The Hotel La Salle Hotel

The lobby of the La Salle Building shortly after the body of Jerry Buckley was removed; the La Salle Building, where WMBC recorded from; and an artist's depiction of the Buckley shooting.

Bowles tried running in the election called to replace him but was defeated by John C. Lodge and exited office on September 22, 1930. He later unsuccessfully tried running for the U.S. Senate, the Michigan Senate, and once more, Detroit Mayor.

Following the failure of Bowles' mayoral term, the KKK influence began to wane. As they were evicted from their quarters and their furniture sold to pay their delinquent bills, the Klan had faded away by 1935.

Bowles was married twice, first to Ruth Davis, with whom he had a daughter, Helen. He remarried when Ruth died in 1935 but divorced three years later. He continued to practice law until his death in 1957. He was interred in the Evergreen Cemetery Mausoleum in Detroit.

Charles Bowles in Evergreen Cemetery Detroit Mausoleum

C HAPTER FIFTY-ONE—FRANK MURPHY—SUPREME COURT JUSTICE, ATTORNEY GENERAL, GOVERNOR, MAYOR

Frank Murphy, Mayor of Detroit 1930-1933

William Francis Murphy (1890-1849) was born on April 13, 1890, in Harbor Beach (the name had just been changed from Sand Beach) in Huron County, Michigan. He was the son of Canadian John F. Murphy, and Mary Brennan Murphy, who met her husband while working in her brothers' music store. John Murphy was a University of Michigan Law graduate of 1881 who opened a law office in Sand Beach in 1882, and practiced law there until his death in 1926.

John's son Frank Murphy went to the local Harbor Beach school, which was described as "the best graded school and the best school-building in the county."

Upon graduation Frank entered the University of Michigan in 1908. He received a bachelor's degree and in 1914, a law degree from the U of M law school. He practiced law until 1917, when he served in the Army during World War I and rose to the rank of captain.

Murphy Museum complex in Harbor Beach includes John Murphy's law office, and the childhood home that Frank Murphy grew up in.

Michigan District Attorney and Ossian Sweet Judge

Upon his honorable discharge, Murphy became a Michigan District Attorney in 1919. In 1922 he again practiced law on a private basis until 1924, when he became a U.S. Recorder's Court Judge.

In 1925 he was the judge for the landmark case of Ossian Sweet, who was on trial for murder when he and eleven friends were defending his 2905 Garland Street home in Detroit. Ossian, a black physician, had moved to a white neighborhood, much to the chagrin of the whites living nearby. With NAACP-appointed Clarence Darrow as their lawyer, Dr. Sweet and friends were acquitted after two trials (the first was a hung jury), and it became a landmark civil rights case.

Victorious Mayoral Run

Largely due to the popularity garnered due to his handling of the Sweet case, Murphy was encouraged to run in the run-off election called to replace deposed mayor Charles Bowles in 1930. Murphy was victorious, beating Bowles 106,637 to 93,985. Three other candidates had smaller vote tallies. Murphy ran for reelection in 1931 and beat Harold H. Emmons 166,748 to 91,657.

He became Mayor just in time to open the Detroit-Windsor Tunnel on November 1, 1930. This is an underground tunnel, going under the Detroit River, connecting Detroit to Windsor, Ontario, in Canada, and was the first traffic tunnel between two nations.

The Detroit-Windsor Tunnel

Murphy campaigning for Mayor and Murphy being sworn in by Judge (later Mayor) Richard Reading

Dealing with the Great Depression

Instead of the gangland violence that marked the previous regime, Murphy's term was dominated by the Great Depression. As a reform Mayor, he insisted that no one go hungry. He created the Mayor's Unemployment Committee, to supplement the Department of Public Welfare. Emergency shelters ("lodges") for homeless people were maintained, the unemployed were registered, and a "thrift-garden" was started.

Murphy's mayoral term ended when he accepted a position from Franklin Roosevelt to be the Governor-General of the Philippines. From there, Murphy moved on to become the Governor of Michigan.

Governor of Michigan

While Governor, Murphy sent the National Guard to protect the workers in the 1936 Flint Sit-Down Strike. Murphy was told to use the Guard to end the strike, but he refused to do so, and instead had them protect the workers from any further violence by the auto companies. The strikers had already been subjected to beatings, fire hoses, and more. There were 27 people injured, 13 by gunshot. Murphy then mediated an end to the strike.

After he was Governor, FDR appointed Murphy to be the Attorney General of the U.S., where he started a Civil Rights Unit within the Department of Justice.

Supreme Court Justice

FDR then appointed Murphy to the U.S. Supreme Court as a Justice. As a Justice, he opposed the Japanese internment camps of World War II. He wanted to help more during World War II and so would volunteer as an infantry officer at Fort Benning, Georgia, when court was not in session.

While on the Supreme Court Murphy authored 199 opinions. He supported so many opinions in favor of the oppressed, including African-Americans, Native Americans, aliens, dissenters, women, and workers, that the phrase "tempering justice with Murphy" became popular.

He never married and had no children. Murphy died in his sleep on July 19, 1949 of a coronary thrombosis at Henry Ford Hospital. He was 59. His remains were buried in the family plot in Harbor Beach. In Detroit, the Frank Murphy Hall of Justice is named for him.

FDR with Frank Murphy with James Couzens with Murphy

Frank Murphy Hall of Justice

Murphy's cemetery plot in Lady of Lake Huron Catholic Cemetery in Harbor Beach, Michigan

CHAPTER FIFTY-TWO
—FRANK COUZENS—
SON OF A COUZENS

Frank Couzens, Mayor of Detroit 1930-1933, 1935-1937

Frank Couzens (1902-1950) was, at 31 years old, the youngest Mayor of Detroit at the time. He was the son of former Mayor of Detroit and U.S. Senator James Couzens and Margaret Manning Couzens.

Frank Couzens was born in Detroit on February 28, 1902. He went to the Newport Prep School in Hackensack, New Jersey, and went to Detroit Public Schools. At the age of 18 he quit his formal schooling and joined an architectural firm.

After three years he was the assistant superintendent of the business. He later joined with John Frazer to form a construction firm which was not dissolved until 1941.

He married Margaret Lang from Kitchener, Ontario. Frank's father-in-law was also from Canada—Chatham, Ontario. The Couzens had seven children. Frank was very civic-minded and served as Chairman of the Board of the Children's Fund of Michigan and was a board member of the Crippled Kids Association, the Boys Club of Detroit, and the Round Table of Catholics, Jews, and Protestants. He was also in recreational associations for golf, riding horses, yachting, and bowling.

Appointed to Planning Commission at Age 21

Couzens was appointed to the Detroit City Planning Commission in 1923 when he was just 21. He was appointed to the Department of Street Railways in 1929 and then in 1931 he made a successful run for Detroit's Common Council, of which he was elected President.

Couzens family home at 610 Longfellow, in the Boston-Edison area of Detroit.

As President of the Common Council, Couzens, at 31 years

old, became Acting Mayor in May 1933 when Mayor Frank Murphy resigned to become Governor-General of the Philippines. Couzens ran as a Democrat in the election to replace Murphy and won, defeating Philip Breitmeyer 141,811 votes to 76,450. He was reelected two years later, beating Joseph Schemansky 130,339 to 30,503.

Providing Financial Stability for Detroit

When Couzens took office in 1933, Detroit was in default of its bond payments and was paying city employees with scrip. Couzens restored the city to financial stability, reducing the city's debt by $45 million and balancing the city budget. When Couzens left office the city's bonds were so improved that they were selling at a premium.

Couzens also successfully lobbied for an improved streetlight program, improved traffic regulations, and the installation of a $20 million sewage disposal system.

City of Champions

During Couzens' term, Detroit became the "City of Champions," when, in 1935, Detroiter Joe Louis won the heavyweight crown, the Detroit Tigers won the World Series, the Detroit Red Wings won the Stanley Cup, and the Lions won an NFL championship! The newspaper across the river, the *Windsor Daily Star*, called the championships the "...the most amazing sweep of sport achievements ever credited to any single city." Governor Frank Fitzgerald declared April 18 as "Champions Day" in commemoration of the achievement.

1934 World Champion Detroit Tigers

1934-1935 Stanley Cup Winners Detroit Red Wings

Detroit's Joe Louis, Heavyweight World Champion in 1935

Detroit Lions, 1935 NFL Champions

During the early years of the 1930s, the Black Legion, an offshoot of the Ku Klux Klan, terrorized the city. The group was anti-trade unions, among other things. Membership was not always voluntary and was a life commitment. Detroit was said to be the headquarters of the Black Legion. Following a wave of convictions in 1936, the group petered out.

Policemen wearing the captured "uniforms" of the Black Legion.

Couzens declined to run for a third term as Mayor in 1937. Entering the private sector as a banker, he founded the Wabeek State Bank of Detroit. The bank later merged with the bank founded by Frank's father, James Couzens, the Wabeek State Bank of Birmingham. In 1937 Frank was also president of a real estate firm, the Wabeek Corporation. It was named for Wabeek Lake in Bloomfield Township, Michigan.

During World War II Couzens was in the U.S. Army and served as the chief of the production service branch of the Detroit Ordnance District.

Tragically, Frank Couzens died of cancer on October 31, 1950, at the age of 48. He was interred in the family mausoleum in Woodlawn Cemetery in Detroit.

Alan Naldrett

Couzens Mausoleum in Woodlawn Cemetery.

CHAPTER FIFTY-THREE—RICHARD READING—DOUBLE DIP RICK

Richard Reading, Mayor of Detroit 1938-1939, Richard Reading and sons, Clarence and Ralph.

Richard William Reading (1882-1952) was another Detroit mayor who was associated with the mobsters and gangsters of Detroit. He was born in Detroit on February 7, 1882, one of eight children of Richard, an electrician, and Louise Reading. He was educated in Detroit Public Schools and then took night classes at Detroit College (now the University of Detroit).

Little Dick the Wrestler

In his youth he was very fit, becoming a semi-pro wrestler —even though he was only 5 foot, 3 inches. He later boxed and "kept fit" by golfing and running. His short stature earned him the nickname of "Little Dick."

Reading started working for the *Detroit News* as a "printer's devil," or apprentice, at $3.00 a week, mixing vats of ink and retrieving type. After he completed his apprenticeship, he quit the *News* and in 1901 went to work for the *Detroit Today*, later to be the *Detroit Times*. This was the same year he married his high school sweetheart, Blanche White. They had four children, sons Richard, Clarence, and Ralph, and daughter Marion. After a while, Reading worked his way up to become the business manager at the *Times.*

From Newspapers to Real Estate

In 1918, Reading quit the newspaper business to go into real estate. He became a successful realtor and was active in the community, as a member of the Oddfellows, Eagles, Elks, the Masonic Order, and the Congregationalist Church. He was also in the Detroit Boat Club, Detroit Athletic Club, the Detroit Golf Club, the Detroit Real Estate Board, the Detroit Board of Commerce, and the Detroit Yacht Club. The *Detroit News* commented that, "He never missed a banquet, a smoker, a saengerfest or a wiener roast. He joined everything he could get into." A "saengerfest" is a singing contest.

Mayor Frank Couzens noted his civil activities and real estate success and appointed Reading to be the City Assessor in 1921. He served as the assessor until 1924, when he was named the City Controller. In September 1925 he resigned to run for City Clerk. He won the election and served as City Clerk until 1937, when he ran for Mayor.

On November 2, 1937, Republican Richard Reading defeated Democrat Patrick O'Brien 261,048, to 154,048 votes. Upon victory, Reading declared, "The victory was one of all the people, the rank and file of our city, determined to preserve nonpartisan, clean progressive government here." However, it wasn't long before he was engaged in graft, the practice of selling political offices.

Need for New Limo

One of his first acts after taking office was to request a new $6,000 limousine for his personal use. When he was informed that many of the city police and fire cars needed replacing,

Reading countered with, "Gentlemen, I intend to take this mayoring seriously, and I need that car."

As soon as he got his limo, Reading set out on a misguided mission to weed out welfare fraud and city money mismanagement, an investigation that never uncovered any apparent fraud.

Reading helping out the Newsboys.

Anti-Labor Mayor

Reading was considered anti-labor union, bragging that he won the election without the backing of the CIO. At the time of his election in 1937, the mayoral salary was $15,000 a year, or about $1,200 a month, and the Mayor appointed the heads of over 70 city departments, including the police force.

Reading was involved in union-busting and consented to

companies lowering their wages and firing many workers, contrary to union regulations. When the workers of the Federal Screw Company went on strike, Reading had 400 police officers escort thirty strike-breakers into the factory. Violence on the picket lines followed, with workers from other unions joining in.

When the American Brass Company went on strike a short time later, Reading told the Welfare Department to have relief workers come to the factory and be strikebreakers. Reading provided 600 police officers for protection of the strike-breaking relief workers.

As the newspapers printed stories of Reading's corruption, Democrat Edward Jeffries, President of the Common Council, beat Reading by a landslide in the 1939 election, 226,181 to 108,993 votes.

Arrested and Jailed for Bribery, Graft, and Selling Protection
In 1940, ex-Mayor Richard Reading was indicted for taking bribes from Detroit underworld mobsters, selling protection to numbers racketeers, and promotions to police officers. Demanding kickbacks in order to do business, one of Reading's nicknames was "Double Dip Dick" because he had demanded kickbacks to be paid to his sons as well as for himself. It was estimated that he made over $55,000 a *month*, far outstripping the $1,200 most mayors earned. This would have been about the equivalent, in modern dollars, of about a million dollars a month.

Reading was convicted in 1942 and sentenced to five years in prison, serving three, in Jackson Prison. The first spotlight on the corruption in the city came when Janet McDonald, the girl-friend of a mobster, dressed her 11-year old daughter Pearl in a pink party dress before killing her and then killing herself. McDonald left a suicide note confessing that her boy-friend was a bagman for the mob. She named names of some of the well-known residents of Detroit, causing the most widespread corruption scandal of its day. It became even more of a smoking gun when Mayor Reading tried to block any further investigation.

Besides the ex-mayor, 150 others, including the county prosecutor, city council members, the county sheriff, and 80 police officers were found guilty of various forms of corruption.

The Greatest Injustice Since the Crucifixion of Christ

When he was convicted, Reading said, "This is the greatest injustice since the crucifixion of Christ!" The *Detroit Free Press* editorial page, on his parole three years later, said, ""He and his worthless son ... worked together to corrupt the Police Department, the Council and every other branch of our city government. This newspaper does not know the politics behind the release of this foul prostitute of public oath. But we go on record as saying that the parole of Dick Reading makes a mockery of all law and justice. Never in the story of Detroit has there been a more contemptible crook, because he traveled under the guise of respectability."

Reading fought the conviction all the way up to the Michigan Supreme Court. But after two years, Reading was ordered to begin serving his sentence. He was also sued by the Federal Courts and was fined $10,000 for income tax evasion. He was in Jackson Prison from January 1944 until he was paroled in February 1947. He retired to White Lake, Michigan after prison.

On December 9, 1952 Reading died of a heart attack at the age of 70, in Mallus Hospital in Brighton, Michigan. He was buried in Detroit's Grand Lawn Cemetery.

Ex-Mayor Reading is Fingerprinted.

Hey Kids! See what kind of gravestone graft and corruption will buy?

C HAPTER FIFTY-FOUR-EDWARD JEFFRIES—CAREER POLITICIAN AND MAYOR

Alan Naldrett

Edward Jeffries, Jr., Mayor of Detroit 1940-1948

Edward John Jeffries, Jr. (1900-1950) was a career politician who was Mayor during much of the 1940's, after the city's previous, graft-ridden mayoral administration.

Jeffries was a hometown boy, born in Detroit on April 3, 1900 to Minnie and Edward Jeffries, a Detroit Recorder's Court Judge for 35 years. He went to Northwestern High School and graduated in 1917. He went to college at the University of Michigan, earning an A.B. degree in 1920 and and LL.B. in 1923. During this time he worked at the Ford Rouge Plant, giving him a pro-labor and pro-union outlook. He then did post-graduate work in London, England at Lincoln's Inn, studying Roman and British constitutional law.

In 1923 he was admitted to the Michigan bar and began practicing law in Detroit, in partnership with Paul E. Krause. In 1929 he became general counsel for the Maccabbees religious group, a position he held until his death.

Serial Club Joiner

In 1930 he married Florence Bell, whose father was the Director of the Detroit Conservancy of Music. In 1940 they adopted their only child, three-year-old Gary. Jeffries was active in a lot of groups, including the Odd Fellows, the Eagles, the Moose Club, the Detroit Golf Club, the Michigan Bar Association, the Detroit Athletic Club, the Maccabees, and the Delta Theta Phi and the Alpha Sigma Phi fraternities.

Jeffries ran for the Detroit Common Council in 1931 and won. He was on the Common Council from 1932 until 1940, serving as President from 1938 to 1940. This constituted four 2-year terms.

Defeating the Corrupt Reading

In the 1939 mayoral election, Jeffries, or "Jeff" as he was affectionally known, beat incumbent Mayor Richard Reading, 226,181 votes to Reading's 108,993. Reading was arrested for graft soon thereafter.

Jeffries was a popular Democratic mayor, and was re-elected to four consecutive terms. In 1941 he defeated Republican candidate Joseph Gillis 219,338 to 72,041. In 1943 he beat Frank Fitzgerald 207,821 to 175,360 and in 1945 Richard Frankenstein lost to Jeffries, 275,159 to 217,425 votes. He was the longest serving mayor of Detroit until Coleman Young.

Race-Baiting

Unfortuneatly, in a few elections Jeffries ran on a race-baiting platform. Some of his campaign litereature read "FITZGERALD VICTORY MEANS STRATHMOOR AND COOLEY HIGH GET NEGRO FLOOD." His opponent was Frank Fitzgerald, later Governor of Michigan. Other similar items were released, aimed at white voters wanting to block blacks from moving into their neighborhoods.

Alan Naldrett

Sign supporting neighborhood covenants, trying to ban non-Whites

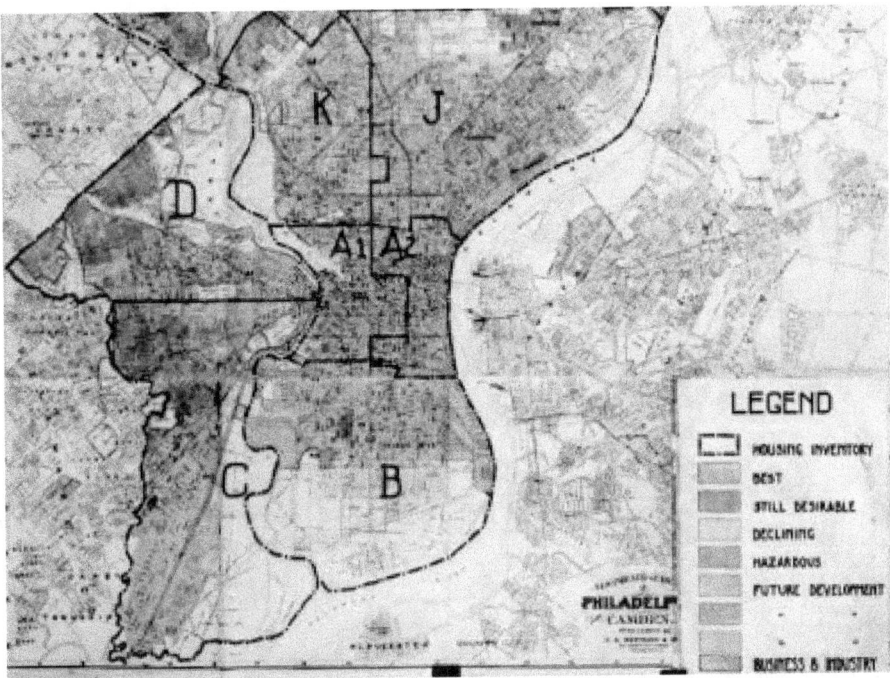

Neighborhood map produced by the Home Owners Loan Corporation showing redlined communities

The ultimate expression of Detroit's racism was the erection of a wall called the Detroit Eight Mile Wall in northwest Detroit, separating the section of black homeowners from the white. This misguided attempt at stabilizing the housing market was the brainstorm of the Home Owners Loan Corporation. Whites were continually fearful of blacks moving into "their area" because they were afraid their property values would go down. The wall, it was thought, would "protect" the neighborhood's property values. Today, the wall is painted with murals denoting racial justice, including later Detroit resident Rosa Parks getting arrested for not going to the rear of the bus in Montgomery, Alabama.

In 1941 to 1943, Detroit had over *400,000* immigrants from the U.S. South—White and African-Americans—as Detroit geared up to become the Arsenal of Democracy for World

War II. The city was short on housing, and racial discrimination and unemployment were rampant. Racial tension was stoked by the predominantly white, and racist, police force.

The Detroit 8-Mile Wall in 1941 and as it looks today in the area of Alfonso Wells Memorial Playground. Photo courtesy of Király-Seth.

Slum Clearance and Race Riot

While mayor, Jeffries launched an extensive slum clearance on the city's east side and adopted Detroit's first city-wide zoning ordinance. Although housing was razed, no equivalent places were built for the displaced residents to live.

Amid this charged atmosphere, the Race Riot of 1943 occurred, starting down by the Belle Isle Bridge. On a hot June

20, 1943, fighting youths actions were intensified as black and white groups began fighting each other. A false rumor among the black population—that a group of white folks had thrown an African-American woman and her baby into the water off the Belle Isle Bridge—helped feed the riot, which then spread further into the city. A similar false rumor spread through the white community that some black men had raped a white woman on the Belle Isle Bridge.

The fighting was exasperated by white youths that came from out of the suburbs to fight African-Americans. People were pulling blacks off buses and attacking them. The fighting lasted for three days. Most of the damage was confined to the black area, Paradise Valley. Mayor Jeffries called out federal troops to restore order and 6,000 responded. By the end of the riot, 34 people were killed, mostly by police, and over 600 injured, most of them African-American.

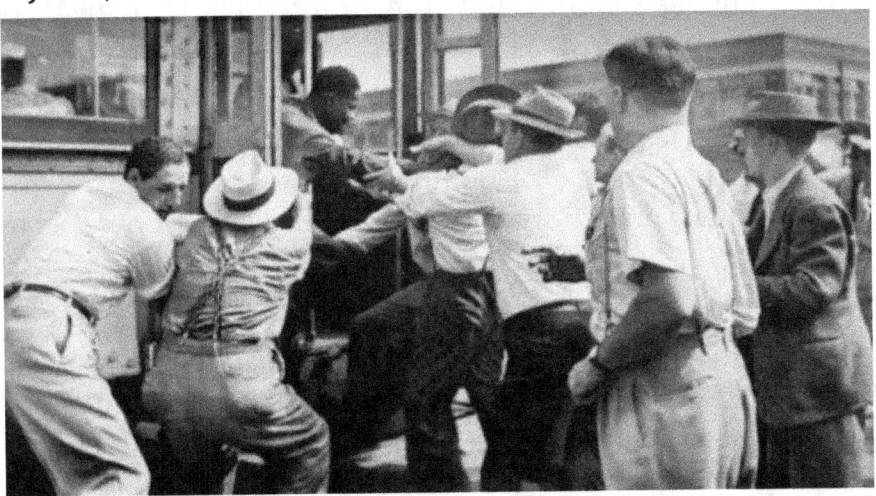

Detroit rioters assault bus rider in 1943.

An earlier melee started when an argument about a canoe rental escalated with a black man getting arrested and beat up by cops. Later, another riot occurred at the opening of the Sojourner Truth Housing Project as a crowd of whites assaulted a crowd of black people moving into the building. The white police force arrested mostly black people.

Misplaced Blame for Riot

Many citizens, black and white, were concerned about the wholesale killing of rioters by police and their resentment spilled over into the elections. Jeffries lost most of his African-American support when he said, "Negro hoodlums started it, but the conduct of the police department, by and large, was magnificent." This was blatantly false.

Besides racial violence, there were still massive struggles between the automakers and auto unions. Racial and union tensions increased as management used blacks as strikebreakers. Indeed, the reason most blacks gave for staying in Detroit was that for all its tribulations it was still better than the South in the treatment of African-Americans.

Jeffries set up a city insurance reserve fund that saved the city lots of money and Jeffries also was mayor when the city's expressway system was begun. A branch of the freeway is named for him. During Jeffries tenure, the Davison Expressway, the first urban freeway in the U.S., was opened.

While Jeffries was Mayor Detroit once again transformed itself into the "Arsenal of Democracy" during World War II, manufacturing munitions, weapons, and war machines.

Jeffries was instrumental in organizing the Michigan Conference of Mayors. As the President of the conference, he successfully lobbied for an amendment that provided cities and schools with a portion of the state's sales tax revenue. In 1948 Jeffries was defeated for reelection as mayor by Republican Eugene Van Antwerp, 224,310 to 205,543.

Jeffries was reelected to the Common Council in 1949 but he died of a heart attack shortly into his term. His death was on April 2, 1950, one day before his 50th birthday. He died while vacationing in Miami Beach, Florida and was buried in Detroit's Woodlawn Cemetery next to his father, John Lodge, Sr. The Lodge Freeway in Detroit was named for him.

Edward John "Jeff" Jeffries, Jr. gravesite in Woodlawn Ceme-tery.

Eugene Van Antwerp (Courtesy of Monica Harris), Mayor of Detroit 1948-1950

C HAPTER FIFTY-FIVE—EUGENE VAN ANTWERP— ENGINEER MAYOR

Eugene Ignatius Van Antwerp (1889-1962) was born in Detroit July 26, 1889 and went to Detroit St. Peter and Paul Parochial School. He then entered the University of Detroit, graduating with a degree in Engineering. In 1910 and 1911 he worked as an English instructor at Gonzaga University in Spokane, Washington and then returned to Detroit and briefly worked for the Detroit Police Department. Following that, he did engineering work for the Michigan Central Railroad and the Grand Trunk Railroad.

He married Mary Frances McDevitt in 1911 and they had eleven children. When World War I began, he joined the United States Army Corp of Engineers as a Captain and served in the Army from 1917 to 1919. He was in the Allied Expeditionary Force and was one of the first to land in France. After the war, he returned to working for the Grand Trunk Railroad.

Chief Engineer for the Army

From 1926 to 1928 Van Antwerp was the Chief Engineer for the National Survey Service and then went into private practice as an engineer and surveyor. He started his political career when he was elected to the Detroit City Council in 1932. He served from 1932 to 1948. He was also the Commander of the Veterans of Foreign Wars (VFW) in 1938 and 1939.

Van Antwerp campaign sign, and John F. Kennedy with Van Antwerp.

In 1931 Van Antwerp was elected to the Detroit Common Council and was reelected seven more times. He went on to run for Mayor. In 1949 Van Antwerp beat Edward Jeffries for the Mayor of Detroit position, 224,310 to 205,543 in 1947 and served one term.

As Mayor he lobbied for closer control of slum landlords, and taxi-dance halls. A taxi-dance hall was an establishment where men paid to dance with women. He was opposed to police speed traps and banned the wearing of dark glasses at Common Council meetings. "They're as effective as a mask" Van Antwerp said.

While he was Mayor, the Detroit Red Wings hockey team, with Sid Abel, Ted Lindsay, and Gordie Howe, began a run that led to winning the Stanley Cup or coming in second all through the 1950s.

Gordie Howe (center) examines the Stanley Cup.

In 1949 the only floating post office in the United States started its service on the Detroit River. The J. W. Westcott II is the name of the ship that delivers to the lake freighters and other ships on the river. It has its own zip code, 48222, and to send a letter to one of the ships you address it to: "Vessel Name, Marine Post Office, Detroit, Michigan, 48222."

When Van Antwerp ran against Cobo for reelection, he stressed his successful budget and the low crime and high morale of the city. Cobo's winning platform was all about him being a treasurer and accountant, just what was needed to turn the city around. When the heavy voter turnout caused Cobo to get the most votes, with George Edwards second and Van Antwerp third, Van Antwerp was out of the main election. By Detroit's bylaws, the top two vote-getters run against each other in November.

Van Antwerp returned to the Detroit City Council in 1950, winning the special election to replace Edward Jeffries who had just died. His service on the City Council continued until his death in 1962. He unsuccessfully tried running for county auditor in 1935, state highway commissioner in 1952, and the U.S. Congress in 1955.

The floating post office J.W. Westcott II on the Detroit River in front of the Ambassador Bridge. Courtesy of Sara Hattie.

Van Antwerp died of a heart attack on August 5, 1962 and was buried in Holy Sepulchre Cemetery in Southfield, Michigan. Van Antwerp Park and Van Antwerp Avenue in Detroit were named for him.

Van Antwerp gravesite in Holy Sepulchre Cemetery in Southfield, Michigan

C HAPTER FIFTY-SIX— ALBERT COBO—COBO HALL AND ARENA

NAMESAKE

Alan Naldrett

Albert Cobo, Mayor of Detroit 1950-1957

Albert Eugene Cobo (1893-1957) was Mayor of Detroit for much of the 1950's and was the second mayor to die in office.

Candy Stores Opened

Cobo was born October 2, 1893 in Detroit to August, a marine engineer, and Elizabeth Cobo. He went to Amos, Craft, and McKinstry Elementary Schools, and graduated from Western High School, all part of the Detroit Public Schools system. He went to the Detroit Business Institute for a year, and then graduated from the Alexander Hamilton Institute after finishing a correspondence course. He started working in 1910 at the Detroit Copper and Brass Rolling Mills as an office-boy. In 1911 he formed a partnership with his brother Edward to manufacture ice cream and candy. The brothers owned and operated two candy stores in Detroit.

In 1918 he started working at the Burroughs Adding Machine Company as a junior salesman, working his way up to senior salesman in a year. In 1929, after a 3-year period as manager at the competing company Sundstrand Adding Machine Company, he returned to Burroughs and was put in charge of all government and utility accounts in Detroit.

In 1914 Cobo married his childhood sweetheart, Ethel Christie, and the couple had two children, Elaine and Jean. Cobo was a member of a number of organizations, including the Masons, the Elks, the Optimists, the Detroit Economic Club, the Great Lakes-St. Lawrence Association and the President's Civil Defense Advisory Council. The family attended the Mount Hope Congregational Church.

Special Adviser and Detroit City Treasurer

In 1933 Cobo became a special adviser to city government in order to help out with a financial crisis. He was named Deputy City Treasurer in the same year. When City Treasurer Charles L. Williams died, Cobo was named to the senior position. He developed a seven-year-tax plan for property owners that made it possible to forestall foreclosure for many Detroiters.

Multiple Mayoral Terms

While still Treasurer, Cobo ran for Mayor as a Republican and beat Democrat George Edwards 313,136 to 206,134. He was reelected in 1951, defeating Democratic candidate Edgar M. Branigin 168,453 votes to 113,824. His first two terms were for two years.

In 1953 Cobo was elected to the first four-year mayoral term. He beat Democrat James H. Lincoln, 237,357 to 159,330.

One of the things Cobo did as Mayor was arranging for the city to build a $112 million convention center. Once finished, it was named Cobo Hall, and then Cobo Center in his honor. Besides other events, the International Auto Show has been held there for many years.

While Cobo was mayor many of the older factories in the city closed. From 1953 to 1960, ten plants closed, taking over 70,000 jobs with them. Some of the plants included the Packard Plant, Studebaker, Murray Auto Body, and Hudson. Due to the loss of the factories that sustained them, in 1957

46 stores along E. Jefferson Avenue, between Connor and Alter Street, went out of business, leaving all the storefronts vacant.

Cobo at the future Cobo Hall in 1953 and in his office.

Cobo also took the initiative in the development of a revenue-bond financing system, making it possible to complete twenty miles of expressway in the city in seven years instead of the predicted fifteen years.

Cobo unsuccessfully ran as the Republican candidate for Governor of Michigan against Democrat G. Mennen Williams in 1956.

Segregation Mayor

After his death, there has been controversy regarding Cobo and his effect on the city. His platform was to keep Detroit segregated, and Cobo constructed the plans that tore down the black areas of Detroit without providing replacement housing. Although the reason given for the destruction was freeway construction, much of the land was never used and stood vacant for decades. This is one of the main reasons there is a movement to rename the Cobo Center for boxer Joe Louis. Louis had an auditorium named for him, but it was torn down, so the city could build a new hockey arena.

All through the 1940s and 1950s, whites formed neighborhood organizations to "protect" their properties from integration by black people wanting to move to a different part of the city. These community organizations were some of the strongest supporters of Mayor Cobo and helped him get elected Mayor twice.

Cobo had a fatal heart attack right at the end of his mayoral term on September 12, 1957. He was interred in the Woodlawn Cemetery Mausoleum. The head of the Common Council, Louis Miriani, was called upon to finish the last few months of Cobo's term.

Mayor Cobo is interred in the Woodlawn Mausaleum next to his wife Ethel.

Albert Cobo in Woodlawn Cemetery's Main Mausoleum, Section: 232, Unit: 4, Crypt: D-1

Cobo Center

Louis Miriani, Mayor of Detroit 1957-1962

C HAPTER FIFTY-SEVEN—LOUIS MIRIANI—THE 'MIRIANI CRACKDOWN' AND TAX EVASION

Louis Charles Miriani (1897-1987) was mayor of Detroit from 1957 until 1962, and along with Richard Reading and Kwame Kilpatrick, was one of the mayors of Detroit to do time after their term.

Miriani was born in Detroit on January 1, 1897 to Roman Catholic Italian parents, Caroline and Charles Miriani, who was a laborer. Louis went to Detroit Public Schools and graduated from Eastern High School. He entered the U.S. Navy, serving 1918 to 1919. He then did various jobs to help his family, including working as a bank clerk and in the post office.

Social Legislation Lecturer and ABA Chief Counsel

Miriani went to the University of Detroit Law School and received the LL. B law degree in 1923. He also attended Wayne State University, where he later lectured on social legislation. He began practicing law and then in the late 1920s began working for a branch of the Detroit Bar Association, the Legal

Aid Bureau. He worked there as chief counsel from 1938 until 1954.

He married Verona Vachon in 1929 and they had two daughters, Delores and Carol. After marriage he became more active in civil affairs, serving as a member of the Detroit Street Railway Commission, the State Welfare Commission, chairman of the Regional War Labor Board, and president of the Detroit Welfare Commission.

Common Council and Acting Mayor

In 1947 he ran for and won election to Detroit's Common Council. From 1950 to 1957 he was the Council President. As the President, he became Acting Mayor when Mayor Cobo had a heart attack in 1952-1953, and then again when Cobo died in 1957.

In 1958 Miriani ran for Mayor and soundly defeated Republican John J. Beck, 290,947 votes to 48,074. During his term, he concentrated on finishing projects that other mayors had begun. During his term, the $70 million Cobo Hall and Convention Center was completed, freeway construction was continued, and efforts were continued to revitalize downtown Detroit. Detroit's population had begun to decline as workers began moving to the suburbs. The city lost federal aid due to population losses in the 1960 census.

More Slum Clearance

However, in an act that would have later repercussions, Miriani continued slum clearance, which essentially meant tearing down the black areas of Detroit. This included the Black Bottom area (originally named for the rich black soil in the area), and Hastings Street. Hasting Street had been the Jewish area of Detroit until the 1930s when the Jewish population moved to the Oakland area. Also destroyed was the Paradise Valley area, which contained the black entertainment district, with many famous people of the day passing through and playing in the many clubs in the district.

All the black areas were obliterated without any replacement housing being built for the 140,000 residents. The only housing erected was in the newly constructed Lafayette Park, which was more expensive than most of the former Black Bottom residents could afford. Other areas became part of the I-75 freeway or often, just vacant lots.

Black Bottom District of Detroit in the 1950s before demolition.

The people of the area referred to urban renewal as "Negro Removal." Not only were most of the black areas demolished, but in 1961 the city also tore down the first Chinatown in Detroit at Third Street from Porter to Abbott, displacing the city's 2,600 Asians. By 1958, 2,222 buildings had been torn down to make way for the Lodge Freeway, and the Edsel Ford Expressway caused the razing of about 2,800 more buildings.

Mayor Cobo had continually promised preservationists that he wouldn't tear down the old City Hall. But after Cobo's death, Miriani had wrecking crews start taking down the City Hall in the dead of night, before an outcry could be raised. The space became a parking lot.

The Old City Hall by Campus Martius that Miriani had torn down in 1961.

Detroit Skid Row

The "skid row" area of Detroit was on Michigan Avenue, between the Lodge Freeway and Cass Avenue. This was the area where the worst drug and alcohol abusers hung out. Miriani had the whole area bulldozed, but the area's inhabitants just moved farther down Cass Avenue, creating a new skid row called the "Cass Corridor."

Demolition of City Hall in 1960.

Miriani's "slum renewal" exasperated the already bad housing crunch in the city and the fact that most areas of the city were effectively closed to blacks and Asians. It would be up to the next mayor to deal with the negative repercussions of the repressive treatment of the black and other minority citizens of the city.

Area near Van Buren and Detroit Streets c1959; Lower East Side 1950s housing.

Miriani reduced the city budget by $27 million per year and eliminated 2,000 jobs in Detroit. Although he was considered the favorite for reelection and was endorsed by the United Auto Workers (UAW), he got 158,679 votes versus 200,773 for Democrat Jerry Cavanaugh, who had large support from the beleaguered African-American community.

Motown Records Forms

In 1959 one of the most well-known institutions of Detroit started when Berry Gordy, Jr. formed Motown Records (the first label name was Tamla) in 1959. The record company went on to produce countless popular records and make many Detroit singers famous.

Motown's first chart record was "Shop Around" by Smokey Robinson and the Miracles. The first number one song for Motown was by the Marvelettes, "Please Mr. Postman." Soon, top hits by the Supremes, Four Tops, Stevie Wonder, Marvin Gaye, Martha and the Vandellas, the Jackson 5, the Commodores, and many others kept Motown's "urban hits" a top force all through the 1960s and the early 1970s. It was not until the company moved to Los Angeles in 1972 that they slowed down.

Not only did it slow down the company, the moving of

Motown Records affected Detroit deeply. The way Motown relocated to Los Angeles was considered shoddy—they abandoned the city that had made them, taking only a few acts with them. Later, the executives admitted that it was the worst mistake they could have made.

The original Motown studios are now a museum.

Claimed Meeting Islam and Soviet Leaders "Not in the Public Interest"

An Arab community began in Detroit in the late 1950s. Miriani was not popular in the growing Islamic community when he refused to greet delegates to an Islamic convention held in the city. He gave the excuse that he felt that some speakers were "anti-American." In 1959 a top Soviet official was visiting Detroit, but Miriani refused to meet him, stating it was "not in the public interest."

Miriani Crackdown

Miriani was not popular with the African-American community, especially when the "Miriani Crackdown" began. This was the result of two murders, one white woman and one black, both said to be killed by a black man. This caused Miriani to require all police officers to work a six-day week until the culprits were found. Over 1,000 people in the black community were interrogated by the white police force. One black community leader said that the police picked up "anyone black who wasn't where they were supposed to be." This caused more general outrage in the black community of Detroit of 1960 as many leading members were wrongly jailed.

After his defeat by Cavanaugh, Miriani became executive vice-president of the Aronsson Printing Company of Detroit from 1962 until the mid-1970s. He was also on the Board of Trustees of Mercy College. In 1965 he was reelected to the Common Council and served until 1970.

Mysterious Income

Although his mayoral salary was $25,000 a year, Miriani was able to acquire over $261,000 while Mayor—money that he never paid taxes on. In 1966 he was indicted on charges of avoiding taxes on $259,495 of income from 1959 to 1962, the years he was Mayor of Detroit.

Miriani was convicted in 1969, but through appeals was able to hold off going to prison until 1970, when he served 294 days and was released in 1971. He was also fined $40,000. He retired from public life upon his release and quietly moved back to Detroit.

On October 18, 1987, Louis Miriani died at age 90 in Pontiac after a long illness. He was interred in a mausoleum in Holy Sepulchre Cemetery, Southfield, Michigan.

Louis Miriani is interred next to his wife Vera in Holy Sepulchre Cemetery in Southfield, Michigan

Jerome Cavanagh, Mayor of Detroit 1962-1969

C HAPTER FIFTY-EIGHT—JEROME CAVANAGH—CIVIL RIGHTS AND RIOTS

Jerome Patrick Cavanagh (1928-1979) was an unexpected winner in the 1961 Detroit Mayoral Election. Defeating Louis Miriani 200,773 votes to 158,679, Cavanaugh began his term in 1962, at age 33, becoming the second youngest Mayor of Detroit. Frank Couzens and Kwame Kilpatrick are tied as the youngest Detroit mayors at 31 years of age.

Jerry Cavanagh was born in Detroit on June 16, 1928 to steamfitter Sylvester and his wife Mary Cavanagh. He attended St. Cecilia High School and then the University of Detroit, earning two degrees, a Bachelor of Philosophy (Ph.B.) in 1950, and a law degree (LL. B) in 1954. **Deputy Sheriff and IBM Sales Rep** Ca-vanagh became chairman of the Wayne County Young Democrats in 1949 and 1950, and was a deputy sheriff, and a sales representative for the IBM Corporation. He was appointed as an administrative assistant with the Michigan State Fair Authority and then was appointed to the Metropolitan Airport Board of Zoning Appeals for two terms. He was a delegate to state and county conventions of the Democratic Party. **Marriage at the State Fair** In 1952, Cavanagh married Mary Helen Martin, who was a secretary from Kokomo, Indiana. He met her when both of them worked at the State Fair—she was secretary to the fair's general manager. They had eight children—Mark, Patrick, David, Mary Therese, Christopher, Philip, Jerome and Elizabeth Angela. In 1955, he became a member of the Sullivan, Romanoff, Cavanagh and Nelson Law Firm. He practiced law until 1961 when he ran for Mayor of Detroit against incumbent Louis Miriani.

Mayor Louis Miriani had a lot of support in Detroit—the endorsement of the UAW, which was important in a union town like Detroit, the Detroit Chamber of Commerce, and both the Detroit Free Press and the Detroit News. But working against his popularity was the "Miriani Crackdown," where Detroit Police were instructed to shake down the black neighborhoods because of a couple of sensational murders supposedly committed by black men. The black community was thrown into turmoil as over 1,000 black persons, mostly men, were picked up by the police, interrogated and held for hours, sometimes overnight and then finally released without being charged with anything. **Successfully Courting the Black Vote** On the other hand, Cavanagh, who had never previously run for office, courted the black vote. He went to black churches and civic events. He chastised Miriani on the city's budget shortfall, the dwindling population, and its handling of race relations. In a "major upset," as the newspapers called it, Cavanagh beat Miriani 200,773 to 158,679. Cavanagh was initially a popular mayor, reforming the police department, and in June 1963, in a giant Detroit Civil Rights Rally, the Detroit Walk to Freedom, walked arm-in-arm with Martin Luther King, Jr. down Detroit's Woodward

Avenue along with 100,000 others. Martin Luther King gave a preview of his "I Have a Dream" speech for this June 23, 1963 rally.   **Detroit is Model City**
Major successes for Cavanagh in the early months of his term included getting Detroit included as part of the "Model Cities Program" which was a component of President Lyndon Johnson's Great Society and War on Poverty initiative. The program endowed federal money for city improvements. Detroit was emboldened by its good reputation to make a bid for the 1972 Olympics (its seventh unsuccessful attempt, a record).   Detroit built some new skyscrapers with some of the federal money it received from the Model Cities Program. These included One Woodward Avenue, 211 West Fort Street, and 1001 Woodward. The Jeffersonian Apartments and 300 Lafayette East Cooperative were completed during Cavanagh's term. In 1965 Detroit received an award given by the American Institute of Architects for urban redevelopment.

Cavanaugh was praised throughout the national media for his urban affairs successes. Articles about him appeared in Life, Newsweek, and Time Magazines and he appeared on TV on Meet the Press. He was named to the "Outstanding 100 People in the US" list.   **Happy Days Are Here Again**
The following quote appeared in the *National Observer*, referring to conditions in Detroit towards the middle of Cavanagh's administration: "Retail sales are up dramatically. Earnings are higher. Unemployment is lower. Physically Detroit has acquired freshness and vitality. Acres of slums have been razed, and steel and glass apartments have sprung up in their place." The Cavanaghs hosted many big functions, including dinners for John Wayne, Frank Sinatra, and President John F. Kennedy, who he was often compared to, since both were young, Irish Catholic, and charismatic leaders. Cavanagh was the first mayor to inhabit the residence donated to the city by Alex Manoogian for use as a mayor's residence.

Cavanaugh's first term could not have gone better for him.

When he ran for reelection in 1965, he beat Republican opponent Walter C. Shamie 295,992 to 144,866 votes. In 1966 Cavanaugh was President of both the United States Conference of Mayors and the National League of Cities.

City Income Tax

Cavanagh instilled a city income tax on residents and people who worked in the city. This helped erase the city's $34.5 million debt. He reduced taxes on property and businesses and achieved a Prime rating for Detroit's municipal bonds. Cavanagh appointed blacks to many high-level city positions and attained federal financing for training high school dropouts, for housing, water and sewer programs, and for a new North Wing of the Detroit Institute of Art (DIA). The North Wing was later named for him.

The 1967 Detroit Riot

And then on Sunday, July 23, 1967, it all unraveled. In the early morning hours, Detroit Police raided a blind pig at

9125 12th Street. Expecting just a few revelers, police were surprised to find over 80 people in the illegal club, celebrating the return home of a couple of soldiers from Vietnam. The police decided to arrest everybody and while they were waiting for transportation a crowd gathered. At first verbally taunting the officers, someone threw a bottle at them and the melee began. As soon as the police left, the crowd began looting a nearby clothing store. They soon began looting the rest of the neighborhood and as the word spread, more people joined in.

The riot began spreading and by mid-afternoon, at 12th Street and Atkinson, a grocery store was torched. Soon, the skyline was filled with smoke as more buildings burned. The tensions of the many years of "urban renewal" in black neighborhoods and the racially-divided neighborhoods caused repressed feelings to erupt.   The ensuing riot lasted for three days, with 43 deaths, 1,189 injured, and over 7,200 arrests, predominantly black. More than 2,000 buildings were destroyed. The National Guard and U.S. Army were called to restore order, which they finally did on Thursday, July 27.

The July 1967 riot on 12th Street.

The riot was one of many that happened during what was dubbed the "Long, Hot Summer of 1967." Riots also occurred in Newark, Atlanta, Boston, Tampa, Buffalo, N.Y., Birmingham, Alabama, Chicago, New York, Milwaukee, Minneapolis, New Britain, Conn., Rochester, N.Y., Plainfield, New Jersey and Cincinnati during the fateful summer.

White Flight

One of the main effects of the riots was "White Flight" increase—the moving of white people out of the city limits into the suburbs. The "ring suburbs" were the ones closest to Detroit, and the first ones Detroiters took flight to. Cities like Livonia, Wyandotte, East Detroit (now Eastpointe), Roseville, Warren saw big increases in population, while Detroit lost people.   Before the 1967 Riot, over 22,000 people had already left the city. In 1968, 66,000 people left, and in 80,000 in 1969. Another 40,000 left in 1970—over 345,000 white people moved out of Detroit from 1960 to 1970, over a third of the populations! Many homes were abandoned without being sold as whites left the area.   As neighborhood covenants gave way to new federal anti-discrimination laws, more and more all-white neighborhoods were integrated. Although many whites moved out, some of the wealthier enclaves dealt with it positively, with whites accepting new blacks into a harmonious neighborhood. Some of the areas that accepted integration were Indian Village, Palmer Park, the Golf Club subdivision, Rosedale Park, East English Village, and the University District Community.

Public Divorce

After the riot, Cavanagh was accused of taking too long to try to stop the insurrection. His life got even worse as he and his wife had a very public divorce in 1968. The newspapers reported that the Mayor said that his wife Mary threw coffee and eggs at him and was a "sloppy housekeeper." Mrs. Cavanagh said her husband "drank excessively."

The riot irreparably damaged Cavanagh's reputation as an urban planner and racial problem solver. He declined to run for a third term and largely retired from public life, except for a failed run for Governor of Michigan in 1974 and for the Senate in 1966. He resumed private practice of the law and lectured at the University of Michigan and the Massachusetts Institute of Technology.

After his divorce, in 1972 Cavanaugh married Kathleen Disser and they adopted a daughter, Katie. On November 27, 1979 he was in Lexington, Kentucky to see a legal client and suffered a fatal heart attack at the age of 51. He was buried in Mt. Elliott Cemetery in Detroit.   The Cavanagh name continued to be involved in public life. His son, Mark, became a Michigan Court of Appeals Judge, Philip, David and Christopher were Wayne County Commissioners, and Jerome was a Wayne County judge. Cavanagh's brother Mike was a Michigan Supreme Court Justice and Chief Justice.

Cavanagh's gravesite in Detroit's Mt. Elliot Cemetery

CHAPTER FIFTY-NINE-ROMAN GRIBBS—GRIBBS NOT GRZYBS

Roman Gribbs, Mayor of Detroit 1970-1974

Roman Stanley Gribbs (1925-2016) was born in Capac, Michigan on December 29, 1925 to Roman Grzyb, an automobile worker, and his wife Magdalena. They separately moved from Poland and met and married in Detroit. The couple bought a 100-acre farm near Capac, Michigan in St. Clair County, where Roman and his brother John were born. John was later Mayor of Capac in 2016.

Anglicizing Name

Roman attended public schools in Capac and worked on the farm. Before World War II, he anglicized his last name to Gribbs. He served in the Army from 1944 to 1948 and was a sergeant upon his honorable discharge.

He went to the University of Detroit in 1948 and graduated with a Bachelor of Science degree, majoring in accounting and economics, in 1952. The same year he married Katherine

Stratis who was an airline hostess. The couple had five children—Paula, Carla, Christopher, Rebecca, and Elizabeth.

Store Salesman and Law School Instructor

While attending the University of Detroit Law School, Gribbs worked as a store salesman, as well as teaching law and accounting to undergraduate students. He received his LL.B. law degree in 1954, graduating third in his class.

Gribbs went to work as an assistant Wayne County Prosecuting Attorney from 1956 to 1964 and practiced law privately from 1964 to 1966. In 1966 he was appointed a presiding referee in Detroit's Traffic Court until 1968. He replaced Peter L. Buback as Wayne County Sheriff, serving Buback's remaining seven months on his term. He was then elected in his own right, as a Democrat, for Sheriff in November 1968, serving until December 1969.

Last-Minute Filing, Mayoral Victory

Gribbs decided to run for Mayor of Detroit in 1970, filing only 24 hours before the deadline. Stressing "crime in the streets" as Detroit's number one problem, he narrowly defeated Richard Austin, the black Michigan Secretary of State. The vote was 258,010 to 251,816.

The "Renaissance Center" was meant to signal a rise for Detroit and was built during Gribb's mayoral term.

Gribbs trimmed city services and eliminated a $20 million-dollar city budget deficit. He achieved a budget surplus upon leaving office. While Gribbs was Mayor, neighborhood police stations were founded, and crime was reduced.

The most controversial aspect of Gribbs' mayoral term was the incorporation of the STRESS ("Stop the Robberies, Enjoy Safe Streets") unit of the police department. They were mostly an all-white police squad that was responsible for many shootings of blacks.

Gribbs also had the unenviable position of being Mayor when the Supreme Court ordered forced busing to integrate schools in 1971. Judge Stephen Roth ruled that the segregation was so bad in Detroit that blacks would have to bused to suburban schools and whites to schools in the city. Roth became the most hated man in the city and three years later when he was dying in the hospital, even though the Supreme Court ruling was overturned, he still got notes hoping he had a "happy bus ride to hell."

Renaissance Center and Ethnic Festivals

While Gribbs was Mayor, a billion-dollars of new construction was started, including the complex on the river comprising multiple large buildings called the "Renaissance Center," now the World Headquarters for General Motors Corporation and the tallest hotel in North America. Gribbs also started riverfront ethnic festivals.

Gribbs was President of the National League of Cities in 1973 and President of the Michigan Conference of Mayors. He was a trustee of the U.S. Conference of Mayors.

Gribbs declined to run for reelection in 1973 and joined a law firm in 1974. He was a director of the Bank of the Commonwealth and a trustee of the University of Detroit. In 1975 he was elected as a Judge to the Wayne County Circuit Court until 1982, when he started serving on the Michigan Court of Appeals. In 1990 he was divorced and married Leola Barr. He retired from the court in 2001. He was later on the Board of Directors of the Piast Institute, a research center devoted to Polish American Affairs.

On April 5, 2016, he died of cancer at the age of 90 at his home in Northville, Michigan and was buried in Northville.

Background. Born in Detroit, 1925; raised on farm in Emmett, Michigan. Sergeant in Army. Worked his way through University of Detroit, earning a Bachelor of Science degree. Majored in Economics and graduated Magna Cum Laude. Third in his class at U. of D.'s Law School, and taught accounting there for three years, including final year in law school.

Experience.
1953
Instructor at University of Detroit
1955
Appointed Assistant Prosecuting Attorney
1964
Entered private law practice
1965
Appointed Traffic Court Referee
June, 1968
Appointed Interim Wayne County Sheriff
Nov., 1968
Elected Wayne County Sheriff

Leadership. As Wayne County Sheriff, Roman Gribbs supervises a staff of 500 employees and directs the spending of a $6,000,000 budget. He is responsible for the county jails, and supervises all the police services at Metropolitan Airport, ranging from traffic to crime control; administers police road patrols in 280 square miles of Wayne County, and is responsible for all officers present in Detroit's circuit courts. He is also one of the city's outstanding trial lawyers.

Know-how. Roman Gribbs is the only candidate who has been—successfully—a teacher, attorney, prosecutor, tax accountant and sheriff.

Vote
Roman
GRIBBS
for
MAYOR

CITIZENS FOR ROMAN GRIBBS
FORT SHELBY HOTEL
DETROIT, MICHIGAN 48226

Vote
Roman
GRIBBS
for
MAYOR

Coleman Young, Mayor of Detroit 1974-1994

C HAPTER SIXTY— COLEMAN YOUNG—LONGEST REIGNING MAYOR

Coleman Young speaking by the Detroit Riverfront.

Coleman Alexander Young (1918-1997) was the first black mayor of Detroit and at twenty years, the longest-serving. Young was controversial, and strong arguments have been made, both pro and con, about whether Young was good for the city.

"In Detroit, Mayor Coleman Young rejected the integrationist goal in favor of a flamboyant, black-power style that won him loyal followers, but he left the city a fiscal and social wreck" was a quote by political scientist James Q. Wilson.

On the other hand, Mayor Dennis Archer, Young's successor, said, "Mayor Young was simply one of the greatest mayors in American history. His legacy is the spirit and the soul of Detroit."

By the time Coleman Young was elected, the city had suffered "white flight" for the past twenty years, as white people avoiding integration and race riots moved to the suburbs. Blacks went from 43.7% of the population to 67.1%

from 1970 to 1980. A popular joke (among people who had left) was, "Would the last person leaving Detroit, please turn the lights off?"

Young, or "Coleman," as he is more commonly called, was born May 24, 1918 in Tuscaloosa, Alabama to Coleman, a dry cleaner, and Ida Young. When Coleman was five in 1923, his family, including four younger siblings, moved to Detroit in the Black Bottom neighborhood. His father set up a dry cleaner's shop and got a second job working for the post office.

"Black Bottom" neighborhood, where Young grew up.

Young grew up working odd jobs in gambling houses and blind pigs during the Depression. One gambit he engaged in was diving in the Detroit River, looking for liquor dropped by bootleggers when running from the cops.

Young went to a Catholic parochial school up to high school, when he was barred from attending any further due to learning while black. He went to the public school instead, Eastern High School, graduating with honors in 1935.

Young's youth was fraught with many other circumstances thrust upon him due to racial prejudice. He was barred from Boy Scout excursions and from going to Bob-lo, an island re-creation and amusement park.

Union Organizing

After high school he joined the United Auto Workers and started working for Ford Motor Company at the River Rouge plant. He participated in the UAW 1937 sit-down strike and was thereafter prevented from working at Ford again. That and hitting one of Harry Bennett's Service Department agents with a metal rod (in self-defense, Coleman said).

Coleman got a job with the post office and with his brother George Young, Coleman organized the post office workers into a postal union.

In World War II Young was a member of the Tuskegee Air-men, the 477th Medium-Bomber Group of the United States Army Air Force. He was a navigator, second lieutenant, and bombardier.

In 1945 he led a group of African-Americans in Seymour, Indiana, protesting segregation in a whites-only officer's club. Over 160 African-Americans were arrested. The incident was later lauded as an important step in a fully-integrated armed forces and was considered a model for the right way to conduct civil disobedience.

Officers of the 477ᵗʰ at Freeman Field in Indiana, including Coleman Young, wait to be transported to Godman Field, Kentucky to face charges in April 1945.

Young was a member of the United Auto Workers and the National Negro Labor Council. He supported the Progressive Party and candidate Henry Wallace in 1948. Young continued to protest segregation in the Army and the UAW. This made him a target to be called to testify to the House Un-American Committee (HUAC), which was then headed by Wisconsin Senator Joe McCarthy.

Appearance at House Un-American Committee

Coleman Young made a famous appearance on February 28 and 29, 1952, as he refused to back down in the face of predatory questioning. He was told that he wasn't personally under investigation but was only there to give names of acquaintances involved with "subversive groups." Here is part of the exchange:

Coleman Young (center, with mustache) appearing before the House Un-American Activities Committee (HUAC) in 1952.

Mr. Young: Mr. Tavenner, I would like to say this: First of all, I have understood, from official pronouncements of this committee, and yourself, that this is a forum; you call it the highest forum in the country, being that of the Congress of the United States. I have, been subpoenaed here. I didn't come by my own prerogative.

Mr. Tavenner. I understand.

Mr. Young. I can only state that in being interviewed and being asked questions, that I hope that I will be allowed to react fully to those questions, and not be expected to react only in such a manner that this committee may desire me. In other words, I might have answers you might not like. You called me here to testify; I am prepared to testify, but, I would like to know from you if I shall be allowed to respond to your questions fully and in my own way.

Mr. Tavenner. I have no objection to your answers, if they are responsive to the questions.

Mr. Young. I will respond.

Mr. Tavenner. But I desire to ask you the question which I have asked other witnesses: Are you now a member of the Communist Party?

Mr. Young. I refuse to answer that question, relying upon my rights under the fifth amendment, and, in light of the fact that an answer to such a question, before such a committee, would be, in my opinion, a violation of my rights under the first amendment, which provides for freedom of speech, sanctity and privacy of political beliefs and associates, and, further, since I have no purpose of being here as a stool pigeon, I am not prepared to give any information on any of my associates or political thoughts.

Mr. Tavenner. Have you been a member of the Communist Party?

Mr. Young. For the same reason, I refuse to answer that question.

Mr. Tavenner. You told us you were the executive secretary of the National Negro Congress.

Mr. Young. That word is "Negro," not "Niggra."

Mr. Tavenner. I said, "Negro." I think you are mistaken.

Mr. Young. I hope you'll speak more clearly.

Mr. Wood. I will appreciate it if you will not argue with counsel.

Mr. Young. It isn't my purpose to argue. As a Negro, I resent the slurring of the name of my race.

Mr. Wood. You are here for the purpose of answering questions.

Mr. Young. In some sections of the country they slur...

Mr. Tavenner. I am sorry. I did not mean to slur it. I was mistaken, in referring to your leaving you said you were the executive secretary of the National Negro Congress; but, I will ask you a question, if you were, at any time in the past, executive secretary of the National Negro Congress?

Mr. Young. I refuse to answer that question under the fifth amendment.

Mr. Tavenner. Your position is that to answer any question with relation to your connection with the National Negro Congress might tend to incriminate you, is that your position?

Young. The National Negro Congress, as I understand it, has been labeled by not only the Justice Department, but by this committee, which also labeled the National Association for the Advancement of Colored People as subversive, and I don't intend to discuss any organization that, properly or improperly, has been designated by you or any other committee as subversive.

Mr. Tavenner. Were you, at any time, a field organizer for the National Negro Congress?

Mr. Young. The same answer will apply in regard to the National Negro Congress.

Mr. Tavenner. I understood you to state—you answered a moment ago that this committee had labeled the NAACP as a subversive.

Mr. Young. That is correct.

Mr. Tavenner. When was such action taken?

Mr. Young. I refer you to the Negro Yearbook of 1949.

Mr. Tavenner. Can you refer to a record of the committee which has so designated the NAACP?

Mr. Young. I am sure this committee is in possession of its own records. I would suggest a search of those records.

Mr. Tavenner. It is on record? You are sure I have evidence of such designation with regard to the NAACP, a national organization?

Mr. Young. I refer you to...

Mr. Tavenner. There was a local in Hawaii which had some special problem, but, as far as the national organization is concerned, this committee has not so cited it, nor has the Attorney General's office, in my opinion."

Mr. Young: I am not here to fight in any un-American activities, because I consider the denial of the right to vote to large numbers of people all over the South un-American." I happen to know, in Georgia, Negro people are prevented from voting by virtue of terror, intimidation and lynchings. It is my contention you would not be in Congress today (said to the Congressman from Georgia) if it were not for the legal restrictions on voting on the part of my people. Congressman, neither me or none of my friends were at this plant the other day brandishing a rope in the face of John Cherve, a young union organizer and factory worker who was threatened with repeated violence after members of the HUAC alleged that he might be a communist, I can assure you I have had no part in the hanging or bombing of Negroes in the South. I have not been responsible for firing a person from his job for what I think are his beliefs, or what somebody thinks he believes in, and things of that sort. That is the hysteria that has been swept up by this committee."

Young gained a lot of respect from the civil rights community and the many enemies of Senator Joe McCarthy for standing up to the committee. A vinyl record of Young's testimony was pressed, sold and widely circulated in the black community.

Post Office Worker, Insurance Salesman, and Michigan State Senator

Young got his post office job back after his military service and worked there from 1947 to 1950. He went on to different jobs, including a spot cleaner at a laundry, butcher's assistant, and taxi driver. However, his chief activity during the 1950s was union organizing and helping to stop discrimination in the auto industry. From 1957 to 1964 he worked as an insurance salesman and in 1964 he was elected to the Michigan State Senate. He served until 1973, becoming floor leader and representing Michigan on the Democratic National Committee.

While serving in Lansing, he worked for open housing legislation and busing to integrate schools. Due to his activity he became well-known in Detroit and in 1973 announced his candidacy for mayor of Detroit. His Republican opposition was Police Chief John F. Nichols, running on a "law and order" platform. Young called out the police force as "white and racist" and promised to hire more black officers.

In particular, Young promised to eliminate the police unit called S.T.R.E.S.S. ("Stop the Robberies, Enjoy Safe Streets"), the unit formed to handle crime, partly in response to the Detroit Riot of 1967. The squad would use decoys to draw out criminals. As a result, police shootings of black men was widespread. The police unit was composed almost chiefly of white officers.

Coleman Wins First of Five Terms

With 92% of the black vote, Young defeated Nichols 233,674 to 216,993, a margin of 17,000 votes. He would go on to win four more terms, for a total of five.

Detroit had garnered a rough reputation for the large number of homicides there and began to be known as "Murder City." One of the main reasons was that Detroit was having an epidemic of crack cocaine.

"Hit Eight Mile"

Once mayor, Young took a hard line on crime, stating, "I issue an open warning now to all dope pushers, to all rip-off artists, to all muggers. It's time to leave Detroit. I don't give a damn if you are black or white, or if you wear Super-Fly or blue uniforms with silver badges! Hit 8 Mile Road!" (Eight Mile is the dividing road between Detroit and the suburbs.) This caused turmoil among the suburbs, where people interpreted his remarks to mean he was telling all the undesirables to move to the suburbs.

Young's relations with the suburbs never improved, and Detroit continued to lose population and businesses. Unfortunately, crime increased after the elimination of the S.T.R.E.S.S. units. Young's plan for a mass transit system ended up a much smaller system than planned, the "People Mover," which had a downtown route only. Lack of cooperation with surrounding municipal units caused the project to fizzle.

The Arab Embargo of Oil sent the United States reeling in the late 1970s, and especially in Detroit, the Motor City. As the car companies produced less cars, they laid off more workers, increasing unemployment and discontent in the city. With all these factors working against Detroit, it's probably true that anybody who was mayor could do little to stop Detroit's decline.

In October 1986 Detroit was presented by *Sports Illustrated* magazine with the "Monument to Joe Louis," which is a giant replica of the fist of Joe Louis. It is more generally called "The Fist." Coleman presided over the dedication.

The Fist, at Jefferson and Woodward Streets in downtown Detroit and its inscription.

The inscription on the Fist reads:

MONUMENT/TO/JOE LOUIS/BY ROBERT GRAHAM/A GIFT FROM SPORTS ILLUSTRATED/TO THE PEOPLE OF THE CITY OF/DETROIT. THE DETROIT INSTITUTE OF/ART AND ITS FOUNDERS SOCIETY/ON THE OCCASION OF THE MUSEUM'S/CENTENNIAL 1885-1985

Young was known for using "salty language" and saying whatever was on his mind. There was even a popular book about Young's quotations, with content like Coleman Young commenting on the "Donut Theory" of Detroit. The theory was that Detroit was surrounded by suburbs but had nothing but a hole in the middle. Young said," We need to consider ourselves a German chocolate layer cake, or, lest someone take offense a French vanilla layer cake. Solid, with no holes, and sweet parts and good parts for everyone."

When accused of stealing politician Tom Barrow's platform, Coleman said, "How could you steal something that doesn't exist?" He didn't care for Ronald Reagan and called him "Pruneface." But once Reagan became President, Coleman changed it to "President Pruneface."

When a reporter for the Revolutionary Worker was interviewing him and accused him of working for the "corporate elite," Young said, "You can just revolution your ass on out of here."

During the mid-80's, a new genre of music emerged from Detroit—techno! The city holds a Techno Festival each year during Memorial Day weekend to commemorate it.

African-American Museum

Beginning in his youth, Dr. Charles Wright started collecting documents and artifacts dealing with the African-American community, such as Elijah McCoy's notes and inventions. In 1965 Wright used his collection to open the International Afro-American Museum on 1549 W. Grand Boulevard in Detroit, in a building he owned. It was one of the first African-American Museums in the U.S.

In 1985 the museum was moved to the city's Cultural Center, near the Detroit Institute of Arts, Detroit Historical Museum, and the Detroit Public Library. It was renamed the Charles H. Wright Museum of African-American History and Coleman presided at the opening.

The Charles H. Wright Museum of African-American History

Developing the Waterfront

In Young's term a lot of positive changes occurred—the Renaissance Center was built on the waterfront, and further development of the waterfront started, including Hart Plaza on the Riverfront. When he was reelected in 1977, Coleman planned low-cost public housing and wanted to enlarge the city's tax base.

He passed a rule requiring all police officers to live within the city limits and opened police "mini-stations" in high-crime areas. He brought two new auto factories, one Chrysler and one General Motors, into the city through use of tax abatements. He built Joe Louis Arena downtown, keeping the Detroit Red Wings hockey team from moving out of the city.

Young served as the vice-chairman of the Democratic National Committee from 1977 to 1981. In 1980 he was the chairman of the Democratic Convention Platform Committee and led the National Democratic Conference of Mayors. He led the United States Conference of Mayors from 1981 to 1983.

Unfortuneatly, Coleman also presided over a Detroit heroin epidemic in the 1970s, presided over by gangs like the Errol Flynns. In the 1980s, the crack epidemic took hold, with gangs like the Young Boys, Inc. on the West Side of the city. They were called "Young Boys" primarily because the gang used underage juveniles to sell their crack cocaine. If busted, the youngsters would only get juvenile sentences. On the East Side of the city the Chambers Brothers (not the Time Has Come Today band) controlled the crack trade.

In spite of the problems, Young continued to soundly win over any opponents who challenged him as mayor. He refused Washington, DC Cabinet appointments in order to stay Mayor of Detroit. Finally, he retired in 1994 and spent his time lecturing as an adjunct Professor at Wayne State University and writing his autobiography, *Hard Stuff: The Autobiography of Coleman Young.*

Twice divorced, Young had a son, Coleman Young, Jr. who ran for Mayor against Mike Duggan in 2014 and lost. The son had been unknown to the public and not raised by Coleman. Coleman, Sr. had long suffered from emphysema and heart problems. He was hospitalized for pneumonia and went into a coma. On November 30, 1997, he died of respiratory failure and was buried in Elmwood Cemetery.

His funeral was a mammoth affair with speakers from all over and hundreds waiting in the snow for a last viewing. Aretha Franklin was the featured singer in the funeral held in the Second Baptist Church of Detroit.

In Detroit, there is a Coleman Young Elementary School, the Coleman Young Community Center, the Coleman A. Young International Airport, the Coleman A. Young Municipal Center, and the Coleman A. Young Foundation.

Coleman Young in Elmwood Cemetery.

Alan Naldrett

Dennis Archer, Mayor of Detroit-1994-2001

C HAPTER SIXTY-ONE-DENNIS ARCHER—MAYOR BEFORE THE KWAME MELTDOWN

Dennis Wayne Archer (1942-) was born on New Year's Day, January 1, 1942, in Detroit. His parents were Ernest James and Frances Carroll Archer. Right after his birth the family moved to Cassopolis, the county seat of Cass County in Michigan.

After graduating from Cassopolis High School in 1959, Archer worked as a golf caddy, washed dishes, and other jobs, to earn enough money to attend Western State University in Kalamazoo. He graduated in 1965, earning a Bachelor of Science degree.

In 1967 he married Trudy Duncombe and they had two children, Dennis Archer, Jr., and Vincent Archer.

Teaching the Learning-Disabled

After graduation from Western, Archer taught learning disabled schoolchildren in Detroit Public Schools from 1965 to

1970, attending the Detroit College of Law at the same time. He graduated in 1970 with the J.D. law degree.

Archer joined the bar and practiced trial law in Detroit. From 1972 to 1978, he taught as an associate professor at the Detroit College of Law, and from 1984 to 1985 he was an adjunct professor at Wayne State University College of Law. Serving on the Detroit Bar Association Board of Directors, he was also President of the American Bar Association from 1983 to 1984 (the first African-American to hold that position) and President of the State Bar of Michigan from 1984 to 1985.

Most Respected Judge

In 1986 Governor James Blanchard appointed Archer to the Michigan Supreme Court in 1986. He stepped down in 1990 and was named "most respected judge in Michigan" by Michigan *Lawyer's Weekly* magazine.

In 1993, following Coleman Young's retirement, Archer ran for Mayor as a Democrat. He had competition from the candidate that Young endorsed, Sharon McPhail, but triumphed in the primary and went on to win in the General Election, beating out many candidates testing the waters after Coleman Young's departure from his 20-year reign as Mayor. A few of the candidates included long-time U.S. Congressman John Conyers, and singer Sixto Rodriguez, later famous as the star of the award-winning documentary, *Searching for Sugarman*.

"Tool of the White Suburbs"

In the campaign between McPhail and Archer, McPhail tried to position herself as the best black candidate, while Archer was a tool of the white suburbs. Archer beat out the 19 other candidates with 149,838 votes, which was 56.63% of the total. The candidate closest to him, McPhail, had 47,965 votes.

Archer's mayoral term won him awards. He managed to balance the budget after only one year and wrangled the city a grant for $100 million in empowerment funds from the federal government. While he was mayor, Ford Field for the Detroit Lions and Comerica Park for the Detroit Tigers were built in the city.

Casinos Come to Detroit

The first Detroit casino, the MGM Grand Detroit, opened in 1999, during Archer's term. It was, at the time considered the first luxury casino resort hotel in a major city. The Motor City Casino, and the Greektown Casino opened in 2000. The casino question had been around for a while, with dissension on both sides of the issue.

Archer ran for reelection in 1997 and handily defeated Ed Vaughn, 137,811 to 27,853. In 1999, an unsuccessful recall campaign was waged against Archer. Some of the reasons given were that Archer privatized city jobs, paid little attention to Detroit's neighborhoods, and wouldn't bargain with unions. The recall was unsuccessful but had a lot to do with Archer declining to run again in 2001.

Upon leaving as mayor in 2002, Archer joined law firm Dickinson Wright and was appointed chairman. He joined the Board of Directors of Compuware and became a member of the Executive Committee of the National Democratic Party. In 2017 he released a book, "Let the Future Begin," which was a memoir of his public life.

Motor City Casino at night.

CHAPTER SIXTY-TWO-KWAME KILPATRICK-HIP-HOP FELONIOUS MAYOR

Kwame Kilpatrick—Mayor of Detroit 2002-2008

Detroit has had its share of corrupt mayors—Bowles, Reading, Miriani, but most agree that Kwame Kilpatrick was the worst.

Kwame Malik Kilpatrick was born on June 8, 1970 in Detroit. His parents were Bernard, a former Wayne County Commissioner and semi-professional basketball player, and Carolyn "Cheeks" Kilpatrick, a member of the U.S. House of Representatives.

Wins Seat in Michigan House of Representatives

Kwame graduated from Cass Tech High School, and then received a Bachelor of Science degree in Political Science from Florida A & M University in 1992. In 1996, he ran for, and won, his mother's seat in the Michigan House of Representatives after his mother resigned to successfully run for the U.S. House of Representatives. Kwame claimed that the whole campaign only spent $10,000, without endorsements from anyone.

From 1968 to 2000, Kwame was the minority floor leader for the Michigan Democratic Party. In 1999 he received a Juris Doctor degree from the Detroit College of Law, now the Michigan State University College of Law. He became the House Minority Leader in 2001, the first African-American to hold that position.

Successfully Runs for Mayor, Defeats Beverly Hills Cop Actor Gil Hill

In 2001 Kwame successfully beat Common Councilman Gil Hill, who famously appeared as Inspector Todd in the *Beverly Hills Cop* franchise. At 31 years old, Kwame tied Frank Couzens as the youngest Detroit Mayor, and became the youngest elected one. He was called the "Hip-Hop Mayor" and sported a sartorial look with an earring in one ear. He became the big hope of the city looking for a revival; a young, charismatic black gentleman with big ideas to revitalize Detroit.

Kwame and Obama

At the 2004 Democratic Convention, Kwame left a dynamic impression when he spoke right before Illinois Senator Barack Obama.

Barack Obama and Kwame Kilpatrick at the 2004 Democratic Convention.

In his first term Kwame closed the century-old Belle Isle Aquarium and the Belle Isle Zoo, justifying it by saying the city couldn't afford them. He wanted to cut funding to the Detroit Zoo also, but was overridden by the Common Council, which appropriated $700,000 for the zoo. (Belle Isle has since become maintained by the Michigan State Park Service, and the aquarium reopened.) He had "pension obligation bonds" issued that only forestalled the financial problems that were facing Detroit and added $1.4 billion to the city's debt.

Using City Funds for Personal Expenses

Kwame's first big scandal occurred when he was discovered to be using city funds to lease a car for his wife. What's more, Kwame was found to have charged $210,000 to the city credit card for such personal items as massages, golf clubs, extravagant dining, and expensive wines. Kwame paid back only $9,000 of the $210,000. This was one of the reasons a 2005 issue of Time Magazine named him as one of the worst mayors in America.

Manoogian Mansion Party

The next big scandal for Kwame were the rumors of a wild, drug-filled party that had been held in the mayoral residence, the Manoogian Mansion. Kwame's wife Carlita was supposed to be out of town with the couples' three sons, Jalil, Jelani, and Jonas.

However, Carlita returned to the mansion unexpectedly and caught one of the strippers, "Strawberry," giving Kwame a lap dance. Carlita first slugged and slapped her, and then picked up an object (variously reported as a fireplace poker, baseball bat, and a table leg) and hit Strawberry with it. Reports say Strawberry left in an ambulance. Later, Strawberry, real name Tamara Greene, was killed in a drive-by shooting. The Kwame administration denied the party ever happened.

The Citizens for Honest Government

Amidst the turmoil, Kwame was up for reelection in 2005 and was predicted to lose. He had a group supporting his reelection, *The Citizens for Honest Government*, that generated controversy by claiming that the newspapers and media were "lynching" Kwame, trying to undermine his candidacy. Kwame came in second in the primary leading up to the General Election, but then unpredictably beat his opponent, Freeman Hendrix, garnering 53% of the vote.

Kwame Strikes Again

Kwame's second term started out with his removal in 2005 as Administrator of the Water Board. This was due to him awarding contracts to unqualified friends. On top of that, when the 2005-2006 city audit is 14 months late, it costs the city an additional $2.4 million in penalties.

A couple of police officers, Harold Nelthrope and Gary Brown, insist on investigating the party rumors and other indiscretions by Kwame's administration and security detail, the Executive Protection Unit (EPU). The officers are fired by Kwame. Suing under the Whistleblower's Act, saying they were fired because they were investigating the Mayor's office, the officers win and are awarded $6.5 million dollars in 2007.

Kwame Caves on Court Award After Threatening Appeal

At first Kwame vows to appeal—he blames the verdict on the "white suburbanites" on the jury. However, he changes his mind when it's revealed that an appeal would cause his text messages to be released. He quickly approves the financial award without consulting the Common Council. The award includes additional funds that include a gag order about talking about the text messages.

The Mayor's attempt to keep the texts and the gag order secret is foiled when the *Detroit Free Press* obtains all of the text messages under the Freedom of Information Act, since the texts were transmitted on city-issued devices.

The newspaper reporters win a Pulitzer Prize when it's revealed, via the over 14,000 texts, that Kwame is conducting a tempestuous affair with his Chief-of-Staff, Christine Beatty. Other wrongdoing is revealed, such as construction jobs, or just some of the money from them, being shunted to Kwame's best friend, Bobby Ferguson.

Here are the transcripts of some of the texts retrieved by the Detroit Free Press between Kwame (KK) and his chief-of-staff, Christine Beatty (CB).

KK: They were right outside the door, they (bodyguards) had to have hear everything

CB: So, we are officially busted! LOL

CB: "Have you and your wife been back on a regular sex life?

KK: "We had sex 1 time this year, not regular at all."

KK: "I really believed that I had not chance to be with you. I've wanted to have sex with you since I was 17 yrs. old. I believe it was my only opportunity."

CB: "I still remember in the days when I was scared to touch you. How I spent my day dreaming when and how to say I love you … a million days in your arms is never too much."

CB: "I have wanted to hold you so badly all day, but I was trying to stay focused on work. So, I promise, not to keep you longer than 15 minutes."

KK: "Don't promise (N-word.)"

CB: "I'm in my office. Do you want me to come to yours or you coming to mine?"

KK: "I'm coming down there ... LOL ditto. Freaky Chris!"

CB: "You told me that you would be my boyfriend every day until I was your wife. Are you reneging?"

KK: "Hell no! Don't start none. Won't be none ...! LOL".

CB: "I can't see living this way with us being a 'secret' forever. I love you so much and I want to tell somebody, someday! (Smile)."

KK: "In this important and somewhat confusing time in your life, please know with all our hearts and soul that I love you. And you will never, never be alone."

CB: I really wanted to give you some good head this morning and i didn't know how to ask you to let me do it. I have wanted to since Friday

KK: "Next time, just tell me to sit down, shut up and do your thing!"

CB: "Will you marry me?"

KK: "YES. WHEN?"

CB: "I don't know when, all I know is I want to be your wife! I want you to be my husband. So whenever our lives permit, just say you'll marry me."

KK:" YES. YES. YES. I REALLY KNEW I WOULD BE WITH You SINCE 12TH GRADE. JUST A MATTER OF TIME."

CB: "I will wait on it! ..."

KK: "You Too! I was about to jump your bones in Ford Field! LOL."

CB: "I'm sorry that we are going through this mess because of a decision that we made to fire Gary Brown. I will make sure that the next decision is much more thought out. Not regretting what was done at all. But thinking about how we can do things smarter."

KK: It had to happen though. I'm all the way with that!"

CB: "I love how you can make me feel by just looking at me!"

KK: "At that time I was trying to make a teenage fantasy come true!"

KK: "Nobody has ever, I mean ever, excited me like you."

"I love how you can make me feel by just looking at me!"

Other texts sent between the two had them recalling the first time they had sex after Christine returned from Howard University. There was even one from Kwame's wife, Carlita, saying, she "had a bad dream last night ... that you had a girl-friend."

Common Council Votes to Have Kwame Resign

Upon having his affair and steamy texts revealed in the media, Kwame went on TV with his wife and family to give a sentimental appeal and candid confession in hopes of restoring his reputation. However, once some of the spicier and incriminating text messages were made public by the news-paper, the Common Council voted 7 to 1 to ask Kwame to re-sign. Kwame responded by saying that the Common Council doesn't have the authority. The Common Council then passed a resolution asking Michigan Governor Jennifer Granholm to remove Kwame from office.

Kwame Indicted on Eight Felony Counts Due to Text Message Scandal

Due to the information revealed in the texts (during the Whistleblower Trial Kwame and Beatty had both denied having an affair), Wayne Prosecutor Kim Worthy indicted Kwame and his Chief of Staff Christine Beatty on eight felonies, including perjury, obstruction of justice, conspiracy, and misconduct in office.

Kwame posts bail, and then goes to Windsor, Canada for the

weekend with his wife and kids, staying in a posh hotel. He is subsequently arrested for violating his probation by leaving the country and spends the night in Wayne County Jail.

Kwame Convicted and Sentenced to Four Months in Wayne County Jail

Kwame is convicted of two felony counts and accepts a plea agreement to spend four months in the Wayne County Jail, receive five years' probation, not run for public office during his probation period, surrender his law license, pay $1,000,000 restitution to the City of Detroit, and resign as Mayor.

Kwame resigns as Mayor and serves four months in the Wayne County Jail. He then leaves Michigan and moves to a Texas mansion larger than the Detroit Manoogian Mansion the Kilpatrick family had been occupying while Kwame was Mayor.

Inquiry into Kwame's Finances Opened

When Kwame pleads that he is unable to make his restitution payment, an inquiry into his finances is opened. Kwame is supposed to be working as a salesman for the Compuware firm. But research reveals he hasn't made any sales. Kwame claims ignorance of where his money is coming from, or even if his wife is working anywhere, but a secret fund raised by Compuware and Roger Penske to give to Kwame in exchange for his leaving office is uncovered. Kwame must return to Detroit and spend another 120 days in jail for his probation violations. But his problems are just beginning as he finds out that he has been under surveillance for the last few years by the F.B.I. and the S.E.C.

Kwame Indicted on Nineteen Federal Counts

Kwame is indicted in June 2008 on 19 federal counts, including three counts of wire fraud, five counts of filing a false tax return, one count of tax evasion, and ten counts of mail fraud. Each count of fraud carries a maximum sentence of a

20-year imprisonment and a fine of $250,000 and each tax count carries a maximum sentence of three to five years.

Kwame is taken into custody.

It is uncovered that Kwame Kilpatrick used "civic" organizations, the Kilpatrick Civic Fund, Detroit 3D and U.N.I.T.E., to pay for personal and elections expenses. These expenses included paying for summer camp for his children, leases on luxury cars, a crisis manager for overseeing his public image, moving expenses, focus groups, and purchasing personal items.

Other items of contention included Kwame using his influence to have a priest's prostitution arrest dropped, funneling state grant money to an account his wife controlled, and hiring over 100 of his friends and family, giving them preferential treatment in the awarding of city jobs. It was proved in court that millions of dollars were funneled from the awarding of construction and other city jobs to Kwame's friend Bobby Ferguson. Also involved was Kwame's father, Bernard Kilpatrick, who would help co-ordinate the illegal cash.

Kwame Sentenced to Federal Prison with 28-Year Sentence

Kwame's father Bernard was sentenced to 15 months, his friend Bobby Ferguson to 21 years, and Kwame received a 28-year sentence. Kwame, Prisoner # 44678-039, is not eligible for parole until August 1, 2037 when he will be 67 years old. His appeal to the Supreme Court was denied in 2016, and his pleas for pardons from Presidents Obama and Trump have been ignored. It was ruled that any profits from his book, "*Surrendered: The Rise, Fall, & Revelation of Kwame Kilpatrick*," must be used to pay his fines.

Was there any good that came out of Kwame's mayoral term? The Book-Cadillac Building had been derelict. Kwame helped pull strings to get it renovated. This led to many of the downtown buildings having a revival. Also, a two-mile paved walkway in Detroit called the "Dequindre Cut" was built.

CHAPTER SIXTY-THREE—KEN

COCKEREL—CITY
IN CHAOS

Ken Cockrel, Acting Mayor of Detroit 2008-2009

Kenneth Vern Cockrel, Jr., (1965-) was the head of the Common Council when Kwame Kilpatrick resigned, and under the city charter, became the interim mayor on September 17, 2008.

Kenneth, or "Ken" as he was officially known, was born October 29, 1965 in Detroit. His father was Kenneth Cockrel, Sr., a renowned attorney and city council member, and his mother Carol was a schoolteacher. Ken Jr. graduated from the St. Florian Church High School in Hamtramck, Michigan, and graduated from Wayne State University with honors.

Journalist for Various Newspapers

After graduation Cockrel was a print journalist for the *Detroit Free Press, Grand Rapids Press,* and the *Cincinnati Enquirer.*

In 1994 he successfully ran for the Wayne County Commission as a Democrat and was reelected in 1996. In 1997 he was elected to the Detroit Common Council and again in 2001 and 2005. In 2001 he was named the Council President Pro Tem and Council President in 2005. He helped pass an ordinance requiring Detroit to pay contractors and vendors within 45 days.

He married Kimberley Cockrel and they have two sons, Kenneth III and Kyle Vincent, and three daughters, Kennedy Victoria, Kendal Imani and Kayla Lanett.

Quotes Star Trek in Inaugural Address

When Kwame Kilpatrick pleaded guilty to obstruction of justice and resigned, Cockrel became Acting Mayor because he was Council President. In his inaugural address he quoted the movies *Terminator 2* and *Star Trek*.

As mayor Cockrel helped cancel an agreement Kwame made with Windsor, Ontario officials, ceding total control of the Detroit-Windsor Tunnel to them, in return for a $75 million-dollar loan to Detroit.

Cockerel had to deal with a Common Council that included Monica Conners, wife of long-time U.S. Representative John Conners, later convicted of bribery. Also, on the council was Martha Reeves of the Motown vocal group Martha and the Vandellas. Their hits included "Dancing in the Streets," "Heatwave," "Quicksand," and "Jimmy Mack."

One Common Council caper had the board singing Onward Christian Soldiers, while Monica Conyers referred to Acting Mayor Cockerel as "Shrek."

Cockrel ran for mayor on May 5, 2009, but narrowly lost to basketball All-Star Dave Bing. Bing got 52% of the vote to Cockrel's 48%. After the election, Cockrel returned to his council seat as President. In 2013 he announced he wouldn't be running for reelection for Common Council. In 2016, he was named the Executive Director of Habitat for Humanity.

Ken Cockrel receives the Michigan Municipal League (MML) Award of Merit in 2010.

CHAPTER SIXTY-FOUR— DAVE BING—ALL-STAR MAYOR OF A BANKRUPT CITY

Dave Bing, Mayor of Detroit 2009-201

Bing 1968, 1971 & 1972 Basketball Cards

David Bing (born 1943) took over as Mayor of Detroit at a tough time—not long after Kwame's scandalous mayoral terms and Cockrel's dealing with a rebellious city council. And then he had to endure being mayor while the city was in the hands of a reciever.

For Bing, getting elected to Mayor of Detroit was just the third act in a very successful life. Act One was Bing's basketball career. He was an All-Star and considered one of the 50 greatest players who ever played. Act Two for Bing was when he went on to start successful industrial businesses. When he got to Act Three, running and winning the election for Mayor of Detroit, at a very difficult time in the city's history, he was once again successful.

Dave Bing was born November 29, 1943 in Washington, D.C. to father Hasker, a bricklayer, and his mother, Juanita, a housekeeper. When he was five, he injured his eye when he suffered a poke in it with a rusty nail, while playing on a makeshift hobby horse. He had diminished eyesight in the left eye thereafter, but it never slowed him down.

Better at Basketball than Boyhood Pal Marvin Gaye

Bing was good at basketball when young, but was told by other kids that he was too small to ever be professional. One of the neighborhood people he played with was future Motown star Marvin Gay(e) (Marvin added the "e" at the end of his name later), although not necessarily the one who give Bing the bad advice about making it in the pros. Gaye and Bing remained lifelong friends.

Another neighborhood resident was future basketball pro Elgin Baylor, who played 14 seasons with the Minneapolis Lakers, moving with the team when they became the Los Angeles Lakers. When Baylor first achieved fame in the 1950s as a collegiate star in Seattle, and then made it to the majors, many of the neighborhood residents started seeing basketball as a way out of the ghetto.

Although one could get into a lot of trouble on the streets of D.C., Bing's exceptional parents Hasker and Juanita gave him a solid base from the start. Bing and his older sister Dorothy and younger sister Brenda and younger brother Hasker, Jr. were active in the New Mount Olive Baptist Church and spent a good part of their Sundays there. The kids went to Sunday School, and Dave sang with his dad in the choir.

Bing's family was close, and would often have family events, such as picnics, with the large, extended family of grandparents, aunts, uncles, and cousins. Bing's dad often took him fishing in the Potomac River.

Bing's parents were always supportive. The first baseball game that Hasker went to of Bing's, Bing hit three home runs to win the game. After that, Hasker was Bing's greatest booster.

Bing worked part-time as a bricklayer with his father and told a story about his dad and doing a job right. When he was 14 he helped his bricklayer father by building a wall. When Hasker leaned against it, it fell over! The lesson was a job worth doing is worth doing right. Not to mention, everything needs a solid foundation.

Because he *thought* he couldn't make it in basketball, when he was younger Bing concentrated on baseball. He followed the Brooklyn Dodgers, the major league team that drafted the first black player, Jackie Robinson. Bing excelled in baseball and in 1959 started attending Springarn High School, where he made the team and did well, despite his fuzzy vision.

His high school team was known as the "Green Wave" and had many Washington, D.C. city championships under its belt. The team coach was William Roundtree, and he was a big influence in Bing's life. By this time Bing had reached his full 6 foot, 3 inches height and head coach William Roundtree encouraged Bing to resume playing basketball. Bing did, and started scoring 10 or more points per game *right out of the starting gate.*

Roundtree encouraged his players to do well in school, make something of themselves, and have a spiritual life also. The coach encouraged his students to work as a team, not trying to hog the glory for themselves. Bing took the advice to heart, becoming the Green Wave's leader in scoring *and* assists in his Senior year. Bing, who became the team Captain, was always looking to see if a team player has a better chance to score before attempting the shot himself. This led to Bing becoming one of the pros with the most assists and scores!

Bing polished his basketball skills after school at the Watts and Kelly Miller Recreation Centers. He continued playing both baseball and basketball until his senior year of high school. When he had two tournaments at the same time, one in baseball and the other in basketball, he chose basketball, thinking it might give him a better chance at a college scholarship. He was right.

All-American Basketball Player

Bing led his team to victory and won MVP honors for the tournament. He also made the All-American team for high school. When it came time to choose a college, he was offered over 100 college scholarships! Bing was the complete deal: a great athlete, a well-adjusted young man, and an honor student. Ironically, the only college that didn't accept him, Princeton University, was his #1 choice.

Bing was welcomed at his next favorite choice, Syracuse University. The rural atmosphere of Syracuse, with its farms and lakes, was very different from the mean streets of Washington, D.C. where Bing grew up.

Bing at Syracuse University & the Orangeman of Syracuse.

Bing led the Orangemen of Syracuse in scoring his sophomore, junior, and senior years, averaging over 20 points per game. When Bing was on the freshman team, they would regularly win when scrimmaging with the Varsity. Bing won All-American college honors, was named to *The Sporting News* All-America First Team, and other honors, including Syracuse University's Athlete of the Year Award. He managed to break nearly every basketball record Syracuse had.

Bing would lead in both points and assists throughout his career. He was never one to hog the ball, but a true team player. He always looked to see if a teammate had a chance at a better shot before taking it himself.

Bing married his high school sweetheart Aaris and moved into a Syracuse apartment. The Bing family grew to include three daughters, Cassaundra, Aleisha, and Bridgett.

Dave Bing as a Detroit Pison

Hall of Fame Pro Basketball Career

Bing had no problem going pro, signing with the Detroit Pistons in 1966 for $15,000 per year, a far cry from today's million-dollar salaries. He was recruited for Detroit by Earl Lloyd, who became one of the first African-Americans on a pro basketball team in 1950. Lloyd spotted Bing and brought him to the attention of the Pistons. Bing was chosen in the draft by Detroit, who luckily for them, got to pick second because of their previous bad season.

Bing, Aaris, and daughters moved to the Detroit area. In his first professional game, Bing didn't score at all! But the next game he scored 37 points against the Los Angeles Lakers, leading the Pistons to victory. He averaged 20 points per game by the end of the season and was named Rookie of the Year for the American Basketball Association (ABA) in 1967.

In 1968 he led the ABA, averaging over 27.4 points per game. It was unusual for a guard to lead the league in scoring, but Bing did it! Bing played on *seven* straight All-Star teams while with the Pistons. In 1968 he was the Piston's Most Valuable Player while on his way to becoming a Pistons legend.

Because of yet another poke in the eye, Bing played sporadically during 1971-72, missing about half the season while recuperating.

National Bank of Detroit logo

With a growing family, pro basketball did not pay very much back in the 1960s and the 1970s. It was especially insufficient for a family with three daughters. Most players worked during the off-season in the days before million-dollar salaries became the norm. Bing worked in the intern program of the National Bank of Detroit during his time off from basketball starting as a teller and became a manager with the bank.

The team logos of the three pro teams Dave Bing played for—the Detroit Pistons, the Washington Wizards, and the Boston Celtics.

In 1974 Bing was traded to the Washington Bullets, playing with them for two years and once again named an All-Star in 1976. He helped a debut team become a solid pennant contender and was given the All-Star MVP award in 1976.

Bing spent his final season with the Boston Celtics and retired at the end of the 1977-1978 season. He had a lifetime average of 20.3 points for his 12 years of professional play and scored over 18,000 points during his pro career.

National Minority Small Business Person of the Year
Bing's All-Star pro basketball career was just Act One in an inspiring life. At first Bing was in a training program run by

Chrysler Corporation to teach about becoming an auto dealer. In 1978 Bing worked for *Paragon Steel* in Detroit, learning the ins and outs of the steel business.

In 1980 he opened his own company, Bing Steel, to do steel processing. Working in a rented warehouse with just four employees, Bing at first lost all his money. Through perseverance he worked the firm back up to become a $4.2 million-per-year company.

In 1984 he was awarded the National Minority Small Business Person of the Year by President Ronald Reagan.

In 1985 Bing started another company while still running Bing Steel. The new company was Superb Manufacturing, which made steel parts for autos that were used by Chrysler and General Motors.

In 1990 Bing was named to the Naismith Basketball Hall of Fame in Springfield, Massachusetts, and in 1996 was named one of the NBA's 50 Greatest Players. His jersey number was retired by both the Detroit Pistons and the Washington Bullets. He was inducted into the Afro American's Hall of Fame in 1978.

In 1998, the Bing Group was named Company of the Year by *Black Enterprise Magazine.*

He was given the 1985 "Humanitarian of the Year" from the City of Detroit and February 11, 1991 was declared "Dave Bing Day" in Detroit in recognition of Bing's accomplishments and exceptional charity work.

Bing's mother Juanita had always told him, "If you see anybody you can help, you try to help them." Bing took this to heart, never one to shy away from helping civic organizations. He worked for the March of Dimes, participated in the Big Brother program, the Dave Bing All-Pro Basketball Camp, the Boy Scouts, the Boys and Girls Club, Junior Achievement, and many other charities.

Bing raised $600,000 (with the help of Michigan State's

Magic Johnson) to save the sports programs at Detroit Public Schools in 1989. He has been a major donor and contributed his time to the Michigan Minority Business Development Council and the Detroit Black United Fund.

Although he divorced Aaris and also had another wife he divorced, Yvette, he stayed on good terms with both women and is very close with his daughters and grandchildren.

In 2009 he sold the assets of Bing Steel and transferred the balance to his new conglomerate, the Bing Group. Bing Group clients include General Motors and other auto concerns. The company provides metal stampings to the auto industry.

Bing on his Election Eve.

Detroit Mayoral Election Victory

In October of 2008 Bing announced he would be a Democratic Party candidate for Mayor of Detroit in the February 2009 election. In January of 2009 Bing received the National Civil Rights Museum Sports Legacy Award and in Febuary he came in first out of fifteen candidates.

In May 2009 the two top candidates, Bing and Ken Cockrel, faced off and Bing won with 52% of the vote. This election was to fill out the rest of Kwame Kilpatrick's mayoral term, which ended December 2009. Bing ran in the next election, winning a full four-year term as Mayor. In May of 2013, Bing announced that he wouldn't run for another term.

Detroit Bankruptcy

Detroit declared Chapter 9 Bankruptcy during Bing's term, the largest major city to do so. Detroit was unable to provide services as population and the tax base declined. The city's debt was estimated to be in the $18 to $20 billion dollar range. The city went into a state of "financial emergency" in March 2013 and Kevyn Orr was appointed as "emergency manager" of the city by Michigan's Governor Rick Snyder. With the Emergency Manager running the city, this left Mayor Bing with strictly ceremonial duties.

After his term, he returned to managing his businesses with an office at 11500 Oakland Avenue, Detroit, Michigan. His Bing Youth Institute helps young people of Detroit.

Dave Bing, upon his 1990 induction into the Hall of Fame, Oscar Robertson said, "Dave is the perfect example of professionalism, class, dignity, and humanity. He cares. He gets involved with the world." That seems like a great way to end Mayor Bing's chapter.

C HAPTER SIXTY-FIVE—MIKE DUGGAN—A SOLVENT CITY AGAIN

Mike Duggan, Mayor of Detroit 2014-2019+

Michael Edward Duggan (born July 15, 1958) was born in Detroit to Patrick Duggan, a United States District Judge, and Joan Duggan. Michael graduated from Detroit Catholic Central High School and went to the University of Michigan in Ann Arbor, earning an A.B. degree in 1980 and a J.D. degree from the University of Michigan Law School in 1983.

Wayne County Deputy Executive and Prosecutor

In 1986 Duggan became the Wayne County Assistant Corporation Counsel. From 1987 to 2001 he was the Deputy County Executive for Wayne County and was elected Prosecutor in 2000.

In 2004 Duggan became the President and CEO of the Detroit Medical Center until 2010 when the company was sold.

Duggan at his victory party after winning the mayoral election.

In 2012 Duggan moved to Detroit from Livonia, with intentions of running for Mayor of Detroit. He missed the residency requirement by two weeks to be on the ballot, so he conducted a successful write-in campaign, garnering 52% of the vote in the August 2012 primary.

In the November election he had won a place on the ballot as one of the two top vote-getters in the primary. He ran against Wayne County Sheriff Benny Napoleon, who had received 29% of the votes in the primary.

Elected While White

Duggan's campaign slogan was "Every neighborhood has a future." He promised a financial turnaround, economic development, and reduction of the crime statistics. He won in the general election, with 55% of the vote, becoming the first white Mayor of Detroit since Roman Gribbs in the 1970s.

On December 11, 2014, the city exited bankruptcy and the mayor resumed his normal duties. Duggan was reelected in 2017 over Coleman Young II with over 72% of the vote to Young's 27%.

While mayor, Duggan has presided over Detroit as it is

involved in many renovations. Quicken Loans Dan Gilbert is involved in many projects and has renovated the Book Buildings, the David Stott Building, and the David Whitney Building, among others. The Ford Motor Company has purchased the derelict train station with plans to renovate.

The Detroit Pistons returned to Detroit from Auburn Hills with the opening of Little Caesar's Arena in Detroit in 2017.

Mike Duggan is married to Lori Maher Duggan and they have four children—Carolyn, Eddie, Mary, and Patrick.

AFTERWORD

Besides for a few exceptional differences, a generic biography for the early Detroit mayors of the 19th Century could be easily written. It would start with the future mayor's birth in a New England state, possibly Massachusetts, New Hampshire, Vermont, Maine, or Connecticut. (After the Erie Canal, most immigration came from New York or Pennsylvania. Detroit had 11 mayors born in New York, and 7 that were born in Pennsylvania.)

The future mayor would then attend public schools and maybe attend college and study law. Most likely he would study law in somebody's law office and study on his own until he felt confident enough to pass the bar. That was the way it was done in the 19th Century. Once the future mayor passed the bar, he would practice for a while and then move to Detroit. Many of the early mayors had military service, with many serving in the early wars of the area, including the Civil War, Black Hawk War, the War of 1812, or even the Toledo War.

The future mayor's civic-mindedness would then lead him to serve on the Common Council and maybe as Alderman. In his early political days, he might be on the Board of Estimates, Police Commissioner, or the Railroad Board. After he felt he had enough support he would declare that he was going to make a run for Mayor. After a campaign he would either win or lose. If he lost, he would likely be back in a new election next year. If he won, he would then become Mayor! After he became Mayor, he would serve a year or two and then retire to his estate. The 20th Century Mayors of Detroit had more varied backgrounds and stories.

Other places where Detroit Mayors were born include the countries of Germany (William Richert), Scotland (Hugh Moffatt), and Ireland (John Patton). Two were from Ontario, Canada (James Couzens and Alexander Lewis).

After Mayor Maybury in 1897, most of Detroit's mayors were born in Detroit with 20 in all to date, including present mayor Mike Duggan. One mayor was from Wayne County (Oscar Marx). Only one mayor was born in Ohio, John Harmon. Mayors came from several small Michigan towns, including Harbor Beach (Frank Murphy), Marine City (Stephen Grummond), Capac (Roman Gribbs), Lapeer (Marvin Chamberlain), and Yale (Charles Bowles). One mayor (Dave Bing) was born in Washington, D.C. and one was originally from Alabama (Coleman Young).

But after a few decades and many one-year mayoral terms later, the biographies of the mayors became more diverse. The main change was the addition of large-scale merchants and moguls to the lawyers who did their civic duty and served as

Mayor of Detroit.

Some of the occupations of mayors of Detroit include shoe factory owner, which was Hazen Pingree's profession, and medical doctor, which were occupations for Detroit Mayors Dr. Zina Pitcher, Dr. Douglas Houghton, and Dr. Marshall Chapin. Two were wrestlers in their youth—John W. Smith, who wrestled under the name "Kid Smith," and Richard Reading, who was "Little Dick."

Two brothers became mayor—Christian and Frederick Buhl, and they were partners as industrialists, starting with millinery (women's hats), and furs, and then graduating on to Buhl Iron Works and Detroit Copper and Brass Company.

James Couzens, who helped lead the Ford Motor Company into being the largest company in the world, was Mayor, as was his son, Frank, the only father-son combination.

The vices were covered with one mayor a beer brewer (William Duncan), one specializing in producing the malts that go into the beers (George Langdon) while one mayor produced tobacco (Kirkland Barker). Marvin Chamberlain sold both liquor and tobacco, and Merrill Mills sold gunpowder.

One Mayor was a wholesale grocer (William Wheaton), and two owned large shipping businesses (Stephen Grummond and John Pridgeon). Oliver Hyde had a large hardware business, John Ladue sold leather goods, and Hugh Moffat and DeGarmo Jones were builders. John Harmon was a printer and John Patton was a carriage maker. Coleman Young was a Union Organizer while Philip Breitmeyer was a noted horticulturist, helping to found FTD Florists. Oscar Marx was an eye doctor and sold glasses. John Ladue was a tanner and sold leather products.

Two mayors had no pictures available-John Ladue and John Harmon.

It wasn't until 1930 and Charles Bowles that Detroit

began having shady mayors. Louis Miriani, Richard Reading, and Kwame Kilpatrick followed Bowles as less-than-desirable Mayors. But Detroit has had mostly mayors that look beyond enriching themselves and instead wish to serve the citizens and enrich the city instead.

Detroit has many organizations working to help preserve Detroit, including Preservation Wayne, the Detroit Historical Society, and many others. And so once more Detroit rises from the ashes...

Detroit renovated skyscrapers.

APPENDIX

Chairmen of the Detroit Board of Trustees 1802-1824

18 Jan 1802 - May 1803   James Henry

May 1803 - May 1804   James May

May 1804 - May 1805   Solomon Sibley (1st time)

May 1805 - 11 Jun 1805   Joseph Wilkinson

11 Jun 1805 - 24 Oct 1815 The Governors of Michigan and Territorial Judges

- A.B. Woodward
- Frederick Bates
- John Griffin
- James Witherell

Oct 1815 - May 1816   Solomon Sibley (2nd time) (1769-1846)

May 1816 - May 1817   George McDougall (1766-1840)

May 1817 - May 1818   Abraham Edwards (1781-1860)

May 1818 - May 1819   John R. Williams (1782-1854)

May 1819 - May 1820   James McCloskey (d. 1828)

May 1820 - May 1821   James Abbott (1st time) (1775-1858)

May 1821 - May 1823   Andrew Griswold Whitney (1786-1826)

May 1824 - May 1824   James Abbott (2nd time) (1775-1858)

Detroit Skyline 2018

BIBLIOGRAPHY

American Biographical History of Eminent and Self-Made Men (Parts 1 and 2) (1878). Cincinnati,   OH: Western Biographical Publishing Company

Archer, Dennis & Elizabeth Ann Atkins (2017). *Let the Future Begin.* Grosse Pointe Farms, MI: Atkins and Greenspan Writing.

Babson, Steve (1984). *Working Detroit: The Making of a Union*

Town. Detroit, MI: Wayne State University Press.

Bak, Richard (1999). *Detroit: 1900-1930.* Charleston, SC: Arcadia Publishing.

Barnard, Harry (1958). Independent Man: The Life of Senator James Couzens. New York: Scribner's.

Bates, Beth Tompkins (2012). *The Making of Black Detroit in the Age of Henry Ford.* Chapel Hill, NC: The University of North Carolina Press.

Beasley, Norman & Stark, George W. (1957). *Made in Detroit.* New York, NY: Van Rees Press.

Bingay, Malcolm W. (1946). *Detroit is My Home Town.* Indianapolis, IN: The Bobbs-Merrill Company.

Bingay, Malcolm W. (1949). *Of Me I Sing.* Indianapolis, IN: The Bobbs-Merrill Company.

Blum, Peter H. (1999). *Brewed in Detroit: Breweries and Beers Since 1830.* Detroit, MI: Wayne State University Press.

Burnstein, Scott M. (2006). *Motor City Mafia: A Century of Organized Crime in Detroit.* Charleston, SC: Arcadia Publishing.

Capeci, Dominic J. (1996). Detroit and the "Good War," The World War II Letters of Mayor Edward Jeffries and Friends. Lexington, KY: The University Press of Kentucky.

Cash, Asher (1931). Sacred Cows, A Story of the Recall of Mayor Bowles. Self-published in Detroit.

Chaffets, Ze'ev (1990). *Devil's Night and Other True Tales of Detroit.* New York, NY: Random House.

Clark, Anna (editor) (2014). *A Detroit Anthology.* Detroit, MI: Rust Belt Publishing.

Desjarlais, Mary (2008). Beauty on the Streets of Detroit: A History of the Housing Market in Detroit. Self-published.

Fine, Sydney (1989). Violence in the Model City: The Cavanagh Administration, Race Relations, and the Detroit Riot of 1967. Ann Arbor, MI: University of Michigan Press.

Fine, Sydney (1985). *Frank Murphy: A Michigan Life.* Ann Arbor: Historical Society of Michigan.

Fisher, Silas (1889). The History of Detroit and Michigan, or the Metropolis Illustrated: A Chronological   Cyclopedia of the Past and Present. Detroit, MI: Silas Farmer & Co.

Franck, Michael S. (1996). *Elmwood Endures: History of a Detroit Cemetery.* Detroit, MI: Wayne State University Press.

Gavrilovich, Peter & McGraw, Bill (editors) (2000, 2006). *Detroit Free Press Detroit Almanac: 300 Years of Life in the Motor City.* Detroit, MI: Detroit Free Press

George, Sister Mary Karl (1969). *Zachariah Chandler: A Political Biography.* E. Lansing, MI: Michigan State University Press.

Haig, Robert M. (2013). *Ten Little Chiefs: A Detroit Police Story.* West Conshohocken, PA: Infinity Publishing.

Harrington, Michael (1997) *The Other America: Poverty in the United States.* New York: Simon & Schuster.

Harris, Walter L. (2011). Badge of Honor: Blowing the Whistle: The True Story of a Mayor's Bodyguard. Shelbyville, Ky.: Wasteland Press.

Henriksen, Wilma Wood (ed.) (1991). *Detroit Perspectives: Crossroads and Turning Points* Detroit: Wayne State University Press.

1930s postcard of downtown Detroit with old City Hall. From the Historic Elmwood Cemetery & Foundation (2018). Detroit, MI. [pamphlet}.

Holli, Melvin G. (1969). *Reform in Detroit: Hazen S. Pingree and Urban Politics.* New York: Oxford University Press.

Holli, Melvin G. and Jones, Peter d'A. Jones (1981). *Biographical Dictionary of American Mayors,* 1820-1980. Westport, CN: Greenwood Press.

Holli, Melvin G. (1993). *The Best and Worst Big-City Mayors.* University Park, PA: The Pennsylvania State University Press.

Jackson, Kenneth T. (1967). *The Ku Klux Klan in the City 1915-1930.* New York: Oxford University Press.

Lodge, John C. and Quaife, M. M. (1949). *I Remember Detroit.* Detroit, MI: Wayne State University Press.

Marden, Orison Swett (1905). A Good Shoemaker Becomes Detroit's Best Mayor and Michigan's Greatest Governor. New York: The Success Company, 1905.

Martin, Brian (2018). The Detroit Wolverines: The Rise and Wreck of a National League Champion, 1881-1888. Jefferson, NC: McFarland & Company, Inc.

Miles, Tiya (2017). *The Dawn of Detroit.* New York, NY: The New Press.

Palmer, Friend (1906). *Early Days in Detroit.* Detroit, MI: Hunt and June.

Poremba, David Lee (1999). *Detroit: 1930-1969.* Charleston, SC: Arcadia Publishing.

Poremba, David Lee (editor) (2001). *Detroit in its World Setting: A Three Hundred Year Chronology, 1701-2001.* Detroit, MI: Wayne State University Press.

Report on Detroit Street Railway Traffic and Proposed Subway, Made to Board of Street Railway Commissioners, City of Detroit (1915). Detroit: Barclay, Parsons & Clapp.

Roberts, Robert E. (1855). Sketches of the City of Detroit, State of Michigan, Past and Present. Detroit: R.F. Johnstone & Co.

Schleichert, Elizabeth (1995). *Dave Bing: Basketball Great with a Heart.* Springfield, N.J.: Enslow Publishers, Inc.

Sharp, Jim (2013). *Dave Bing: A Life of Challenge.* Windsor, ON: Human Kinetics.

Stanton, Tom (2016). *Terror in the City of Champions.* Guilford, CN: Rowman & Littlefield.

Streeter, Floyd Benjamin (1918). *Political Parties in Michigan 1837-1860.* Lansing: Michigan Historical Commission.

Taragano, Martin (1991). *Basketball Biographies.* Jefferson, NC: McFarland & Co.

The Real Detroit / prepared by the Detroit News; in cooperation with the Mayor's Committee for Economic Growth. (1960). Detroit: Detroit News.

Warner, Robert and Vanderhill, C. Warren (eds.) (1974). *A Michigan Reader: 1865 to the Present.* Grand Rapids: William B. Eerdmans Publishing Co.

Williams, Jeremy (2009). *Detroit's Black Bottom.* Charleston, SC: Arcadia Publishing.

Woodford, Arthur M. & Frank B. (1969). *All Our Yesterdays: A Brief History of Detroit.* Detroit: Wayne State University Press.

The Manoogian Mansion, home of the mayor of Detroit.

ABOUT THE AUTHOR

Alan Naldrett started one of the first used vinyl record store (also featuring—cassette tapes!) while attending Michigan State. Much to the surprise of his professors, he graduated and moved to California where he was an advertising exec and insurance broker.

Returning to Michigan, he got a master's degree in library and Information Science and a few years later a master's degree in Archival Science. He has helped organize the archives for his township, a museum, a college, and other entities.

After writing his first book during slow times at the Reference Desk, in retirement Alan has written fourteen more to date. His most popular book so far has been *Lost Car Companies of Detroit*. Others include *How Detroit Became the Motor City, Michigan's Great Thumb Fires, Michigan's C. Harold Wills, Lost Towns of Eastern Michigan, Forgotten Tales of Michigan's Lower Peninsula (Toledo War), Michigan's Great Small Towns, 50 States of American Autos, Putting the Vice in the Vice-Presidents,* and *Michigan's Forgotten Celebrities.*

Old City Hall and Early Map of Detroit

The main exhibit building of the Detroit
International Exposition of 1889

Nightime in the Motor City.

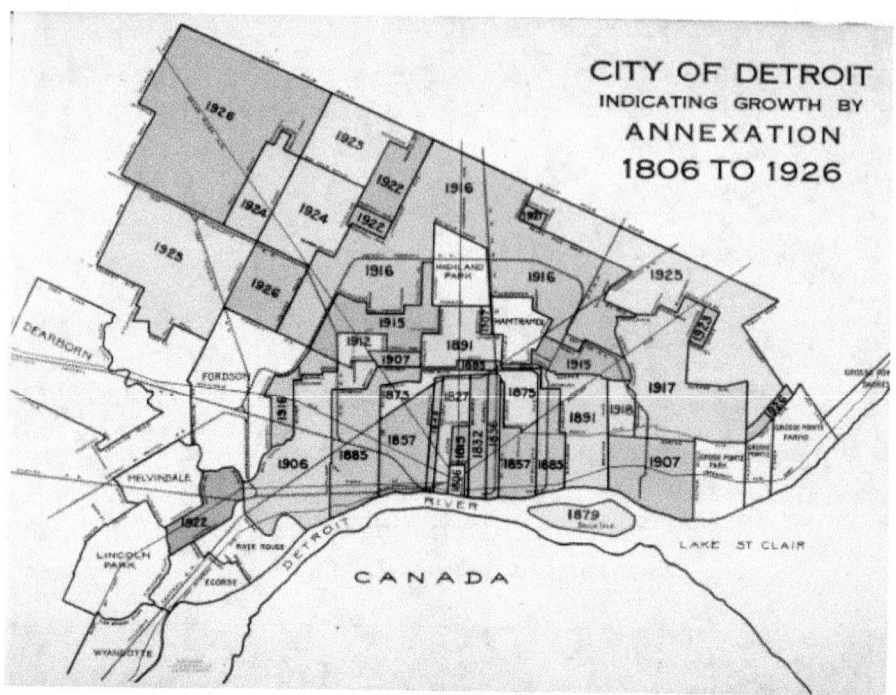

Map detailing when sections of the city were annexed.

Old City Hall in downtown Detroit

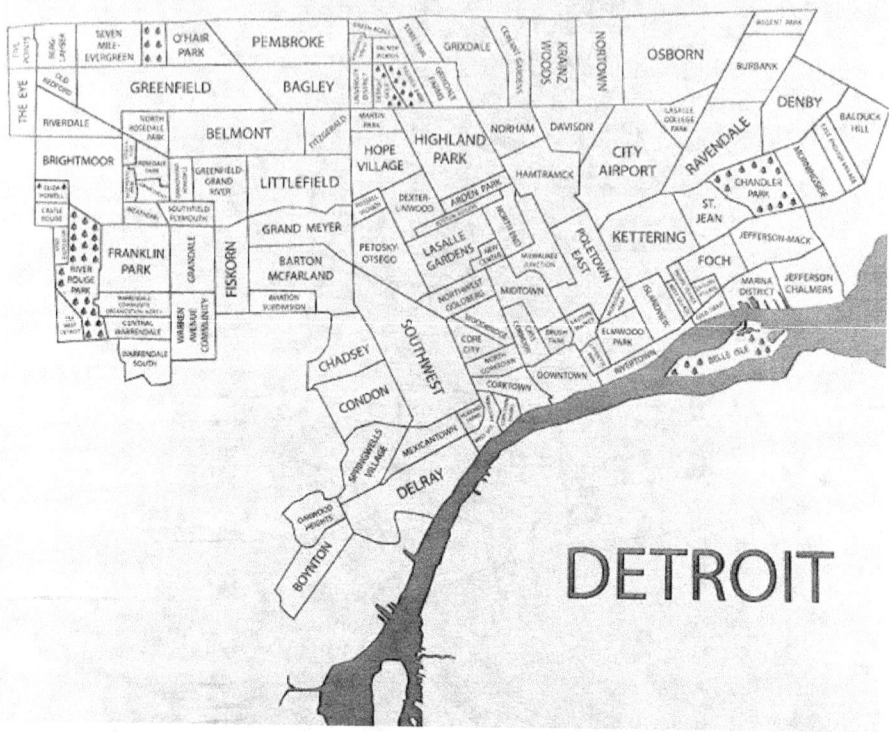

Neighborhood map of Detroit

The Seal of the City of Detroit